AF521656

SCHOLARS ON THE RECORD

Insightful Interviews on Bible and Archaeology

Hershel Shanks
Editor

Biblical Archaeology Society
Washington, DC

Library of Congress Cataloging-in-Publication Data

Scholars on the record: insightful interviews on Bible and archaeology /
Hershel Shanks, editor.
p. cm.
1. Biblical scholars—Interviews. 2. Archaeologists—Interviews. 3. Bible—
History of Biblical events. 4. Bible—Antiquities. I. Shanks, Hershel.
BS501.A1.S36 2009
220.9'3—dc22

2009033311

Designed by Sean Kennedy/SPK Designs, New York, NY

All interviews previously appeared in *Biblical Archaeology Review* or *Bible Review*

ISBN 978-1-935335-23-8

CONTENTS

INTRODUCTION

Although the interviews in this book were culled from two different magazines (*Biblical Archaeology Review* and *Bible Review*) and each was published independently without relation to any of the others, they nevertheless form a kind of natural flow when gathered together between two covers. They will not only provide the reader with intriguing and varied personal stories of leading biblical scholars and archaeologists, but also highlight their shared concerns about critical scholarly investigation of the Bible and its world.

The very first interview cuts to the chase: Four prominent scholars talk about their personal religious faith—their belief in God. Paradoxically, a Baptist minister (James Strange) and an Orthodox Jew (Lawrence Schiffman) seem to agree with each other more than they agree with a (former) Christian (Bart Ehrman) and a Jewish convert who began as an evangelical (William Dever). But even Strange and Schiffman acknowledge that it is no easy thing to have faith. They too struggle as we all do. And even Dever recognizes that he cannot say God does not exist. Both Dever and Ehrman have simply turned to other questions, though oddly enough, their questions are still situated in a religious context.

In the second interview, one of the nation's leading—if not *the* leading—feminist Bible scholars, Phyllis Trible, talks about how she approaches what might seem like difficult passages in an admittedly patriarchal book. She too struggles with the text and, without compromising her feminist principles, still creatively manages to find inspiration and value even in difficult biblical passages.

In the third interview, two scholarly giants—Frank Cross and Elie Weisel—meet each other for the first time. For each, the Bible is at the center of his life, but they both come to the text—at least professionally—from entirely different perspectives. But each scholar also has another take on the Bible, a more personal perspective, which brings him around to the viewpoint of the other. Their different perspectives have a kind of chiastic relationship: What is personal for one is the professional interest of the other. And vice versa. In the end, they both relate to the Bible in similar ways.

It is in this interview that the subject of the biblical minimalists (scholars who contend that the Bible contains little, if any, history) is raised for the first time in this book. Cross notes that several minimalists are active in Denmark and in England and "unhappily, out of Tel Aviv." He is no doubt referring to Israel Finkelstein, a prominent archaeologist at Tel Aviv University. The next interview is with Finkelstein who claims he is a centrist, not a minimalist. As a centrist, he says, he is attacked from both the left (the minimalists) and the right (the traditionalists). Finkelstein contends that much of the archaeological evidence that has been attributed to King Solomon is actually much later, thus depriving Solomon of almost all of his glory. Moreover, the biblical texts, he says, were written much later than the events they describe, and reflect the concerns of the time they were written rather than the concerns (or history) they purportedly narrate.

In the next interview, we meet two of the world's best known biblical minimalists, Niels Peter Lemche and Thomas Thompson, as they face off against two scholars with more traditional views of the Bible and biblical archaeology—Kyle McCarter and William Dever. In this interview, we come as close to fisticuffs as we get in this book. But we learn more than simply the intensity of academic disputes and academic relationships. We learn how each side uses the same evidence differently and why the field is beset with controversy.

The next interview brings together Israel's most famous archaeological couple, Trude and Moshe Dothan (Moshe has passed away since this interview), often known as Mr. and Mrs Philistine. Trude tells us what it was like in the early days of the state, when archaeology too was budding, and how she juggled being a professional archaeologist and a mother at the same time. She also gives vignettes of some of the founders of Israeli archaeology—Yigael Yadin's father E.L. Sukenik and Benjamin Mazar. She also recalls the *grande dame* of British archaeology, Kathleen Kenyon, as well as the highly respected biblical scholar Père Roland de Vaux, who was both an archaeologist and a comedian.

In the second installment of their interview, Moshe and Trude wrestle with some larger questions, both procedural and substantive: How we know what we know from the archaeological mire we call an excavation, how we know about the Philistines from archaeological evidence, the differing ways in which Philistines and Israelites are identified in the archaeological record, and, finally, what part the Bible plays in archaeological interpretation.

In the next interview, we hear from an extraordinarily broad and brilliant scholar, Cyrus Gordon, who was an acknowledged maverick (Gordon passed away shortly after the interview). Some of Cyrus Gordon's insights were absolutely brilliant and only recognized years later by scholars who followed him. Other positions, like his insistence that Linear A was a Semitic language, he held largely alone. How does the layperson—or even the scholar—decide which is which? Even Gordon's wildest ideas he held with passion and some rational support. This interview also gives the outsider a sense of the viciousness and intensity of disagreements in the academic world. Gordon was also one of the few scholars who still had personal memories of such iconic figures in the history of biblical archaeology and Bible scholarship as Sir William Flinders Petrie and William Foxwell Albright.

The interview with Israel's most illustrious archaeologist, Yigael Yadin, taken two years before his death in 1985, presents what would today be considered a maximalist position with regard to archaeology and the Bible. Yadin makes a powerful, yet measured case. The man's greatness shines through. He is nothing if not broad; he is concerned with everything from the smallest detail to the grandest hypothesis. One also feels in his words the magnetism of his personality. He was a scholar and a man writ large.

Each of the final two interviews has both a personal and scholarly aspect. David Noel Freedman (recently passed away) was born a Jew but converted to Christianity. Geza Vermes, although born a Jew, became a Catholic priest before returning to Judaism. Both are great scholars, and, to this, their personal religious beliefs are irrelevant—but nevertheless interesting.

Substantively, Freedman discusses the differences between the Christian Old Testament and the Hebrew Bible and what the differences imply doctrinally. Christians and Jews interpret much the same text in very different ways and this difference is reflected in how the two traditions ordered the books of their respective Bibles. This much seems clear and is undisputed. But Freedman goes on to explain how the Hebrew Bible itself developed as a book. His insights are profound (and make a good deal of sense), although, as in most issues related to the Bible, proof "beyond a reasonable doubt" eludes us.

We end with the Dead Sea Scrolls. In the final interview, Geza Vermes (pronounced Ver-MESH) tells us that his translation of the scrolls has sold 300,000 copies, and doubtless many more have been sold in the years since the interview. His translation has become the international standard. Vermes also had an important role in encouraging the release of the scrolls. He is also widely known for his work on the historical Jesus. In this interview, he explains why a background in Second Temple Judaism is fundamental to understanding Jesus and his message. And that is where the scrolls fit in. They are some of the most important documents of Second Temple Judaism. There is much doctrine that Christianity and the scrolls share.

These 11 interviews would not have been brought together under one cover, however, were it not for the vision and commitment of the staff of the Biblical Archaeology Society. Our president, Susan Laden, skillfully guided the project from start to finish, while long-time BAS editor Steven Feldman provided insightful counsel on which of *Biblical Archaeology Review's* and *Bible Review's* countless interviews should be included in the final book. The original manuscripts and images from the interviews were ably edited into a single volume by Joey Corbett, who was assisted and guided along the way by editors Bonnie Mullin and Dorothy D. Resig. Production manager Heather Metzger diligently oversaw the book's transition from computer documents to finished product. The design and layout was brilliantly handled by Sean Kennedy/SPK Designs. We hope that the quality of this book can, in some measure, reflect the greatness of the accomplished scholars it presents.

Hershel Shanks
Editor, *Biblical Archaeology Review*
Washington, D.C.
August 2009

CHAPTER ONE

LOSING FAITH
Who Did and Who Didn't?

From left: Bart D. Ehrman, William G. Dever, James F. Strange and Lawrence H. Schiffman.

Media reports that Bart Ehrman, a leading expert on the apocryphal gospels and one of our most popular lecturers, had lost his faith as a result of his scholarly research led us to raise a question that is not often talked about, but seemed well worth a discussion: What effect does scholarship have on faith? We asked Ehrman to join three other scholars to talk about this: James F. Strange, a leading archaeologist and Baptist minister; Lawrence H. Schiffman, a prominent Dead Sea Scroll scholar and Orthodox Jew; and William G. Dever, one of America's

"Losing Faith: 2 Who Did and 2 Who Didn't" appeared in BAR, March/April 2007

best-known and most widely quoted archaeologists, who had been an evangelical preacher, then lost his faith, then became a Reform Jew and now says he's a non-believer.

Hershel Shanks: *Bart Ehrman, how did your scholarship affect your faith?*

Bart D. Ehrman

Bart Ehrman: First, I lost my fundamentalist faith because of my scholarship. Like Bill Dever, I have a fundamentalist background. I had a very high view of Scripture as the inerrant word of God, no mistakes of any kind—geographical or historical. No contradictions. Inviolate.

My scholarship early on as a graduate student showed me that in fact these views about the Bible were wrong. I started finding contradictions and finding other discrepancies and started finding problems with the Bible. What that ended up doing for me was showing me that the basis of my faith, which at that time was the Bible, was problematic. So I shifted from being an evangelical Christian to becoming a fairly mainline liberal Protestant Christian.

What ended up making me lose my faith was kind of related to scholarship. When I was at Rutgers University, I taught a course on the problem of suffering in biblical traditions, where I dealt with issues of theodicy throughout different biblical books, both Hebrew Bible and the New Testament—

Shanks: *What is theodicy?*

Ehrman: Theodicy is the question of how God can be righteous, given the amount of suffering in the world. The issue as it's usually put today is that if God is all-powerful and is able to prevent suffering, and is all-loving so that he wants to prevent suffering, why is there suffering? This problem isn't ever expressed that way in the Bible, but biblical authors do deal with the problem by asking: Why do the people of God suffer? In teaching this course, the thing that struck me is just how different the answers are. Depending on what part of Job you read, you get one set of answers. If you read the Prophets, you get a different set of answers. If you read apocalyptic literature, you get still a different set of answers.

This made me think more deeply about my own understanding of why there's suffering in the world. Finally, because I became dissatisfied with all the conventional answers, I decided that I couldn't believe in a God who was in any way intervening in this world, given the state of things. So that's why I ended up losing my faith.

Shanks: *I want to separate a couple of issues. You talked about how you, as a young person, believed in the inerrancy of the Bible, that every word was accurate and divine. I really want to separate that from what we're talking about.*

Is it fair to say that no one here believes in the inerrancy of the biblical text?

James F. Strange

James Strange: I think so. Yeah.

Shanks: *Larry?*

Lawrence Schiffman: Yeah, it's fair. Inerrancy assumes a kind of literalism never adopted in Jewish tradition.

Lawrence H. Schiffman

Shanks: *Okay. That's a different question from what I want to discuss. I want to discuss the second issue: What your scholarship has done to your faith. Faith, I take it, is not a rational thing that we arrive at, not an argument that we win. It comes from another source, and we've just heard what his scholarship has done to Bart's faith.*

Jim Strange, you're a Baptist minister. Has your scholarship, your excavations and your archaeology deepened your faith? Or has it caused you to question it? Are you still a Baptist minister?

Strange: Yeah, I'm still a Baptist minister. I don't have a pulpit. The only thing I do every now and then is a wedding for someone—or a funeral. Maybe now it's more funerals. [Laughs] I bury more than I marry.

But to answer you more directly, I just don't see the connection. My faith is not based upon anything like a propositional argument. When I indulge myself in all this scientific research and explication, I'm not doing anything about faith.

Shanks: *What is your faith based on?*

Strange: My faith is based on my own experience—a good old Protestant principle.

William G. Dever

William Dever: Very Protestant.

Schiffman: It's a form of existentialism.

Strange: Yes, it is. I love the existentialist philosophers. I love to read them, not because they're giving me any testable facts. It's because it's like reading a really good poet. It does something to you that propositional truth never does.

Shanks: *What do you mean by propositional truth?*

Strange: Propositional truth is like: There is a loving God that intervenes upon the earth. That's a proposition. It's testable or it's not. If it's not testable, then you can't falsify it; you can't know if it's true or not. If it really is testable, then the way you test it is to start checking out a list of experiences people have—and suffering is a prime one human beings have in common. So you end up saying, "I've tested the hypothesis and it is now wanting." Suffering tends to disconfirm the hypothesis.

Shanks: *You say your faith is not based on this proposition?*

Strange: That's correct.

Shanks: *What is it based on?*

Strange: Based on my own experience with God. For a lot of people, this makes me sort of a mystic in a cave or something. But I think it's eminently practical and out there. I think that there's as much reason to see the face of God in someone like William Dever.
Dever: Hold on. [All laugh]

Shanks: *Does this God of yours have any attributes?*

Strange: I suppose so, but I'm not really much interested. If I'm passionately in love, I hardly ever want to discuss the attributes of the person I'm in love with. Or if I do, I wind up saying superfluous things for everybody listening. "She's *wonderful.*" "Can you give me some more information?" "Yeah, she's *really wonderful.*" [Laughs] When you're in this state, you don't utter propositions.

Shanks: *Would you say that your scholarship, then, has had really no effect on your faith?*

Strange: Virtually none. I mean I have a wonderful intellectual time with my scholarship. I get the same existentialist thrill out of touching the dirt when I'm excavating as I do holding my wife's hand.

Shanks: *You love the earth that you're excavating really?*

Strange: Yes.

Shanks: *Does that have anything to do with your faith?*

Strange: It has something to do with the center of my being. But I don't know how to express that like a philosopher. I have a B.A. in philosophy, which doesn't make me much of a philosopher. I grew up in east Texas, where the choices were you believed in the Bible literally or you didn't believe in the Bible literally. That was it. I didn't. So it's my own experience with God that tipped me over on the other side. My best analogy is falling in love.

Shanks: *Bart, do you have any reaction to what he says?*

Ehrman: Yeah, I do. It seems to me that Christianity—Christian faith—has always been grounded in certain historical claims, for example, about Jesus. One thing that scholarship did for me: It led me to question historical claims that Christians have made about Jesus.

Shanks: *What historical claims?*

Ehrman: For example, that he was raised from the dead. That's a historical claim. I mean either he was raised from the dead or he rotted in his grave. The kind of Christianity I was in believed in an active physical resurrection of Jesus. That was part of what it meant to be Christian. You had to believe that.

Shanks: *Do you believe it, Jim?*

Strange: I don't believe *that,* but, yeah, I believe in something that means that Christ is alive, and our explanation of that is that there was a resurrection.

I think I'm more or less untouched by the sort of literalist interpretation [Bart is talking about]: resurrection is sort of a metaphor.

Ehrman: If Jesus hadn't been crucified, if he grew up to be an old man and died and was buried in a family plot outside of Nazareth, then for me, when I was a Christian, that would've destroyed my faith.

In other words, the faith is rooted in certain historical claims. As historical claims, they can be shown as either probable or improbable. And I got to a point where the historical claims about Jesus seemed implausible, especially the resurrection. Not the crucifixion—I think Jesus was crucified like a lot of other people were crucified, and I think that, like a lot of other people, he stayed dead. And so, for me, that had a damaging impact on my faith.

Shanks: *Do you feel a necessity to subscribe to the historical claims of Christianity, Jim?*

Strange: In some way I do because in the earliest Christian language there are some of these historical claims. I'm not in any position to be able to check those claims or even decide on their plausibility. I guess I just don't worry about it.

Shanks: *Well, Larry, I take it that you, as an Orthodox Jew, don't believe those historical claims about Jesus.*

Schiffman: No. One of the principles of the Jewish faith is not believing in Jesus. [Laughter] But, like Bart, I of course believe that he lived, preached and was crucified by the Romans.

From a Jewish point of view, these kinds of problems aren't problems. First of all, the Bible was never taken literally in Judaism. It doesn't mean that it's not historical, but it is not taken literally in the Protestant sense. It's not an issue in Judaism. Admittedly there is a literalist strain in a minority of medieval Jewish thinkers and a minority—maybe a growing minority—in modern Judaism, but it's not classical Judaism. The Talmud doesn't take the Bible literally in the Protestant sense.

Jim's approach of taking a kind of experiential approach to the whole thing is one that is much more primary in Judaism.

I get into debates about these historical types of issues all the time, especially within the Orthodox community. I don't want to say they aren't important—they are important. We sit around and debate these kinds of questions all day.

I heard a recent lecture by a rabbi who is becoming a medical doctor. He talked about the problem of creation. And he said, well, evolution is obviously true. What do I do about it if evolution is obviously true? He said that we learn from Nachmanides [a medieval Jewish philosopher and biblical commentator] that nothing in the Bible about creation is intended literally. What's important to me is that I have the experience of God as the creator.

Let's take the problem of evil. Somehow or other, Jews have learned throughout their history the bad news that we can't explain it. We talk about it all the time. We talk about the debate in Job and the various approaches explored there. We see the continuation of these debates in Midrash. But we know that we can't explain evil, especially after the Holocaust. Any person who says that he can give an explanation for the Holocaust is crazy. So the bottom line is that we all go along living with the fact that this horrible thing happened and we can't explain it. Judaism doesn't claim that the individual will get all the answers to everything.

In one of Bill Dever's books, he discusses the historicity of the Exodus, and he throws up his hands. From the Jewish viewpoint everyone says it happened; it's part of our past, part of our history. Somehow or other, it happened. I happen to believe there was some kind of Exodus. But the point I'm making is that the framing of the question, from the Jewish point of view, is very different.

Dever: Which is why I feel comfortable in Judaism. That's where I've arrived—by a long and tortuous path.

Shanks: *Tell us a little about your long and tortuous path, Bill.*

Dever: Well, my father was a fire-breathing fundamentalist. I grew up hearing him preach in tent meetings in the hills of eastern Kentucky and Tennessee. He had a bigger voice than I do. I was ordained a minister at 17, put myself through undergraduate school and on through divinity school, through Harvard, then a congregation. I have 13 years' experience as a parish minister and two theological degrees. For me, it was this typical Protestant conundrum: It's all true or none of it is true. My sainted mother once said to me, "If I can't believe that the whale swallowed Jonah, I can't believe any of it."

When I was writing a master's thesis on the revival of Old Testament theology, I got all excited because at last modern critical scholarship was going to prove the Bible true after all. I discovered the works of George Ernest Wright [a professor at Harvard] and his little book *God Who Acts* (SCM Press, 1960), a classic of the neo-orthodox movement. I still remember to this day the quotation that sort of turned my life around. "In biblical faith," Ernest said, "everything depends upon whether the original events actually happened." And I thought they had, so I went to Harvard to study Old Testament theology with Ernest. I got disabused of that in the first semester, so I shifted to archaeology. The rest is history.

Then, of course, a nice Christian boy like me graduates, and the day after graduation he goes to Israel for a day and stays 12 years. I became the director of archaeology at the Jerusalem branch of Hebrew Union College, a Reform Jewish seminary. I worked on Sunday, my staff was all Jewish; I more or less forgot my Christian background, but I never forgot Ernest's statement.

Then, about 15 years ago, in my archaeological work I began to write about ancient Israel. Originally I wrote to frustrate the biblical minimalists; then I became one of them, more or less. The call of Abraham, the Promise of the Land, the migration to Canaan, the descent into Egypt, the Exodus, Moses and monotheism, the Law at Sinai, divine kingship—archaeology throws all of these into great doubt. My long experience in Israel and my growing uncertainty about the historicity of the Bible meant that was the end for me.

Shanks: *Well, then your scholarship did destroy your faith?*

Dever: Absolutely. Next year will be the 50th anniversary of my first trip to Israel. I worked there for 49 years and let me tell you something: Seeing Judaism and Christianity and Islam up close and personal does not help.

Living in the Holy Land, I became extremely cynical about religion. I began to think, more or less, maybe like all of you, that I had no talent for religion, that faith might be a matter of temperament as well as training. I never had a pious bone in my body. And I realized I was never really a believer, but it just took me 40 years to figure out that it was no longer meaningful. That's when I converted to Judaism. [Laughs] I did it precisely because you don't have to be religious to be a Jew. And I'm perfectly comfortable where I am.

Shanks: *How do you respond to that, Larry? "You don't have to be religious to be a Jew"?*

Dever: That's true of most Israelis.
Schiffman: Yes, that's a fact. A Jew remains part of the Jewish people whatever he or she believes or practices. But in order to be a Jew, you have to have some concept that you believe in Judaism. You have a received tradition from other people—at least *they* believed they received the revelation.
Dever: Absolutely.
Schiffman: You've got to decide: Do I believe there is a God? Do I believe that God communicated some kind of way of life to someone that became Judaism?
Dever: I think Judaism is about practices rather than a correct theology.
Strange: I think precisely that [about Judaism]. Christian tradition, on the other hand, made a mistake because we intellectualized it so much that Christian experience got submerged. Theology was bereft of any kind of experience.
Schiffman: Judaism is different because much of the act of being a traditional Jew is intellectualizing. Study becomes a form of worship.
Strange: Yes, it does precisely.
Schiffman: Study is worship. So a person who claims not to be a believer may be doing worship in some form. You could study the whole Talmud and say, "I don't believe anything."

But I think modern Judaism goes too far with the notion that you don't have to believe anything to be Jewish. You don't in the sense that you're part of the community even if you don't believe. But the question is, doesn't Judaism really have in mind that a person will have certain types of faith commitments that are then acted out in certain ways?

Shanks: *Larry, do you believe in God?*

Schiffman: Yes.

Shanks: *What's the God you believe in?*

Schiffman: I believe in a personal God, but I'm conditioned by the philosophical approach of Maimonides [a medieval Jewish philosopher and biblical commentator]. Does that personal God interfere in the individual's life or not? How would I get close to that personal God? Can I have a mystical experience? These are all debates that Jews have carried on for millennia. So I don't have to have the answer to everyone's questions. I can say there's a lot that I don't know.

An Orthodox Jew can believe whatever he wants and be part of the community, but Orthodox Judaism assumes that a person does believe that there really is a God. There is a force that cannot physically be accounted for. There is a force, even if we don't know how to present what it is in words. Somehow or other God reveals himself or his will to humanity. This revelation and its experience constitute in some mystical way, if not in a physical way, the Torah, the Prophets, the Writings. Otherwise, you could be a Jew, no question, but let's face it, an Orthodox Jew, some way or another, believes that. How you account for that, with the many philosophical issues, theological issues, and scholarly issues and your own perceived experience, I think that's what Jewish theology and philosophy are all about. Obviously, I don't have all the answers.

Shanks: *How do you react to that, Bart?*

Ehrman: It's very interesting, because two of us have remained within our religious traditions and two of us have left our religious traditions. Bill [Dever] and I have both left our original traditions. But there's a difference between Bill and me. Bill adopted another tradition. It seems to me that, as somebody who has left his tradition, I have to decide if I'm going to believe something and what it is I'm going to believe. And even if that isn't expressed propositionally, there still have to be reasons. Once one leaves one's tradition, it isn't an automatic move for me to go from Christianity to Judaism. There are hundreds of religions in the world. Why would I choose one over the other?

Dever: Well, I lived and worked so long in Israel, all my friends were Jews, I was remarrying a Jewish woman; it was obvious to me that's where I should go. I ended up feeling very comfortable.

I will never forget the reaction of Avraham Biran, who was my successor at HUC [Hebrew Union College], when he got the news that I converted. He said, "No-o-o, Dever, I was born a Jew; I didn't have a choice. But you had a choice!"[Laughter]

But I want to make it very clear. I'm not an atheist. I'm an agnostic. I don't know but I'm willing to learn. Right now the Christian tradition does nothing for me and the Orthodox Jewish tradition does little for me. In my own experience, I find this God so distant that it doesn't make any practical difference. And, for me, I guess the final straw probably was the death of my son five years ago. If I had believed in God, I would have been very angry, but I didn't and I survived.

As the Yiddish expression says: "If God lived on earth, people would break his windows." That's been my experience.

Strange: When my eldest daughter was born with a heart defect, I got mad as hell at God. And I told him so. But I didn't say, "Okay from now on I'm not going to believe in you."

Shanks: *Let me ask the two believers: Is one religion truer than another? Is your religion truer than another?*

Strange: We'll never know that.

Schiffman: I don't believe in pluralism. I believe in toleration and mutual respect. But I do believe that certain things are ultimately true or untrue. I believe that my religion is more correct than some other people's religion. But I'm the first to admit that many other people's religions make them better people and that many things taught in their religions are things that I agree with. We share a lot in common.

A guy came to interview me recently for some TV program about Adam and Eve. So I said that the story of Adam and Eve is like a microcosm of human relations between a man and a woman, about people and God, and about good and evil. After about five minutes, the guy turns off the recorder and says, "I don't understand. Everybody else I interviewed is talking about—"Where is Eden?" "Was there really one human being in the beginning?" I said that is not what this is about. There are major challenges to the Bible if you take it literally, but that is not what matters. That isn't what it means to be a believing Jew.

Maybe I'm compartmentalizing. Maybe I'm being apologetic. I don't know. But the bottom line to me is not only that my faith has not been weakened but that it has been strengthened by my scholarship.

Shanks: *Bart, it sounds to me as if all these people kind of agree with you that the historical questions you're raising about the Bible are of very doubtful veracity, but it hasn't destroyed their faith. They're talking about faith that isn't grounded in historical propositions.*

Ehrman: Yes, but even Larry thinks that at the end of the day you have to believe in God. And then your original question about "What kind of attributes does God have?" matters. Just believing in God is for me an amorphous idea. I think belief has content. Without content it's simply some kind of feeling that you have inside. I think that faith has to have substance. But once you start putting some substance onto that, you get into trouble. Faith in the Judeo-Christian tradition has a God who intervenes. That's what the Exodus event is, that's what the crucifixion is: It's a God who intervenes, and when I look around this world, I don't see a God who intervenes.

Dever: Precisely my experience.

Strange: What I can't help but notice is that two people look at precisely the same event and one sees God intervening and the other does not. Apparently the one who has seen God is either fooling himself or there is something genuinely happening that's going on. Bill doesn't see a God where I'm seeing God.

Dever: I'm glad you do. I just don't need to do that. Religion doesn't do anything for me and it hasn't for a long time, and I've decided I don't need its excess baggage.

Ehrman: I have a different view. I would actually like to be a believer.

Dever: I would too. I wish it were true. I really do.

Schiffman: I see the whole thing as a lifelong quest. It's not that either a person believes or doesn't believe. The life experiences of people are very difficult and very complex, and believing in God is itself a challenge. It's not about whether I know the Exodus happened or didn't happen. It has to do with understanding the difficult world that we're in. Faith is a process.

Dever: A dynamic.

Schiffman: It is a dynamic. A person goes through many experiences.

Strange: It's certainly not just a set of beliefs.

Dever: Or a warm fuzzy feeling. If that's all it is, I'm just not interested.

Schiffman: In Judaism there is actually a commandment to believe. What does that mean, a command to believe? Well, it wouldn't be a commandment if it were so easy. There has to be a struggle that a human being goes through in this complex world, in which we don't really know what's going on. That's why the believer can't say of the non-believer, "Oh this guy is some kind of a fool; you're a heretic, an infidel." No, you're a person who has certain experiences. And you react in a certain way to those experiences.

Ehrman: I think what's happened in the case of both Larry and Jim is that they have a tradition that they inherited. That's the way they were born and raised. The experiences they've had they interpreted in light of that background. When I interpret my experiences, I don't have that background anymore because I've left the kind of propositional faith that I used to have. And so the question for me is, "Why should I believe one thing rather than another?" Why should I be a Jew instead of a Buddhist? There are thousands of options out there.

I just think faith, in order to be intelligent, needs to have reasons behind it. I myself just don't have sufficient reasons for believing in the Christian tradition. The same thing, I think, for the Jewish tradition.

Shanks: *All right. How about a final statement: Has your scholarship affected your faith?*

Schiffman: Perhaps because of my intellectual background—the way I understand Judaism in general—the more I've done in scholarship, the more it has strengthened my faith, even though it has refined it in certain ways. There's a non-literalist tradition that I'm coming from. And for this reason a lot of these issues aren't challenges to my faith. They're rather part of the ongoing debate and dialectic.

Dever: At this stage of my life I'm interested only in finding out what it was really like in ancient Israel, if possible, and I find faith an impediment to that.

Strange: I think I would say that faith/unfaith is sort of a false dichotomy. I think faith always contains elements of unfaith and vice versa. So in a way, we can't avoid it. It's just a matter of deciding what fits and what works. And also, where we get hope from.

Shanks: *How about your scholarship, Jim? Has that had any effect?*

Strange: Scholarship doesn't give me hope. Scholarship is a wonderful intellectual exercise.

Shanks: *The last word is yours, Bart.*

Ehrman: Historical scholarship calls into question certain beliefs and can call into question faith. But it can't resolve any faith issues. There are historians who agree with everything that I think about the historical Jesus, about the New Testament, about the development of Christian doctrine, and yet they're professors in theological seminaries training pastors. If you ask them, they will say, "Yes, Jesus is God. Historical scholarship doesn't determine what we believe." So I think what's important is that people engage in historical scholarship. It's better to have a knowledgeable faith than an ignorant faith, and it may be that it will change faith, but it's not necessarily going to lead somebody to agnosticism.

Shanks: *Thank you all very much.*

CHAPTER TWO

WRESTLING WITH SCRIPTURE

An Interview with Phyllis Trible

Phyllis Trible

Phyllis Trible is one of the most distinguished feminist biblical scholars in the world and is considered a leader in text-based exploration of women and gender in the Bible. Her best-known books are God and the Rhetoric of Sexuality *(Fortress Press, 1978) and* Texts of Terror *(Fortress Press, 1984).* Hagar, Sarah, and Their Children, *co-edited with Letty M. Russell, appeared in 2006 (John Knox Press). In this interview, she dis-*

"Wrestling with Scripture" appeared in BAR, March/April 2006.

cusses how she reconciles her feminist principles with the admittedly patriarchal perspective found in much of the Bible. But she also describes how, in her struggle with the text, she still manages to find inspiration and value even in the most difficult biblical passages.

Hershel Shanks: *Was there a moment of crisis for you when the patriarchy of the Bible first hit you between the eyes?*

Phyllis Trible: My life has unfolded in a somewhat gradual way—perhaps like a flower unfolding—rather than having moments of crisis. There are people who talk about their conversion experiences; they know the exact time and place. My story is not like that. I was always a feminist. It's bone of my bones and flesh of my flesh. I didn't always know it, because there was not always a vocabulary for it. But once people started talking about it, it was a gradual unfolding for me.

HS: *When did the vocabulary come up?*

PT: With the second wave of feminism. Betty Friedan wrote *The Feminine Mystique* in 1963. That started something that resonated in the secular world *and* in the religious world. It started us thinking about these issues. By the early 1970s, women in theology were beginning to speak up and to confront the patriarchy of theological education and the patriarchy of the biblical text.

HS: *In one of your most famous books,* God and the Rhetoric of Sexuality, *you say, "I realize that the theology which informed my life was inadequate for addressing the concerns of students. Nor was it still wholly satisfying to me. Ironically, the mighty acts of God in history proved wanting and the ensuing years have heightened that deficiency." That sounds like a crisis of faith to me.*

PT: No, it was not a crisis. I'm always struggling with the Bible. I'm still doing it—even more, perhaps, than when I wrote those words.

The Bible is a mixture of blessings and curses. It doesn't speak with a single voice. It has competing voices, contradictions in it. As it moves through history, it encounters new settings and new occasions, and we're ever called upon to do something with this text.

The story that I use as a model is Jacob wrestling in the night (Genesis 32:24–30) with what? The stranger? Was it a demon? Was it [his brother] Esau? Was it God? Are they one and the same? At the end, when the struggle is over, Jacob goes away limping. He gets a blessing, but he doesn't get it on his terms—and he limps. I see this as my struggle with the Bible, my wrestling with Scripture.

HS: *There are two kinds of struggling with the biblical text. One is to struggle simply to understand and to plumb its depths. The other is to confront something that is offensive to you, something that you find difficult to accept. You spoke a moment ago about the Bible being a combination of blessings and curses. Well, that's okay if the good guys are blessed and the bad guys are cursed. But sometimes a curse is undeserved, and you have to struggle with something you find unpleasant, even offensive.*

PT: Absolutely. It's not a matter of a Deuteronomic view in which good gets rewarded and bad gets punished. It's far more mixed than that.

HS: *What do you do when you hit something in the Bible that's unfair to women, yet it seems to be what's prescribed in the Bible?*

PT: One obvious answer is you produce *Texts of Terror* (probably Trible's best-known work).

HS: *The plight of Hagar, Abraham's concubine (Genesis 21:9–21), is one of the passages featured in* Texts of Terror. *She was treated badly.*

PT: Yes.

HS: *She gave this man his first son [Ishmael] and served his purpose and was then thrown out into the desert, supposedly to die.*

PT: I'm still working on Hagar. The more deeply I get into that text, the more puzzling it becomes and the more stimulating and provocative. She's one of the most amazing characters in all of the Bible. Her distinctiveness is there, but it doesn't jump out. I now have a list of 12 firsts about Hagar. She is the first runaway slave. She's the first divorced woman. She's the first single mother. She's the first person to weep. She's the first woman to receive an annunciation.

The problem set up between Hagar and [Abraham's wife] Sarah has never been resolved, and the Bible really portrays Sarah as less than benign. Her last words are "Cast out this slave woman and her son, for the son of this slave woman will not inherit with my son, with Isaac." Then, shortly thereafter (Genesis 22) comes the near-sacrifice of Isaac. And before that the near-sacrifice of Ishmael [to starve in the desert]. Once Isaac is spared, the text kills Sarah; she dies, as though we've got the son now and we don't need the mother anymore. Likewise the text abandons Hagar; it never says anything more about her. So the problem between those two women is never resolved.

HS: *When you interpret a text like this, as you are doing brilliantly, is there a difference between saying, "Okay, it is put there by the author," or is it the case that it is something that your own insights bring to light, that may or may not have been intended by the author?*

PT: The latter for sure. I would never claim that the comments I make about the text are necessarily the intention of the author.

Traditional biblical scholarship has focused on authorial intentionality, but there has been a shift. And the place where I work is at the intersection of text and reader. The reader can be any number of readers: ancient readers, modern readers, myself.

Authorial intentionality is a problem, because often we don't know the intentionality of the "authors." So what do we do? We take the text and use it to try to discern the intentionality of the author. Then we use what we get from the text as a way of *controlling* the text. So it's a circular pattern. Though that approach has sometimes been helpful, that's not the only way to read a text.

HS: *Why the Bible? What is special about a tale from the Bible? Why the story of Hagar? Why not some very deep novel?*

PT: It could be some deep novel. Whatever one's text is, we all live by myths in the broad sense of some kind of text by which or through which we read the world.

HS: *Myth implies it isn't true.*

PT: No, no, no. That's a popular meaning of myth.

HS: *What do you mean?*

PT: A worldview. A place where we stand. A story by which we live. That's what I mean by myth. For me, the Bible is that major story.

HS: *Is the Bible sacred?*

PT: What does sacred mean?

HS: *That was the next question I was going to ask you. What makes the Bible special—just simply the historical fact that it has shaped Western civilization?*

PT: That's a major reason why it's special. We can't get away from it, no matter how much we try.

HS: *If we can't say whether it's sacred or not, what about a word like "holy"?*

PT: Those words don't really resonate with me, because I don't know where you're going with them, what you intend to do with them. I don't even like using the phrase that the Bible is the word of the Lord. The Bible doesn't use that phrase, except in particular genres. "The word of the Lord" is a prophetic genre, but that phrase does not appear at all in a book like Genesis, so I shy away from it.

HS: *What differentiates the Bible, say, from Shakespeare?*

PT: I ask myself that question, and if I had a clear answer, I'd give it to you.

HS: *You can look at a text from many different perspectives. You can look at it as a woman. Someone else might look at it as a person of color, or as another minority or a Jew who feels the weight of that tradition.*

PT: That's right. And you can have a mix of those things. I look at it not only as a woman but as a feminist and as a white woman. All those things. It's a mix.

HS: *What's the difference between a feminist and a woman?*

PT: Not all women are feminists.

HS: *Can a man do feminist criticism?*

PT: It is difficult, but not impossible.

HS: *Why is it difficult?*

PT: Well, to begin with, most men have grown up in a male culture, and they have absorbed the values of that culture. But there are some who can transcend that. That's always a joy when it happens.

HS: *Can I talk to you a little about Adam and Eve?*

PT: "Eve and Adam" would be better.

HS: *Why?*

PT: It got your attention for one thing. It shifts the whole discussion. It undercuts the concept of order, the man first and the woman second.

HS: *Is there something implied in that, that God didn't create man first?*

PT: Yes, I would hope so.

HS: *Is the text anti-feminist?*

PT: Why would it be considered anti-feminist?

HS: *Because God created man first.*

PT: No, "he" didn't.

HS: *Do you question that in the Bible he created man first?*

PT: I do, I do question it. I do.

HS: *As I read the story, he created man, then he created woman.*

PT: That's the traditional way of reading the story. The text says that "Lord God formed *adam* [אדם, pronounced a-DAHM] from *ha-adamah* [האדמה]." In Hebrew that's a pun. It's very difficult to take a pun and translate it into another language. Traditionally the verse is translated, "Lord God formed man from the dust of the ground" (Genesis 2:7). You lose the pun when you do that. Furthermore, there is nothing in the statement about the sexuality of this creature. Sexuality is based on what happens later. All we are told at this point is that the "creature" (a better translation than "man") is made of dusty earth and divine breath and it has nostrils. ["He breathed into his nostrils the breath of life" (Genesis 2:7).] Now, you tell me how that equals a gender definition.

Why don't we translate it preserving the pun? "God created the human from the humus" or "God created the earthling from the earth"? Already we've made a tremendous difference in how we conceive the story, and we are more faithful to the Hebrew.

I find nothing in the story about human sexuality until God puts that creature to sleep and performs surgery on that creature and out of that creature come two creatures. There is not a word in the story about sexuality until the woman appears. It is when the woman (*isha*) appears that the man (*ish*) appears. Sexuality is simultaneous for male and female.

My purpose is not to promote my view over or against somebody else's view of the text, but to look at the text and see how many ways it can be interpreted. If you want Genesis 2:7 to be an androcentric text, you can have it.

HS: *What does androcentric mean?*

PT: Male-centered. If you want it to be a male-centered text, if you want the traditional view that man was first and woman was second and she's subordinate, you can read the text to fit that interpretation. But there's also another reading—within the text, within its vocabulary, within its syntax, within its order—a counter-reading. No text is locked into a single reading. This raises a big question for us: How do you adjudicate readings? But I never think you have to come out with one reading and say that this is the absolute, the only, the sole reading of the text. Some readings may be better and more persuasive than others, however.

HS: *What about the other story of the Creation (in Genesis 1)? There—and I'm reading your translation from* God and the Rhetoric of Sexuality*—"God created humankind in his image, in the image of God created he him, male and female created he them." The last point in that is "male and female created he them." But before that it says "in the image of God created he him," according to your translation. What do you do with that?*

PT: Yes, that's what the Hebrew says grammatically. And as you know, in Hebrew there's no neuter gender, so you must have either a masculine or feminine. That's a grammatical problem that we can't really solve. But you could say "God created that one," and try to get around it, not using gender-specific language.

HS: *Would the Hebrew bear that translation?*

PT: Yes.

HS: *What about the phrase* ezer k'negdo *in Genesis 2:18? That's traditionally translated as saying that the woman is a "helpmate" or "fitting helper" to the man. What do you do with that?*

PT: A lecture by a teacher of mine, Samuel Terrien, started my thinking about another way to read that garden [of Eden] story, quite different from the traditional reading.

For example, when the woman is having the conversation with the serpent, she is depicted as quite intelligent and informed. Before she eats the fruit, she considers all the possibilities. By contrast, look at the man. He's certainly not depicted the way a patriarch would be. He is passive, bland and belly-oriented.

Another thing that Terrien said: In the Bible that word *[ezer]* most often refers to God. So there the helper is the superior one. Terrien told us that in no way does this word connote inferiority or subordination. So I took that as a clue and then I worked on it. *Ezer k'negdo* is "one who is equal to or like unto—mutuality."

HS: *There is a traditional Jewish interpretation that's very similar to that. As described in the text, Adam is a shlemiel. He needs a strong woman to make a man of him.*

I know your field is not New Testament, but what do you do, for example, with Colossians 3:18: "Wives, be subject to your husbands, as is fitting in the Lord"? Or Ephesians 5:22–23: "Wives, be subject to your husbands, as you are to the Lord. For the husband is the head of the wife just as Christ is the head of the church"?

PT: Yes, pretty bad. Several things come to mind. You probably know the view of some New Testament feminists: that Jesus' circle practiced egalitarianism and then Paul was divided on the subject, neither male nor female. Paul never made up his mind on it, and the post-Pauline church went with the inferior side of it. So you might chart that kind of scheme. What you quoted would be a text that works as curse, not as blessing. You bring texts into conversation, one with another; you can counter one text with another text. Now, the devil can do that as well as other people. In fact, that happens with the temptation of Jesus.

Another observation on those texts is that they are historically conditioned texts. To what extent do they impose upon us (if you think about the authority of the Bible in this connection)? For me, authority does not necessarily mean command or imperative. The Bible is not a "should" book from beginning to end. There is such a thing as the authority of a mirror. You look in the mirror in the morning, and it shows you something you don't particularly like, so it gives you a choice to do something about it. The Bible is a reflection of the whole panorama of life, and therefore places upon us the responsibility to make choices. I find that theology in the Bible itself. I find it in Deuteronomy, not that I accept the whole theology of Deuteronomy, which is so stark; it's either you obey God and are blessed or you disobey and are cursed. It's much more difficult than that. But the concept of blessing and curse is a valuable concept. In the sermon that Moses preaches, God says, I set before you blessing and curse, good and evil, and you choose. So the responsibility is on us to choose. The Bible sets before us blessing and curse, good and evil, and it tells us to choose. It doesn't make the choice for us. The text that in one setting can be a blessing, in another setting can be a curse.

I'll give you an example: The Book of Ruth. I think of the Book of Ruth as a wonderful blessing. But you try telling that to Christian women in Asian cultures that are influenced by Confucianism. Some of the women go berserk because, in their culture, the Book of Ruth is used to control a daughter-in-law by her mother-in-law. In that culture, the whole story functions often as a curse for those women. I'm told that in some Korean marriage ceremonies a young woman has to pledge allegiance to her mother-in-law with the words of Ruth to Naomi. ["Where you go, I will go; where you lodge, I will lodge; your people shall be my people, and your God, my God. Where you die, I will die—there will I be buried" (Ruth 1:16–17).] The Korean version stresses the vow of one woman to another, her mother-in-law. So how can you say the Book of Ruth is always a blessing? No! Setting makes a difference. Reader response makes a difference.

HS: *Why do you think the book is a blessing then?*

PT: I think that it's a powerful story of two women working out their own salvation in an alien and hostile environment. Naomi has nothing. She's bereft of husband and children. And then Ruth makes this radical choice to break with the past and to follow this woman. You see these two women struggling throughout the first three chapters of the book. Then, in the fourth chapter, all their struggles are with men who come in and take over. For a while it's disappointing. But at the very end of the story, the women of Bethlehem come back in, and they claim the story and conclude the story by speaking to Naomi. So I see it as two women struggling for survival in a world that would defeat them or oppress them in some way. I see them as working out their own salvation.

HS: *And Ruth the Moabite becomes the great-grandmother of King David.*

PT: That traditionally has been given a positive interpretation—that Israel is inhabited by strangers and foreigners, beginning with Abraham and Sarah, and that Israel welcomes the stranger and foreigner. Then, you can go to other texts where Israel is not so welcoming of the stranger and the foreigner. In that case you set up a dialogue—a tension between and among texts.

I'd like to go to a second example of a text that can work both as a blessing and a curse. I was lecturing on that horrible story of the unnamed woman in Judges 19, gang-raped through the night, murdered and finally dismembered. Reading a story like that, how could anyone see it as a blessing? After my lecture, a woman came up to me weeping. She said to me, "I didn't know the Bible had a story like that." I expected her to recoil in horror. But she did quite the opposite. She said, "Physically I have not been dismembered, but I have been raped, and I have been psychologically murdered. To know that the Bible is telling my story makes all the difference to me." Right before me, she claimed that story as a blessing for herself, because it was a mirror of what she had experienced. I was just startled by that. It helped me to see that you never throw away any part of the Bible. You never know when and in what situation it will relate to a reader.

HS: *(softly) Wow.*

PT: Yes.

HS: *But aren't you still left with the male language of faith and the dominance of male language in Scripture? Isn't there a bottom line that you have to reject?*

PT: The Bible is too full of its own contradictions and diversities for me to want to do that. One uses the small things to confound the large things, or uses the foolish things to confound the wise things. You live by faith in the remnant. You do acts of subversion. The prophets were subversive figures. There are models like that in the Bible that I cling to. I'm not going to let the Bible go, and I'm not going to let anyone reduce it to one thing; I'm not going to turn it into a feminist document either. It is through and through androcentric, male-centered and patriarchal. Nevertheless, it does not speak with one voice. Readers interacting with it can do things to the text that bring out countervoices within it.

HS: *There's no residue of bitterness in your feelings toward the Bible, is there?*

PT: No.

HS: *Are you Christian?*

PT: Yes.

HS: *What does that mean?*

PT: It means taking the major symbols of Christian faith and using them, appropriating them. But I am so much embedded in Tanakh [the Hebrew Bible] that I see the so-called New Testament as a midrash [an expansion of the text in Jewish tradition] on Tanakh, even as the Talmud is a midrash. I think that the major categories of faith in the Second Testament [New Testament] are derived from the First Testament [Hebrew Bible].

As a Christian, I'm not centered in the Second Testament. If that sounds like a contradiction, so be it. I see Scripture moving from one testament to the other, but I don't see the Second Testament being dumped back onto the First as the controlling voice.

HS: *We haven't spoken about faith.*

PT: Faith is a constant in my thinking, whether I've said it or not. I see this wrestling with the Bible as a wrestling with faith.

HS: *And God?*

PT: Yes...if you want to say faith in God, yes.

HS: *You hesitated.*

PT: Yes, because that's a cliché, faith in God.

HS: *How would you phrase it?*

PT: God...it's hard. Who is that stranger in the night? Is it God? Is it a demon? Are they the same? So yes, I struggle with the divine world, with who we are as creatures. "Creatures" presupposes a creator. All of those things are involved in faith in God. Faith does not come easily or simply, so I worry about it. I do say to whoever that stranger is, I will not let you go unless you bless me. But I don't think that blessing, to follow the story, will come on my terms. So there is an agony in the struggle for faith. I am not with those people who want to rush to the Resurrection to solve everything, because I'm still at the Crucifixion. A theology of the cross—that's where we are, in a world of deep suffering and many unknowns. We somehow have to wrestle to come to some kind of healing and redemption within that world. I think the Bible is a major resource for that wrestling. But the answer is "Not yet."

CHAPTER THREE

CONTRASTING INSIGHTS OF BIBLICAL GIANTS

An Interview with Elie Wiesel and Frank Moore Cross

From left: Elie Wiesel, Hershel Shanks and Frank Moore Cross

Elie Wiesel and Frank Moore Cross, each a towering figure in the field of biblical studies, met for the first time at this interview to discuss their complementary approaches to Scripture. Wiesel, who survived Auschwitz and Buchenwald, is widely considered a universal moral beacon and the conscience of humanity. He was awarded the Nobel Peace Prize in 1986. Cross, now retired from Harvard University, long held one of this country's most prestigious academic chairs and is a leading authority on the Dead Sea Scrolls. Wiesel brings to the Bible the world of traditional Jewish learning, while Cross embodies the most distinguished Western critical scholarship.

"Contrasting Insights of Biblical Giants: BAR Interviews Elie Wiesel and Frank Moore Cross" appeared in BAR, July/August 2004.

Hershel Shanks: *I have known each of you for many years. And I know that the Bible has been a central influence in your lives—but in a very different way. In truth, you inhabit very different biblical worlds.*

Both of you are giants, dare I say nephilim *[giants; see Genesis 6:4; Numbers 13:33], in your world. For 35 years, Frank Cross held one of the most prestigious chairs in academia: the Hancock Professor of Hebrew and Other Oriental Languages at Harvard University. I believe that's the third oldest university chair in the country, isn't it?*

Frank Moore Cross: Yes.

Shanks: *I don't think there is any other professional Bible scholar who is more respected and honored. Now 82—and presumably full of wisdom [all chuckle]—Frank has just been honored with a heavy tome of his professional papers republished under the title* Leaves From an Epigrapher's Notebook: Studies of Ancient Semitic Texts *(Eisenbrauns, 2003).*

Frank is also a leading Dead Sea Scrolls scholar, which he's been since they were discovered more than 50 years ago. He's just completing an edition of one of the most significant scrolls for biblical studies, the Book of Samuel from the Dead Sea Scrolls. And it would be hard to find a more influential book of biblical studies than his Canaanite Myth and Hebrew Epic *(Harvard University Press, 1973).*

Elie Wiesel has for years served as the moral compass of the civilized world. For many of us, including me, he has defined the Holocaust. Awarded the Nobel Peace Prize in 1986, he is also the author of more than 40 books. As relevant as anything to today's discussion are the insights into the biblical texts that are contained in his lectures and books. They include Messengers of God *(Random House, 1976),* Five Biblical Portraits *(University of Notre Dame Press, 1978) and* Wise Men and Their Tales: Portraits of Biblical, Talmudic and Hasidic Masters *(Random House, 2000). As long as I'm giving a little hype, I can't resist saying that Elie has also written a number of pieces for* Bible Review, *for which I serve as editor. Interestingly enough, I think that until today, the two of you have never met. Is that right?*

Cross: Yes.
Elie Wiesel: Except in books.

Shanks: *I have my own ideas about the differing ways you two relate to the Bible, but I wonder if we might begin with a broad-based inquiry: How do you relate to the Bible—as historian, as literary critic, as text critic, as a person of faith, as keeper of a tradition?*

Wiesel: I am not so sure that there is much difference between the two of us. We have a text before us, an ancient text, a living text, and we try to enter it, not only to decipher it, but to penetrate it, to become part of it, similar to the way every student becomes part of a teacher's texture. That's how I see our two differing approaches. We differ simply because of our differing backgrounds. But we have the same fervor, the same passion when in front of us is a page, a unique page—every page is unique—of the Pentateuch. I see history in it. I see revealed truth in it. I see in it human holiness as much as divine inspiration. Wherever you open it, any page, you *know* that you are in the presence of something that exists nowhere else.

Shanks: *Do you agree, Frank? Do you think about the Bible the same way?*

Cross: I think that there is a certain schizophrenic aspect to my own relation to the Bible. In my work, I attempt to deal with the Bible as I would deal with any work of literature. And to treat the history of Israel as I would treat the history of England or Russia or China; that is, an attempt at a scientific, historical approach. I am particularly fascinated with origins. Most of my professional work has been in these areas—as a historical critic, as a literary critic. I've done very little in the history of interpretation [as Elie Wiesel has]. I've been interested in it, but I have not contributed to that field, really.

On the other hand, the Bible is a book that has shaped my life, my beliefs, my ethics, my moral concerns, my religious outlook.

This is not something, however, that I have taught or written about. This has been, if you wish, a private aspect. I've been on a faculty in a university, and I felt it was incumbent on me to deal with the Bible not as something I was attempting to convert people to, or to have them enter into my religious experience, but rather as an academic and scientific discipline. So I think that there are these two very different sides to my relation to the Bible: one, my professional life; the other, a more private concern, interest and fascination with the Bible.

Shanks: *Your father was a minister?*

Cross: Yes.

Shanks: *What denomination?*

Cross: Presbyterian. But I did not take the Bible seriously until I was forced to take Hebrew at McCormick Theological Seminary [in Chicago]. I had to take Hebrew, so I began to read prophetic poetry, and suddenly it became the life I wanted to spend.

Shanks: *Elie, you wrote that as a child you used to tell your grandmother what you had learned the past week. How old were you at that time? You must have been a child, even before entering school.*

Wiesel: Oh, yes, we started very young.

Shanks: *Where?*

Wiesel: In my little town, Sighet, which is in Romania, Hungary-Romania, but a real *shtetl,* a little [Jewish] village—and we began with the Chumash [Pentateuch], probably at age four.

Unlike you, Professor Cross, I do not deal with the text scientifically. I read it, I'm interested in its layers of meaning, but my relation to it is much more an emotional one. It's been my passion almost from my youth. I want to go back to the child I used to be, and to read with the same naiveté. I want to leave science aside and go back to the pure perception offered to me in the text that is waiting there for me year after year.

I remember one day I came home and shouted to my grandmother, "Grandma, Sarah is pregnant!" [All laugh]

Poor Sarah! For weeks before I had read how difficult it was for her to get pregnant. "Grandma! I have news for you!" "What did you learn?" "I have news, Grandma: Sarah is pregnant!" (Genesis 16–21)

Shanks: *Among your other roles in life, Elie, you, too, are a university teacher—at Boston University. And you teach Christian students, as well as Jewish students and perhaps Muslim students.*

Wiesel: Yes, but I really don't teach the way Professor Cross does. I don't teach the text the same way he does. I teach biblical themes, biblical events. I try to see their moral relevance and, of course, to admire the literary beauty of the text. Prophetic poetry: No one has written the way Isaiah does. The royal style, the majesty of the language. He is called the prince of the prophets. *No one* has written like that. I've studied ancient literature, Homer, for example, but it's not the same thing.

Shanks: *That is somewhat different from your university approach, Frank. Just for fun I picked up your* Canaanite Myth and Hebrew Epic, *and looked in the index for the word "Talmud." It wasn't there.*

Wiesel: Your next book.
Cross: I do have it at home. I have a concordance to the Talmud at home, which I have to use.

Shanks: *When Elie was recalling his childhood and his study of the Bible, he said that there was something that was always asked: "Und vos zogt Rashi?" "And what says Rashi?" Who is Rashi, Elie?*

Wiesel: He was the greatest commentator we ever had. [Rashi is an acronym for Rabbi Shlomo ben Isaac; he lived in France from 1040 to 1105, and his commentaries on the Bible and Talmud are an essential part of a traditional Jewish education.—**Ed.**]

Shanks: *Frank, would you ever ask a question like that? Have you ever used Rashi?*

Cross: Yes, I have referred to him on occasion, but I doubt that you will find his name in any of my indices. In my view, he is important in the history of interpretation; and that is a subject I have not approached directly.

Shanks: *Is it fair to say that you are interested more in history?*

Cross: Certainly professionally, yes. And literary criticism, the structure of poetry. But it is primarily as a historian that I work, although text criticism and literary criticism are very much a part of my interests. The history of interpretation is fascinating; but that is something else. It has been said that in order to pursue the history of biblical interpretation, you must include the whole philosophy of the West, which informs it at every stage.

Shanks: *What about rabbinic tradition? That apparently is not part of your focus.*

Cross: No, that belongs to the history of interpretation, as do the Church Fathers.

Shanks: *Elie, I get the feeling—this seems strange to say—but in your approach to the Bible, history doesn't really matter.*

Wiesel: Oh, it does matter. Everything matters. But I have priorities. For instance, for me to know whether there were two Isaiahs or one is less important than the text itself. Of course I read the arguments for and against. But it's not my task in life to say there were two or three authors of Isaiah's book, or how many authors there were of Deuteronomy. This is not what I'm doing.

Shanks: *Is that what you are doing, Frank?*

Cross: Yes, it is. It fascinates me to analyze these things and, yes, to see layers in the texts and the building up of biblical literature. I think this provides insights that one simply does not get by the direct approach. To put it another way, I prefer to have all of this apparatus—historical, literary, critical—and then. beyond initial innocence and naiveté, to try to achieve a new innocence, a new naiveté.

Shanks: *In one of our conversations several years ago, Frank, you told me: "Israel defined its God and its relation to that God in existential, relational terms. They did not, until quite late, approach the question of one God in an abstract philosophical way. If I had to choose between the two ways of approaching the deity, I should prefer the existential relational way, to the abstract philosophical way. I think it is truer, or in any case, less misleading, to say that God is an old Jew with a white beard whom I love, than to say that God is the ground of being and meaning, or to say that God is a name denoting the ultimate mystery. I prefer the bold primitive colors of the biblical way of describing God."* Isn't that close to what Elie is saying?*

Cross: I think so. I think there we meet.

Wiesel: I would surely have been proud to have written this! [All laugh] For me, it's really simple. Because of my own upbringing and past. I remember when I heard the words "biblical criticism" in my town, it was with disdain: "Biblical criticism? How dare you?"

One day—I remember it was a Sabbath afternoon—I came to the synagogue with a book in my hand. I was never without a book in my hand. It was between the afternoon and evening prayers—we were waiting for Maariv [the evening prayer service]—and we had half an hour. So I went to the bookshelves and looked for something to study. All of a sudden, I saw a volume *behind* the others. I picked it up, and I saw a commentary on the Bible by a certain Rabbi Moshe Dessauer, better known as Moses Mendelssohn. An elderly man came up to me—I was then

*Hershel Shanks, ed., *Frank Moore Cross: Conversations with a Bible Scholar* (Washington, D.C.: Biblical Archaeology Society, 1994), pp. 49–50.

maybe 10 or 12. "What are you studying?" he said. "Dessauer's commentaries," I said. So he gave me a slap on my face.

That was the only time in my life that I was punished like that. I developed an anger at Mendelssohn. Later, I read the book. I realized there was nothing subversive in it. Mendelssohn was a religious Jew. I felt sorry for him. I became one of his defenders. But then I heard the words "biblical criticism" again. And, of course, afterward, I studied it more closely. But, in truth, it doesn't touch me. It doesn't change my attitude toward the text. I say to myself, if the text was good enough for my father and grandfather, it must be good enough for me. I admit, that is a rather personal way of approaching the text—or a prayer.

Cross: I grew up in a household in which the Bible played very little role. My father was a Social Gospel, far-left liberal, and to some degree a mystic. But we did not have Bible readings; we had prayers. My father's religious life was not biblically centered. He was a saintly man, whom I could never emulate, so I went into scholarship rather than into the kind of pastoral activity that he pursued. I became intimately acquainted with the Bible only as a theological student.

Shanks: *How does being a Christian affect your relationship to the Hebrew Bible?*

Cross: Happily, I come out of a Calvinist tradition in which the Hebrew Bible carries as much authority as the New Testament. No different weight is given to one or the other.

The Bible is one, Old and New, in my particular tradition. My own interest is far more in the Hebrew Bible. My religion is more personally related to the Hebrew Bible than it is to the New Testament.

Shanks: *What does that mean?*

Cross: I find myself a little uncomfortable in the New Testament environment. And this is also true of what I would call late Judaism, the Judaism of the Second Temple and later. With the

Hebrew Bible, you're living in an austere world. When you come to the New Testament you can't even swing a cat without hitting three demons and two spirits. And magic becomes something that is everywhere. In the Hebrew Bible this sort of thing doesn't go on.

Shanks: *You have miracles in the Hebrew Bible.*

Cross: You have miracles, yes, but they're not the work, normally, of demons.

Shanks: *Elie, you say you're interested in history. I take it neither of you believes literally in Adam and Eve. Is that true, for both of you?*

Wiesel: I first have to ask Adam and Eve.

Shanks: *You've even written about the serpent speaking as if it were a person. Would you ask the serpent?*

Wiesel: At that time the serpent was talking. In Talmudic literature, certainly in the beginning, he was like a human being—except he was a serpent. But he was talking and walking and probably dreaming.

Shanks: *Do you believe that?*

Wiesel: I believe in the story. For me, it's a story.

Shanks: *It is for you, too, Frank?*

Cross: It's poetry. One must interpret it as poetry. The first 11 chapters of Genesis [the Primeval History] are absolutely remarkable.

Shanks: *You would agree with that, Elie?*

Wiesel: Oh, absolutely.

Shanks: *What makes it a holy text? Are they just wonderful stories created by some ancient storyteller with depths of meaning and a lot of tradition behind them, or are they holy?*

Wiesel: What do you mean by holy?

Shanks: *What makes them Scripture?*

Wiesel: What is Scripture? The Hebrew word is *torah.* Torah means teaching, learning. There is no word in Hebrew for religion, by the way. In my town we studied the five Books of Moses, but rarely the prophets. We studied the Talmud so much that I sometimes knew the prophets because of the prophetic quotations in the Talmud. We almost never studied the prophets themselves.

Shanks: *Judaism is in a sense a rabbinic, Talmudic religion, rather than a biblical religion.*

Wiesel: It's both.
Cross: That's too simple, Hershel.

Shanks: *How would you describe it, Frank?*

Cross: The Hebrew Bible defines Judaism. It's certainly true that the Talmudic interpretations become authoritative and normative, but they are interpretations of the Hebrew Bible. So that is *always* there. I would not speak of Judaism as a Talmudic or rabbinic religion. It's a biblical religion.

Shanks: *With the gloss of the Talmud?*

Cross: Yes.
Wiesel: The Bible is interpreted by the Talmud. Except, in rabbinic tradition, a Talmudic law has the weight of the biblical law. Sometimes we say in a prayer, "Blessed are Thou, O God, who has ordered us and commanded us," to do something. But you don't find that "something" in the Bible; you find it in the Talmud. So Talmudic law becomes as important as biblical law.

Shanks: *In Jewish tradition the Talmud is said to have been given on Sinai.*

Wiesel: Yes, it's called the "oral tradition," or "oral law," given at Sinai.

Shanks: *We've sort of agreed that the account of Adam and Eve is a story, but what of the Exodus? That too, is a wonderful story, but from the viewpoint of an historian, it is—to use a word scholars love—problematic. Let's say there are doubts, to say the least, among many scholars, as to whether the Exodus actually occurred. That's a historical issue. Elie, you say you're interested in history, but I would guess that that's an issue that doesn't concern you.*

Wiesel: Not at all. I personally have no doubt that the Exodus occurred. How it occurred, I don't know. But that it occurred, I have no doubt. For nearly 3,500 years it has left such an imprint on people's memories that I cannot imagine it had been invented just as a legend or a tale.

But even if people tell me they have historical proof [that it is not historical], that doesn't really bother me. I read the text; and then I come to the *Shirat ha-Yam,* to the Song of the Sea (Exodus 15), to the poetry. Who could have written such a poem except someone who went through it? It is so full of life, so full of truth, of passion, of concern. And the thousands and thousands of commentaries in the Talmudic tradition that have been written on it. It had to have happened. But even if not, I would attribute the same beauty to the text as I do now.

Shanks: *Frank has written about* Shirat ha-Yam. *You dated it to the very early time of the Exodus itself.*

Cross: Yes. It is one of the earliest, if not the earliest, pieces of biblical literature that we possess. It is much closer to history than later traditions of the Exodus. As you know, I describe this as part of an epic story that has qualities of history and which also has qualities of the mythological, of an epic.

Shanks: *Elie, would you agree that the story has qualities of history and also qualities of the mythological?*

Wiesel: I would accept it simply because I have a tremendous respect for Professor Cross. But, really, it doesn't bother me.

Shanks: *It doesn't bother you that it may be mythological or that you don't really accept it as mythological?*

Wiesel: I accept it as it is, realizing in my subconscious that there are some great scholars who believe that part of it is mythological. This contradiction doesn't bother me.

Shanks: *What about the miracles? Did the sea part? And does it matter?*

Wiesel: It really doesn't.
Cross: If you read Exodus 15 carefully, it describes a storm at sea. This is the old Yahwistic source. In the retelling of the story in the later Priestly source, it is more miraculous: The water stands up on either side like a wall. There are walls of water standing up. As you move back in time, oddly enough, the story becomes more historical.

Shanks: *Elie, do you see that development?*

Wiesel: I see the story in itself. It is meant to be a source of wonder. That is the object of the story, to arouse wonder in us. We read it with awe because of the beauty of the text, and also the cruelty. We come to the death of the firstborn, the tenth plague. You swallow hard!
Cross: But we're both a long way from the position of the so-called biblical minimalists [see Chapter Five, "Face to Face: Biblical Minimalists Meet their Challengers"]. Some of them see no history in the Bible until [the time of King] Josiah [seventh century B.C.E.].

Shanks: *Yes, the minimalists who come out of Copenhagen, and the University of Sheffield in England...*

Cross: And, unhappily, out of Tel Aviv...

Shanks: *And say that there really is no history in the Bible until the seventh century B.C.E.*

Wiesel: I think that's more political than scientific. But, personally, as a student who loves words, who loves texts, I am concerned with finding something in the text from within. I am looking for the word which is there and shouldn't be there. I wonder, why is it there? Or I look for problems: the *Akedah* [the Binding of Isaac—Genesis 22]. It still baffles me. Each time I read it—and I read it at least twice a year—each time I discover new layers in it. *Always.* So this is of more concern to me than the minimalists.

Shanks: *You wrote that there was something terrifying and fascinating about reading ancient texts, something that filled you with awe.*

Wiesel: Absolutely. Take the story of Cain and Abel. Why were we given that story? Scientifically, you may have an explanation for it, but I'm not approaching it from the scientific point of view. I'm saying: Why do we need that? It's a *sordid* story, a depressing story, a dark story. Why should I believe that I'm a descendant of either Cain or Abel? Thank God there is a third son! (Genesis 4:25) [All laugh] Well, I may be a descendant of Seth. I say to myself, "What does it teach me?" So I go back to all the interpretations in the Talmud, which to me are a source of pleasure and joy. Then I say, maybe this story is not for then; maybe it's for now! It's possible for brothers to kill one another in civil wars. But most important, whoever kills, kills his brother. That's a moral conclusion that may not be there; but that must be *my* conclusion. Otherwise, why read it? Whoever kills, kills his brother.

Cross: "Am I my brother's keeper?" There you have the whole biblical understanding that you are your brother's keeper. You also have a whole other understanding in which you are *not* your brother's keeper. And I've heard some extremely bright people take this position.

Wiesel: My interpretation is different. God asks Cain, "Where is your brother Abel?" (Genesis 4:9) And Cain answers *"Lo yadati,"*—"I don't know" or "I didn't know." Then comes a period, followed by "Am I my brother's keeper?"

I would remove the period after "I don't know." The biblical text does not have punctuation marks like periods and question marks. Where we end sentences is a matter of interpretation. In removing the period after "I didn't know" the sentence would continue: "I didn't know that I am [supposed to be] my brother's keeper."

Shanks: *What about the Patriarchs? Did they exist, Elie, or is this not an issue?*

Wiesel: For me they exist. Abraham, Isaac and Jacob exist today. They are people that you see with white beards. I have no doubt of their existence. Whether every story that's there is a historic truth...Again, I'm not concerned. My approach is not a scientific approach. For that, we have greater minds than mine. My approach is: I am in the possession of a text, it has survived so many centuries, and it is my task, my pleasure, to try to decipher it and find all the things that have been said about these few words by generations and generations of commentators. That is what I'm doing. I don't innovate anything. I'm just repeating.

Shanks: *That statement of yours resonates with me. I think of Abraham, who exists for me in a special way. I often think, what would be Abraham's reaction to something that has happened today, to the way we live, to the luxuries we have? So I can appreciate that. Frank, I have a feeling that you take a sort of double-tiered approach. On one level, what Elie says resonates with you, and on another level, you say, well, it's...*

Cross: It's an epic tradition.

Shanks: *Tell us what you mean by "epic tradition."*

Cross: Well, go over to Greece with the *Iliad* and *Odyssey.* These have elements of history, and they have non-historical elements. It's very difficult to pull them apart. And I think there's not much reason to.

Shanks: *What do you mean by that: "There's not much reason to." If we want to know history, I would think there would be every reason to.*

Cross: When I say it doesn't make much difference, I mean in terms of the importance of the piece of literature.

Shanks: *Were the Patriarchs real people?*

Cross: Yes, there are real people behind the stories.

Shanks: *Did they have those names? Abraham, Isaac and Jacob?*

Cross: The story of Abraham and the sacrifice of Isaac are nowhere in any other tradition. How can you put that aside? If you make a determination that it's not historical, do you throw it away? I don't think we can say whether it's precisely, scientifically historical.

Shanks: *Well, certainly Elie wouldn't throw it away!*

Cross: Nor would I!

Shanks: *I noticed you had a Christian way of referring to that story. Christians call it the "Sacrifice of Isaac," and Jews call it the "Binding of Isaac."*

Wiesel: I think it's the most important event in the Bible except for Sinai.

Shanks: *Why?*

Wiesel: Everything is in it: the promise and the hope and the fear and the challenge and the defiance. The test is a double test. Just as God tested Abraham, Abraham tested God: "Let's see if you really want me to go ahead with it and kill my son." Then the angel says, "Do not raise your hand against the boy" (Genesis 22:12). It was the Angel of God who says this, not God. God was embarrassed. [All laugh]

Abraham is trying to obey God, but not to kill. I feel that

moment is one of the defining moments of Jewish faith.

Shanks: *What does a text critic have to say about the text of the* Akedah *[the Binding of Isaac]?*

Cross: This is a major theme of the so-called Elohist [one authorial strand in the Pentateuch]. It is marked by all of his linguistic characteristics, and so on. We cannot determine what is historical and what isn't. As literary critics, we would understand the importance of this for understanding life, destiny. But the historical question must be left with a question mark.
Wiesel: The story is much more a part of theology than of history.

Shanks: *Is this a divine text?*

Wiesel: Why do you want to know? [All laugh]

Shanks: *My own struggle! You don't need to ask that question, Elie, but I do.*

Wiesel: For the purpose of my life, I don't ask the question. First of all, I believe. I think the Five Books of Moses are inspired. Call it divine. I don't know. But I would certainly call it inspired.
Cross: I think there's a danger here. Back in the mists of time is another story, the story of the Tower of Babel. If one attempts to get to heaven and grab the holy...

Shanks: *Grab the holy?*

Cross: Yes, grab the holy.
Wiesel: To unseat God.
Cross: Yes, exactly.
Wiesel: A coup d'etat [of God's realm].
Cross: If one attempts to achieve deity or to have the holy, he is thrown back; he is refused. His language is taken from him. He can no longer even communicate. That's the Tower of Babel.

The Garden of Eden presents the same story: If you want to make yourself gods, you'll find you're akin to the animals. And, so, I'm not quite sure, Hershel, what you want by your question.

Shanks: *That's a very good answer. Elie, when you ask, "Why do I want to know," I'm trying to grab the holy. And I'm getting thrown back. [All laugh]*

Wiesel: You know what Kafka says about the Tower of Babel: In the beginning there were actually many languages, and then as a punishment God gave the world a single language. And then they stopped understanding each other.

Shanks: *I guess what this is reflecting is my own search for answers that I can't find. Frank and I have examined a lot of archaeological materials in the hope of finding out. If I ever write a book on "How True Is the Bible?" I'll have to start out by saying that archaeology is not the way to find out; that it has very little to say. We are thrown back on the text, for the most part. Archaeology can give us background. It doesn't either confirm or disprove the Bible, but it may illuminate it.*

Cross: I find it exciting to get any historical material from the ground. As you know, I love to put ancient Israel and its literature into their ancient contexts. And to rebuild—that is, to me, a very exciting historical task.

Shanks: *I try to look at the texts and say: Is there a way that I can find history in the texts and separate it from what may be the mythological elements, and I don't find any rules for that.*

Cross: I don't think there are any. I think you can, in this early material, find survivals of culture and customs...
Wiesel: Influences, elements of influences...
Cross: Yes. But I don't think we'll get certitude.

Shanks: *Or even likelihood that this element is historically accurate and this element is not.*

Cross: I think we may very well, in many areas, get likelihood, but not certitude. We don't want certitude anyway, do we?

Wiesel: I don't. I surely don't.

Cross: We want to live in ambiguity. This is the human condition.

Wiesel: Nietzche said: "Madness is not a consequence of uncertainty but of certainty."

Cross: I love that.

Wiesel: Occasionally, I come to moments of anguish in the text. You mentioned Josiah [King of Judah]. Josiah has a tremendous reputation in the text. He rediscovered the Book of the Law; you remember how Hilkiah the High Priest somehow found it (2 Kings 22:8). Can you imagine? The book was lost for so many years. And then he decided to celebrate Passover. The text says that "The Passover sacrifice had not been offered in that way...during the days of the kings of Israel and the kings of Judah" (2 Kings 23:22). What do you mean? Not in the days of David and Solomon? Never before? And what of the days of the prophets? What happened? That's what I'm anguishing over. If the Book of the Law could be forgotten for so many years, who knows what was done to it during those years? Maybe it was lost later, too. And another one replaced it, and that one is no longer the original text. These are questions that perturb me much more than whether it's history or not history. What happened to certain books that the biblical text says were lost? Nobody knows. We know, for instance, of "The Book of the Wars of the Lord." It is mentioned in the text (Numbers 21:14). There was a book: Where is it? One day you will dig and you will maybe find it. [All laugh]

Shanks: *Frank approaches that text about the book found by Hilkiah in Josiah's time in a very different way, as do most scholars. Most scholars regard the so-called lost book as an early form of Deuteronomy. It was written at that time, not lost. It went through several editions.*

Cross: Yes.

Shanks: *And the text says it was lost, but you say it was written then.*

Cross: It's more complicated. There was certainly an old law code which stands behind the earliest form of Deuteronomy. Presumably that is what was lost. Furthermore, I think there was, in fact, a celebration of Passover in the era of the Judges in which the epic was recited in the context of the central sanctuary. That tradition was displaced by the Feast of Enthronement beginning in the Solomonic era [tenth century B.C.E.]. So I do think that the Josianic return to the archaic form of the Passover is appropriate and, indeed, historical. Josiah does go back to a different, earlier tradition, the time of a central sanctuary in which the law code was read. But then there were accretions to the Book of Deuteronomy.

Shanks: *I think this discussion has illustrated two somewhat different ways of looking at the Bible. At the beginning you said, Elie, that you and Frank didn't differ so much. I wonder if you'd revisit that question.*

Wiesel: No, I don't think so. We didn't really differ because we have the same love of the text. We share that love.

As for the discipline, we belong to two different disciplines. One involves research and archaeological materials. Mine is more interpretive. But it is the love for the text that is there, and that is what makes the whole adventure of reading and studying and sharing worthwhile.

Shanks: *What do you say, Frank?*

Cross: There are surely many legitimate approaches to biblical literature, and I think that it depends very much on one's experience and temperament which way one deals primarily with biblical material.

Shanks: *How would you define the different approaches, or are they essentially the same, as Elie suggests?*

Cross: I think they are essentially the same. In fact, we're both engaged with the text. We search for different things, we find dif-

ferent things. There is a side of what he does that I'd like to do, a bit more privately. I'm not sure he is as interested in history, as I am.
Wiesel: I am. Absolutely, I am, but not for my work. I respect scholarship. But I don't like to do things half-heartedly. I cannot do both, really. What I do, I want to do with all my being. I have an open mind—I read, I study, I study your work [referring to Cross] and the work of other people with less talent. But that is not what I do in my writing and teaching. Still the love for the text we have in common.

Shanks: *Correct me if I'm wrong, but I sense that what you two share is that you each have a public relationship to the biblical text and a somewhat private relationship to the biblical text. What is public for you, Elie, is private for Frank, and the reverse. That is to say, the inspiration, the interpretive richness of the text is what Elie does publicly, and his interest in history is his private reserve; he knows that he is not an expert in dissecting the text the way Frank does. Frank, on the other hand, publicly dissects the text but he has a private, passionate relationship to the text that he doesn't often speak of publicly.*

Wiesel: Except that a human being is both the public and the private. We are both, private and public in the same person.
Cross: Yes, we're the same.

CHAPTER FOUR

A "CENTRIST" AT THE CENTER OF CONTROVERSY

An Interview with Israel Finkelstein

Israel Finkelstein

A debate rages among biblical archaeologists: Was there a United Monarchy under David and Solomon? Should impressive ancient structures throughout Israel be attributed to Solomon or were they built a century later? How old is the text of the Bible? A key figure in this debate is Israel Finkelstein,

"A 'Centrist' at the Center of Controversy: BAR Interviews Israel Finkelstein" appeared in BAR, November/December 2002.

codirector of the Megiddo excavations and professor of archaeology at Tel Aviv University.

In this interview, Finkelstein discusses his controversial "low chronology" for the archaeology of early Iron Age Israel, defends his view that much of the Bible's history was only written down in the seventh century B.C., and talks about the influence of the so-called biblical minimalists on contemporary archaeological and historical research.

Hershel Shanks: *Israel, how long have you been the director of Tel Aviv University's Institute of Archaeology?*

Israel Finkelstein: Six long years. I hope to retire soon—if possible. [Finkelstein served as director of the Institute of Archaeology until 2002.]

HS: *You're a young man. How old are you?*

IF: An old man. I'm 53 and I should retire soon and write more.

HS: *How about digging?*

IF: Well, David Ussishkin and I are going to continue the excavation at Megiddo. It's an enchanting site. It's been the cradle of archaeology in this country, biblical archaeology if you wish. It's providing us with a window into the history of this country. And there's a nice swimming pool in the kibbutz. So I see no reason why not to continue excavating there.

We have new insights in almost every spot we dig, almost every issue we touch on. We are excavating in six different fields. There's a big advantage in going back to a site that has been excavated before, because you have these windows into the belly of the mound. And you can excavate at the same time in the Early Bronze Age, the Middle Bronze Age, the Late Bronze Age and the Iron Age.

THE IMPOSING MOUND of Megiddo rises 100 feet from the floor of the Jezreel Valley in northern Israel. Because of its strategic location on the Via Maris, an important trade route, Megiddo witnessed numerous conflicts in ancient times. Its bloody history makes it an appropriate setting for the end-of-days battle predicted by the Book of Revelation—the name "Armageddon" derives from the Hebrew *Har Megiddo,* the Mount of Megiddo.

Since 1994, Israel Finkelstein has codirected, with David Ussishkin, a comprehensive re-excavation at the site under the auspices of Tel Aviv University.

Starting from the Early Bronze I (c. 3500–3100 B.C.), we are uncovering the largest temple compound ever excavated anywhere in the country from the entire Bronze Age—a monumental temple with evidence of animal sacrifice. Only one small piece of wall from that building was previously known. We opened the rest of the area.

In Early Bronze I, Megiddo was the largest site in the country; it covered an area of between 50 and 60 hectares [between 120 and 140 acres]. It was a huge site, probably at least partially fortified.

That tells you that as early as the fourth millennium B.C., you probably already had some sort of territorial entity. You need a significant population in order to build a temple like this. You cannot establish something like this with only 300 or 400 people. You must have some sort of a central site with a countryside relationship. You already have some sort of evolution of a territorial entity, call it a chiefdom, call it an early city-state, call it whatever you want. It's the first time that we have, not on the level of theory, but on the level of what we find in the ground, definite evidence for something like this in the late fourth millennium B.C.

The site also flourished in the Late Bronze Age (1550–1150 B.C.). The city was then destroyed at the end of the Late Bronze Age, in the 12th century B.C. This is what we may call Canaanite Megiddo. But, when the city recovered from the shock, from the destruction, it was still Canaanite in its material culture.

HS: *Who destroyed it?*

IF: Possibly one of the Sea Peoples.

HS: *The Philistines? They were one of the Sea Peoples.*

IF: Possibly. There's no way of knowing. We don't have an inscription saying so.

HS: *Could it have been destroyed by another Canaanite army?*

IF: It could have been destroyed by a neighboring city-state, if you wish, but I think one of the Sea Peoples is the best candidate.

HS: *Is there any possibility that the Israelites were the people who did the conquering?*

IF: Well, not according to my point of view.

HS: *Why not?*

IF: I don't know what an Israelite is in the 12th century B.C.

HS: *In other words, archaeologically, you don't feel you can identify an Israelite?*

IF: Yes. If you think that a gang of 'Apiru or Habiru, an uprooted population, or Shasu, or whatever, in the 12th century could be identified as Israel, and, that in the turmoil of the 12th century, they took over a city, then it's a possibility. But I don't believe in a functioning, coherent ethnic entity named Israel as early as the 12th century.

HS: *When would you speak of such an Israel?*

IF: I suppose that in the Canaanite highlands, there were groups who identified themselves as Israel as early as the time of the Merneptah Stele [see "The Merneptah Stele: Israel Enters History," p. 101]. You do have some people identifying themselves—or being identified by the Egyptians—as Israel.

HS: *When was that?*

IF: In the late 13th century, almost around 1200 B.C.

The question, however, is not whether you have a group of people, 'Apiru or Shasu, one of whom is called Israel. The question is when something larger and more significant grew out of that, something that has a territorial aspect to it. When we speak about a territorial entity, I would say definitely by the tenth century and possibly before. But how much before, that's a big question.

The Bible portrays mainly the realities of the time of its compilation (regarding the Book of Joshua, the seventh century B.C.) and a little bit before. It also includes earlier material; there is no doubt about it. The Deuteronomistic history [Deuteronomy, Joshua, Judges, Samuel and Kings] includes material that reflects earlier memories. There is no doubt about that. How early, I don't know. I mean these things are not reachable. They are beyond our knowledge. The Bible may even preserve some sort of a very vague memory or myth or folk tales about the turmoil of the 12th century. Who knows? I always say to my students that I will not go to court to say that there was a Joshua or an Abraham, and I will not go to court to say there was no Joshua or Abraham. There may have been some sort of a figure in the very ancient past. I don't know. I can only tell you that the text we have reflects the realities and needs and, if you wish, also the propaganda, politics, ideology and theology of later periods.

HS: *But archaeology has nothing really to say about whether or not there was an Abraham. You say you would not go to court on that* *question. Isn't it true that archaeology is irrelevant to that question?*

IF: Archaeology is almost completely irrelevant to that. Archaeology is relevant when somebody tells me that the patriarchal material in Genesis reflects the realities of the second millennium B.C. Then archaeology is in full steam to prove that he is wrong. Then, for instance, you can compare the names of the sites; you can go to the sites to see whether they existed at that time. There are things archaeology can contribute, but archaeology cannot recreate Abraham and archaeology cannot deny the existence of a person in the very early past.

HS: *You wouldn't expect to find in archaeology evidence of a particular family.*

IF: Of course not. But the Bible in my opinion doesn't give us any solid information about early Israel in the late second millennium B.C., except for possibly shreds of memories here and there, which I cannot trace. They are irretrievable.

HS: *But what you just said is beyond your expertise as an archaeologist. Maybe you are right, but not as an archaeologist, not based on your archaeological knowledge.*

IF: My dear Hershel, let me remind you that there are two approaches to archaeology. Some archaeologists see themselves as dealing only with material culture; and this is perfectly okay with me. I see myself, however, as an historian practicing archaeology. So I'm looking at matters from a completely different point of view. I'm trying to put together all possible pieces of evidence. Archaeology is one. And from my point of view, of course, it is a central one, maybe the most important one, but not the only one. I'm looking at the same time at the biblical text, and at other ancient Near Eastern texts.

Every text is biased, both the Bible and every other Near Eastern text. They are all written from a particular point of view.

HS: *And the interpretation of archaeological materials can also be biased.*

IF: I agree with you.

HS: *And even with an unbiased approach, there are differences in interpretation of material culture.*

IF: I agree. But again, if you ask me whether archaeology can prove or disprove the existence of a person named Abraham, archaeology is irrelevant. But if you ask me whether archaeology can or cannot shed light on a theory that the material in Genesis depicts realities of the second millennium B.C., then archaeology is very relevant.

HS: *An earlier generation of biblical archaeologists tried to show that the patriarchal age could be fixed, archaeologically, in the early second millennium B.C. This proved not to be the case. They were wrong. But that doesn't mean that there were no patriarchs or that the Bible's patriarchal narratives contain no history. It only means that we have failed archaeologically to place them in a particular period.*

IF: At the end of the day, the patriarchal narratives reflect basically and mainly the needs, the ideology, the perspectives of the time of the compilation of the text.

HS: *You keep coming back to the ideology of a later period when the text was composed, and I keep coming back to the questions that our readers are interested in, and that's the matter of historicity. In the case of the Patriarchs, people sometimes assume that because we can't place the patriarchal narratives in a particular period archaeologically that there was no patriarchal age. But that's not correct. There may or may not have been a patriarchal age. We just don't have archaeological evidence to support it or disprove it.*

IF: No, you are wrong, Hershel. The descriptions are fully immersed into the realities of late monarchic times, into the toponyms of late monarchic times, into the states of late monarchic times, into the realities of the seventh, sixth and fifth centuries B.C. Since the patriarchal narratives are immersed in these realities, we have no reason to go and look for a patriarchal age.

I look at it from the point of view of the composition; it does have importance, great importance and great beauty and great meaning and great value. The value is not whether there was or was not a patriarchal age and the value is not in historicity, either. The value is in the message that you have in the text. There is a historical value to the stories, but the historical value is at the time when the stories were put into writing. I have never understood why this history is less interesting than the history of something that may or may not have happened in the second millennium B.C.

When people ask me what's the difference between the way I understand the history of early Israel and traditional biblical archaeology, I say there are two main differences. The first is that in the classical form of biblical archaeology, archaeology was expected to decorate the story. Archaeology was not expected to give its own testimony. Archaeologists started their investigation from the biblical story, and archaeology was expected to give some sort of illustration, nice slides for a talk. My opinion is that archaeology is not in the business of decoration of any text, a biblical text or another text. Archaeology has its own voice. Archaeology speaks with real-time evidence, and in many cases it provides the most important testimony, sometimes the only evidence. And true, its testimony is sometimes problematic. I'm not saying that archaeology is free of problems and difficulties.

The second difference is about the role of archaeology. In classical biblical archaeology, the idea was that you followed the ancient history of Israel from early to late (in the biblical order of events), with archaeology at times decorating and at times correcting the story. You start with Abraham and the Patriarchs and then you go down to Egypt and then you have the Exodus, the Conquest and so on. My point of view is [and this is the main line of *The Bible Unearthed* (Simon & Schuster, 2001), written with my friend Neil Silberman—**I.F.**] that you have to look at the history of Israel in the opposite direction, from late to early. From the biblical text point of view also, you have to go from late to early: First, you understand the periods of the compilation of the text, and then you try to work back from that point into earlier history, in the opposite direction.

HS: *I start with people who are interested in the Bible as a text.*

IF: Me, too.

HS: *For example, whether the Red Sea parted is not a question of history, it's a miracle. You either believe it or you don't. It's a matter of faith. It's outside the function of archaeology or even of history to demonstrate that this happened or that it didn't happen.*

IF: I agree. It's also beyond the reach of explanations that come from the realm of nature. If the Red Sea parted because there was this natural phenomenon, for the believer, that is blasphemy, because God's power is enough to do whatever God wants without being explained later by all sorts of simplistic natural phenomena.

HS: *On the other hand, someone may reason that the ancients understood a phenomenon like the parting of the Red Sea as a God-given miracle, when in fact there is a natural explanation for it. To such a person who sees this text as sanctified by time and as representative of an early people's understanding of an event, they may ask themselves, "What inspired that understanding in ancient people thousands of years ago?" That is also a legitimate question. I believe there are no illegitimate questions, only illegitimate answers. To such a person, he or she may be interested in whether or not there was some natural event that the ancients understood as a miracle. And to such a person I say, "That's a legitimate question." It may not interest you, it may not interest me—or it may. Would you agree that that's a legitimate question?*

IF: Every question, almost every question is legitimate. I don't want to go into the philosophy of whether every question is legitimate here.

HS: *Getting back to the historicity of events in early Israel, I started with a miracle, the parting of the Red Sea. Let's take another one: God told Abraham to "go forth to a land that I will show you" (Genesis 12). Whether God said that of course is a miracle. That's beyond history. That's a matter of faith. But someone may legitimately ask, "Did Abraham come from the east?" Does archaeology have anything to contribute to that question?*

IF: I'm not sure. I think the question should be, "Why did they tell the story in late monarchic times?"

HS: *That's your question. That may not be someone else's question.*

IF: But the question before was your question.

HS: *That's right.*

IF: Who are you representing? The lawyer Hershel Shanks, are you representing the ancient people?

HS: *No, I'm trying to understand your views.*

IF: Okay, so I'm trying to tell you what my question is.

HS: *That's your question, though.*

IF: You just told me a minute ago that every question is legitimate.

HS: *Yes, your question is legitimate, too. But our readers would like to know whether archaeology has anything to contribute to my question.*

IF: My method is to start with the question of why the story was told. What's the purpose of telling this story in the text, a text that was put into writing only at quite a late date?

HS: *Didn't the people who put together the biblical text use sources?*

They didn't just make up a story, did they?

IF: Definitely not. Do you mean written sources?

HS: *They had some written sources.*

IF: How far back do the written sources go?

HS: *Probably to the tenth century B.C.*

IF: Well, on that we don't agree. Take the Book of Joshua, for instance. I cannot imagine the Deuteronomistic historian, who in my opinion sat in Jerusalem in the late seventh century B.C., inventing stories out of his imagination, to sell to the people as the story of the conquest of Canaan. Had he done that, he would have lost his credibility immediately. Definitely, the stories in the Book of Joshua must reflect some sort of traditions, memories, myths, local legends about the destruction of Canaanite cities.

HS: *Written sources?*

IF: I'm not sure. What the ancient historian wants to do is to tell a story about the "early" history of Israel based on memories, but to present it in a way that will be useful for his ideology and theology. Is that right? I'm asking you.

HS: *Yes. I agree.*

IF: So the question then is whether there are written sources that he is using.

HS: *Right.*

IF: And here I think we don't agree. Here archaeology enters the story. The question now is whether there are written sources and how early they are. Yes, there are written sources, in my opinion. The answer is positive.

HS: *There are written sources?*

IF: I think so. The question is how far back they go. We need to look at Judah, right?

HS: *I would say any sources.*

IF: Okay, but we're speaking mainly about Judah, because Judah is in the center of the whole thing. Judah is the place where the history is compiled. And Judah is also the center, from an ideological perspective. So we're speaking about Jerusalem from the seventh century B.C., and whether there were written sources for the historian to use.

HS: *You're saying the final compilation of the text was centered in Judah, because Israel (the northern kingdom) had been destroyed by that time. [Samaria, the capital of the northern kingdom, was conquered by the Assyrians in 722 B.C.—**Ed.**]*

IF: Right, and also because the text reflects only the ideology of Judah. And then, since you have just mentioned the tenth century B.C., the question is whether the historian, when describing the time of Solomon, rushes to the archive in Jerusalem to ask for tenth-century royal correspondence or histories. The answer is negative.

HS: *The ultimate compiler in Judah may have used Israelite sources, even sources from the United Monarchy*

IF: Israelite, yes. United Monarchy only according to your viewpoint, Hershel. I don't think there are written sources from the time of the United Monarchy. Anyway, we look around to see, first of all, whether we have written material, in Israel or Judah, in the what, twelfth century, eleventh century, tenth century? When do we start getting a flow, a reasonable, a meaningful quantity of written material? This is related to a second question: When do we start getting a flow of official inscriptions, ostraca, etc., that may attest to literacy and real statehood in Judah?

As far as I know, there is no evidence for meaningful writing in

Judah, in Jerusalem, in Israel, before the eighth century B.C. Maybe ninth.*

HS: *What about the Gezer calendar, which is...*

IF: Wait, wait, wait...

HS: *No, no...*

IF: Wait, wait, wait. I mean, yes, theoretically, it's possible that there's a single inscription in the ninth century. The Gezer calendar, in my opinion, is ninth century B.C. [not tenth, as many scholars think.—**Ed.**]. In the second half of the ninth century we do have inscriptions in Moab—the Mesha stela—and in Damascus—the Tel Dan stela [mentioning the "House of David"], which was written by Hazael [see p. 104]. Why not Israel? It's possible. We don't have such an inscription from the Northern Kingdom yet, but we may expect one...

HS: *The Gezer...*

IF: Wait!

HS: *The Gezer...*

IF: Calm down, let me calm you down. I said, it's possible.

HS: *The Gezer calendar indicates that there's probably a school. This is a schoolboy's practice text.*

IF: Yes, in the ninth century. Something is going on at Gezer and

*In 2008, excavations at the tenth century B.C. fortified site of Khirbet Qeiyafa uncovered an ostracon with five lines of ancient Hebrew writing, making it the earliest Hebrew inscription ever found. See Hershel Shanks, "Newly Discovered: A Fortified City from King David's Time," **BAR**, January/February 2009. In addition, an early Hebrew abecedary, or alphabetic list, was discovered in 2005 at Tel Zayit (about 35 miles southwest of Jerusalem) in a stratum dating to the tenth century. See Ron E. Tappy, P. Kyle McCarter, Marilyn J. Lundberg and Bruce Zuckerman, "An Abecedary of the Mid-Tenth Century B.C.E. from the Judaean Shephelah," *Bulletin of the American Schools of Oriental Research* 344 (2006), 5–46.

HEBREW HOMEWORK. The small limestone tablet known as the Gezer calendar describes the yearly agricultural cycle. Because both the language and the script contain archaic elements, the tablet is thought to be one of the earliest extant Hebrew inscriptions. Signs of erasing suggest that it may have been a practice tablet, perhaps belonging to a scribe's apprentice.

Most scholars date the Gezer calendar to the tenth century B.C. Israel Finkelstein, however, assigns the Gezer calendar to the ninth century B.C. In his view, "meaningful writing" did not appear in Israel before the eighth century B.C.

the Izbet Sartah inscription [a student's practice text] is probably a bit older. So what? And I even think that there is a possibility that there were royal [Judahite] inscriptions in the ninth century. My friend Nadav Na'aman pointed out—and I think rightly so—that the [biblical] story of the coup of Athaliah (c. 841–835 B.C.) and then the counter-coup of Jehoash (c. 835–801 B.C.; see 2 Kings 11–12) comes from some sort of a royal inscription. It's a possibility. Why not? But a full flow of writing you get only from the eighth century B.C.; in fact, only in the seventh century. Also from the point of view of state formation and evolution of society in Judah and in Jerusalem, I don't see a reality before the late eighth century B.C. when you would expect to have some sort of major writing industry, if you wish to call it that.

HS: *This is after the time of the United Monarchy of David and Solomon?*

IF: Yes, at least two centuries later.

HS: *So you say that there was no state of David and Solomon in the* *tenth century B.C.?*

IF: That depends on what the definition of a state is. We'll talk about that later.

HS: *What do you do with the texts in the Bible that are dated even before the tenth century B.C., even going back perhaps to the 12th century B.C.?*

IF: Like what?

HS: *Like Exodus 15, the Song of Moses (or the Song of Miriam if you want to call it that).*

IF: I am not expert on this. I don't want to speak about it [though the two are considered by some to be of different source and age—**I.F.**], but personally, I do not think that there is in the Hebrew Bible written material that can be proven to be earlier than the ninth or eighth century, except for vague memories, myths and folk tales. You're speaking about written material, aren't you, Hershel?

HS: *I'm speaking about a particular poem, in Exodus 15, which Frank Cross [of Harvard], for example, and other leading philologists and experts in the history of language date to that very early period.*

IF: But there are other leading experts who say different things. It's like the question as to whether material in the Book of Samuel contains written material from the tenth century B.C.

HS: *Your colleague Baruch Halpern [of Pennsylvania State University] believes that it does.*

IF: I know. And then [John] Van Seters [of the University of North Carolina] comes and says something completely different.

HS: *Wouldn't it be relevant to your inquiry whether the Song of Moses had been written out in that early period?*

IF: You caught me here. I'm not ready to answer you at this point. I should go home and look at what scholars wrote, because I don't remember now. If you give me ten minutes in the library, I'll give you an answer. [Biblical scholars have dated the Song of Moses to anywhere between the 12th and second century B.C.; the early date is advocated by only a few scholars, with most preferring a date in late-monarchic or post-Exilic times.—**I.F.**]

I don't remember the Song of Moses, but I know the Song of Deborah (Judges 5), which is also early. I find it extremely difficult to buy this—that you have 12th or 11th century B.C. written material in the Hebrew Bible. There is no evidence of that whatsoever; not a single inscription.

HS: *Don't you think the Song of Deborah is early?*

IF: I don't think it's as early as that. There may have been oral transmission, but I don't think that it depicts a real, historical situation of the 12th century B.C.

HS: *That's a question that's really central to your inquiry, isn't it?*

IF: And I am answering you.

HS: *Shall we get back to the question about the United Monarchy of David and Solomon? You said we'd come back to that later.*

IF: Okay, let's talk about the United Monarchy. I see the fire in your eyes, Hershel, that you want me to speak about the United Monarchy. How can I let you down? You traveled all the way from Washington to Tel Aviv to sit with me and talk about the United Monarchy. Ask me, please.

HS: *Well, there are a couple of questions. Of course, the historical question relates to whether the United Monarchy existed, whether David and Solomon ruled over a united Israel, and what the nature of this entity was—a state or a chiefdom or some other kind of entity.*

And of course this relates to the question of your now-famous low chronology, in which you date things that were traditionally dated to the tenth century B.C. down to the ninth century B.C. According to you, what was traditionally considered the poor material from the 11th century B.C. now becomes tenth century B.C., the period of the United Monarchy. So we want to see if we can explain to our readers this so-called low chronology of yours.

IF: Let me start by saying that I see myself as a scholar standing somewhere in the center between the more conservative camp, on one hand, and the more critical camp, on the other. Being in the center is a very tricky business. If you stand on one side, you are attacked only from one side; but if you are in the center, you are always being attacked from both sides. So sometimes some of my friends from the more conservative camp accuse me of belonging to the more nihilistic approach (or the very critical approach), denying the existence of the United Monarchy. This is not the case. For many reasons I do not deny the existence of David and Solomon. The Tel Dan inscription is one of them.

There was a memory already in the ninth century B.C. that the founder of the dynasty in the capital of Judah was a person named David. I do not deny the existence in history of a David and a Solomon. I must put this on the table, once and for all, in order to make things clear.

However, I definitely have a different view on the extent, on the nature of the entity which was centered around Jerusalem in the tenth century. There was something there in the tenth century, but exactly what it was is the big question.

In order to understand what was there in the tenth century, we have to go back to the matter of dating.

In Jerusalem itself, regardless of the low chronology, we are in an extremely difficult situation. I'm not saying that there is nothing from the tenth century in Jerusalem. But whether you go with the low chronology or a more conservative chronology—the more conventional dating of 10 or 20 or 30 years ago or for many people even today—you are still in big trouble, because you don't have real monuments in Jerusalem from the tenth century.* You definitely have [pottery] sherds. There definitely was a settlement there in the tenth century, but it was not the monumental, glorious, illustrious city described in the Bible.

Before you ask me about the famous Stepped Stone Structure in Jerusalem, let me answer you. Sure, we have there some sort of terraced construction from the Iron Age I (1150–1000 B.C.) that was renovated in the eighth century B.C. So it was probably used in the tenth century for the village or settlement that was there, but it was not constructed in the tenth century.

The conventional dating that we have been using—I'm not using it anymore, but many scholars are—is the system that was established mainly on the theory of Yigael Yadin based on the results of his excavations at Hazor and Megiddo. Yadin did a great job excavating at Hazor and a great job at Megiddo as well. You and I both knew him very well. He was a great scholar. There's no doubt about it, really brilliant. In the 1960s and the 1950s there was probably no other way to describe the finds at Hazor and Megiddo other than the way Yadin described them. We cannot judge Yadin now from the point of view of what we know in 2002 and go back with this knowledge and try to impose it on the 1950s at Hazor. Yadin stated that he had dated Stratum 10 at Hazor and the contemporaneous material at Megiddo to the tenth century based on stratigraphy, pottery and then the biblical text. But in my opinion, he based it only on the biblical text. Stratigraphy doesn't give you a date; it just tells you what's early and what's late. Pottery? I have not seen a sherd with a label, "I was made by Solomon." Maybe you have. Have you?

HS: *No.*

*Archaeologist Eilat Mazar recently excavated a large building in the City of David which she believes was built as King David's palace in the tenth century B.C. See Eilat Mazar, "Did I Find King David's Palace?" **BAR,** January/February 2006.

IF: Good. So then the whole business of archaeology is to find a way to tie the relative chronology that we have established, from pottery and stratigraphy, to tie it into a system of absolute chronology. How do we do that? In the 12th century B.C. there is no difficulty because you have strata with Egyptian monuments mentioning Ramesses III. [This gives us an absolute date because we know when Ramesses III lived—c.1184–1153 B.C.**—Ed.**] Basically, we know where we are.

In the eighth century B.C., we are in the same situation. We know where we are because we can identify the Assyrian destructions of Tiglath-pileser III (744–727 B.C.) at Megiddo in the north, of Sennacherib (704–681 B.C.) at Lachish in the south, etc.

The question is what we do about the eleventh, tenth and ninth centuries? In these centuries there's no way to tie the relative chronology to an absolute scale. There is the Shishak stela at Megiddo [dated by most scholars to about 925 B.C.], but it was found in a dump [not in a stratified level]. The same kind of thing is true elsewhere.

So the only way for Yadin to establish an absolute chronology was to look at the Bible. There was no other way in the 1950s. So he came up with this idea: You have similar gates at Megiddo, Hazor and Gezer [see "Monarchy at Work?: The Evidence of Three Gates," p. 98]. And the Bible says that King Solomon fortified these three locations (1 Kings 9:15). Solomon lived in the tenth century. Therefore the strata with these gates must date to the tenth century B.C.

This whole paradigm is based on a single biblical verse, 1 Kings 9:15. But this verse may reflect a reality different from the time it describes. It was compiled in Jerusalem in later times. Whether it describes a memory from the tenth century or whether it reflects a memory from the eighth century or the ninth century, we don't know. Now, almost 50 years later, when we look at this, there is ample evidence coming from different directions to tell us that something is wrong here, really wrong. First of all, you have wider theoretical, historical questions that need to be addressed, for instance whether Jerusalem—possibly a limited village at the time, not a very significant settlement, not a very elaborate one—could be the capital of a united monarchy extending over the northern part of the country, with its palaces at Megiddo, not in Jerusalem. It's a question that must be addressed.

Then you have evidence of state formation in the Levant, the western part of the ancient Near East. If you look at Moab, Ammon, Aram Damascus and the northern kingdom of Israel, you see that they developed into real states only in the ninth century B.C. That does not mean there could be no great state before them—in the tenth century. But we need to remember that if you say there was a great state in the southern Levant in the tenth century B.C. centered in Jerusalem, then it's the only one; it's unique, and it left no evidence. Other peoples in adjacent regions did not reach the level of state formation at that time.*

Is that possible? Yes, it is possible, but it's highly unlikely. This is just one set of questions—there are many others—that lead me to the conclusion that the conventional dating must be rechecked.

Then, we have more direct evidence that cannot be brushed under the carpet. The first one is the similarity between the pottery assemblage from Jezreel, which was destroyed apparently in the middle of the ninth century B.C., and Megiddo, which according to the conventional theory was destroyed in the tenth century. There's a problem there—the two assemblages are identical. In my opinion, the only way to deal with this is either to pull one down or to push the other up. Pushing Jezreel up to the tenth century is not an option.

Then there is the similarity in architectural details between the palaces at Samaria (clearly ninth century B.C.) and Megiddo, conventionally dated to the tenth century. Again, you either have

*But recent excavations in southern Jordan have uncovered possible evidence of an early Edomite state in the tenth century B.C. See Thomas E. Levy and Mohammad Najjar, "Edom and Copper: The Emergence of Ancient Israel's Rival," **BAR**, July/August 2006.

to push one down or pull the other up. There's no way to pull the palace at Samaria up to the tenth century. The only way is to push the palaces at Megiddo down to the ninth century.

Some of my friends tell me, "Here you are in a trap, Israel. How can you accept the biblical text ascribing the building of Samaria to the [ninth century] Omrides, yet reject the biblical text ascribing the construction of Megiddo to Solomon?" This was the question of Hershel Shanks also.

Here's the answer: Whoever asks a question like this does not understand the meaning of biblical studies in the last two centuries. The study of biblical history is all about sorting history from non-history; accepting one verse and rejecting another. As for Samaria and the Omrides, on the one hand, and Megiddo and King Solomon, on the other, there are several reasons for a difference. There's a big difference between the tenth century B.C. and the ninth century in our historical and archaeological knowledge. In the ninth century, we have evidence for the greatness and the strength and the prosperity of the Omride dynasty in the northern kingdom of Israel. We have the Assyrians referring to the Omride state as *Beit Omri,* the house or land [dynasty] of Omri, which means they knew there was a monarch named Omri who was the founder of the dynasty and the founder of the capital. So in my opinion there is ample evidence that comes from both extra-biblical texts and archaeology for this understanding of the biblical text.

HS: *So you depend on the biblical text for dating the palace at Samaria?*

IF: Not necessarily, but why not? I'm not rejecting the entire biblical text. I'm a biblical archaeologist, Hershel. Well, I can see now that this will be the title of the interview. "'I am a biblical archaeologist,' says Israel Finkelstein." You see, I gave it to you.

But it's different with the stories of David and Solomon. With the Omrides, the text and the archaeology support one another, so why not use the text? Whoever tells me that I have either to accept all the biblical material or reject it all is talking nonsense, in my opinion.

Then there's the question of carbon 14, radiocarbon dates [of organic material found in excavations]. I think that at the end of the day, this will give us a verdict on the chronology, in maybe 20 years. Not now, because for the time being we don't have enough samples, and we are still far from agreement on the interpretation of the results.

HS: *When you say we may have a verdict in 20 years, does that reflect your own uncertainty or are you saying that you will be shown to be right?*

IF: No, what I'm saying is, that for the time being, the results from Tel Dor, even from Tel Rehov and from Megiddo, support the low chronology. It's more probable, but it's not definite. It's not the end of the story.

HS: *For you, is it an open question as to whether the low chronology is correct, or are you certain it's correct?*

IF: I am certain.

HS: *This is very technical material. I think what our readers would like to know is why so many senior...*

IF: You are stepping into a trap. I'm warning you.

HS: *Many of your remarks seem to be addressed to the fact that I oppose your views. My purpose here is to allow you to expose your views to the readers of* **BAR.** *So okay, I'll step into your trap. Why is it that so many leading scholars do not accept your low chronology—Ephraim Stern of Hebrew University, Amnon Ben-Tor, also of Hebrew University, Amihai Mazar, also of Hebrew University, Americans like Lawrence Stager of Harvard, Seymour Gitin of the Albright Institute in Jerusalem, Timothy Harrison of the University of Toronto? Even your close colleagues at Megiddo, David Ussishkin of Tel Aviv University and Baruch Halpern, have not come out in favor of it. They* *take a more stand-offish view. How do you account for this? Is it that they are obtuse, or have they some motive? What is the source of this intense disagreement?*

IF: There is a difference between intense disagreement and a list of names. It's a funny question, I must say. It's the funniest question you have asked me today because it's not relevant whatsoever. If I'm right, I'm right; if I'm wrong, I'm wrong. It's irrelevant that X and Y and Z and A and B and C are against me, and D and E and F and G and H are for me.

Ten years ago there was a great debate in the archaeology of the Levant about the beginning of the Middle Bronze Age. One scholar argued for one position; the other scholars argued for another position. When all the ammunition was presented by the lone scholar who argued for an earlier date, the final doomsday weapon was to say that this scholar was wrong because everybody was against him. Ten years later, the scholar who stood alone was proven right. And the scholars who accused him for standing alone were proven wrong. What does it mean? It means nothing. There's no relevance to this question whatsoever.

But I'm ready to play your game. You are right about one thing here, that it's a very complicated matter. In my opinion, Hershel, the number of people who really understand what this is all about—not in slogans, but who are really ready to go into the nitty-gritty of the pottery and the texts and the architecture and the scarabs, and the paleography—is extremely limited—maybe 20. You can judge only according to those people who publish articles about this debate, not people who say in an article yes, I support it, or not.

In an article that is going to be published soon in *BASOR* [the *Bulletin of the American Schools of Oriental Research*],* I give a temporary list of those who support the low chronology in one way or

*Israel Finkelstein and Neil Asher Silberman, "*The Bible Unearthed:* A Rejoinder," *Bulletin of the American Schools of Oriental Research* 327 (2002), 63–73.

another. It's a very long list, Hershel. [Since you mention names, let me do the same. The list includes Lily Singer-Avitz, Alexander Fantalkin, Norma Franklin, Ayelet Gilboa, Axel Knauf, Stefan Munger, Nadav Na'aman, Michael Niemann, Tali Ornan, Benjamin Sass, Ilan Sharon, Christoph Uehlinger, David Ussishkin, John Woodhead and Orna Zimhoni—**I.F.**] So in my opinion, I am in the majority. You simply have not acknowledged that yet. You have not understood what's going on. If you take away all the declarations and all the big names, all the small names and whatever, and you really look at people who publish articles on one aspect of the debate or another, either on the pottery or about the architecture or about the stratigraphy, I seem to be in the majority.

There is support for my view on the basis of history, on the basis of paleography, on the basis of amulets and scarabs, and so on, from every point of view, from every angle. Some of my opponents are great scholars, and they do publish, so I accept them fully, and their view is extremely important to me. They are real scholars who know exactly all the small details of this debate. But the number is extremely limited. Incidentally, you, Hershel, think that the world, the entire world, is centered in one place in this country, and maybe one place in America. But the world is more complex than that.

HS: *You mean Jerusalem and Harvard?*

IF: I don't mean anything, I'm just describing your point of view. I will name one other place. It's not an important place. Negligible, on the margin. No real education there, no scholarship, no history writing, no biblical history or criticism there. But maybe it is a little bit important. Its name is Europe. Have you heard the name Europe? Europe is the place between the two places, one in America and one in this country, and over there, for instance, I'm definitely in the majority. So what does that say? Does it say that I'm right? No. It doesn't mean that I'm right. But I'm not impressed by any list of supporters or opponents. I am impressed only by evidence.

And I must tell you that I am definitely impressed by the evidence provided by some of my opponents. Some of them are doing a great job, and putting on the table new material, which is extremely valuable.

HS: *Would you name those people?*

IF: Amihai Mazar, for instance.* He's a great scholar who really understands the problem, including the smallest detail in the debate. I'm not going to go farther than that. There are people who really understand the nitty-gritty, and I respect them. I oppose them; we fight each other in writing; we debate each other in lectures; but I hope that we respect one another. I definitely respect them.

HS: *At one point I remember your saying that Ami Mazar was halfway to your position. Do you still maintain that?*

IF: Well, you have to ask him. I think so.

HS: *In what respect?*

IF: Well, I cannot speak for Ami Mazar. You have to speak to him. But the way I understand his position is, first of all, he understands that there's a real problem with the conventional chronology. Secondly, I think he would admit that some of my arguments are strong and should be addressed. He has published scientific articles on several issues related to the debate, and has provided new information, not only saying, you know, X and Y and Z and D and F are against him, and that's why he's wrong. You'll never get this from Mazar. This is not scholarship, it is name-dropping.

HS: *I take it you know that you are a controversial scholar, that...*

*See John Camp and Amihai Mazar, "Will Tel Rehov Save the United Monarchy?" **BAR**, March/April 2000.

IF: What's the meaning of "controversial scholar"? The meaning is you disagree with me.

HS: *I'm not talking about my view! I'm talking about the world of scholarship. One of the things we haven't spoken about is the debate in biblical studies between the so-called minimalists and the maximalists, the minimalists being the people who tend to deny the historicity of the Bible in general [see Chapter Five, "Face to Face: Biblical Minimalists Meet Their Challengers"]. They're broadly represented by a group in Copenhagen, Denmark, and in Sheffield, England—Niels Peter Lemche and Thomas Thompson from Copenhagen, and Philip Davies and Keith Whitelam, for example, from Sheffield. I know that you are offended sometimes because you are lumped with these minimalists. I don't believe I have done that, but it's often done. I was looking at something from a very respected European archaeologist who recently wrote in a very obscure German publication about the utter skepticism "of the biblical tradition" by those called "minimalists." And then he puts in parenthesis the names of Lemche and Thompson, and, "from an archaeological angle, I. Finkelstein." Now, I assume that you would disagree with this, that you are not a minimalist, yet things like this get into print. There are many such instances. I wonder if you would explain your position.*

IF: First of all, you, Hershel, play a major role in the incitement. You have to admit this. You play a really important role in inciting people against each other. I respect and have respected a lot of what you have done throughout the years. But there are points that I don't respect. You know exactly what they are. We have known each other long enough to know where we disagree. The only problem in the last year or two has been that I felt that the disagreement between the two of us got a twist into a hostile direction that really surprised me.

But let's put this aside for a minute. It's not a matter of being offended or not. I am not offended by being put with the minimalists or with the conservative people. The only question is whether my positions are being portrayed properly.

I think that the minimalists—the people you call minimalists—are good scholars, and they are important scholars, and they have contributed a lot to historical and biblical scholarship. We have to listen to them carefully, even when they are wrong. Sometimes they are right. It depends on what, it depends on where; but they have steered this debate—which is a positive debate, an important one. Whatever the verdict is, the debate is important, and the debate is there, thanks to their publications. So we have to be very grateful for their publications. This has nothing to do with whether I agree or disagree with them, but I respect them and I respect their scholarship in the same way that I respect good scholarship from the conservative side, so it has nothing to do with being offended, this way or that way.

In any event, I think that I stand in the middle. When we speak about right, left or middle, we are speaking about the history of Israel. When we speak about the history of Israel, we are speaking about the text of the Bible. I stand in the middle. On one side you have the conservative camp, which follows basically the lines of the biblical description of the history of Israel, from early to late. On the other hand, you have the minimalist camp. They argue that all or most of the material is Persian or Hellenistic [fourth-third centuries B.C.], and it has nothing to do with the real history of early Israel. What they are saying then is that the text was put in writing in the Persian or Hellenistic period and therefore has no value for understanding the history of Israel in the Iron Age.

My position lies between the two. What I'm saying is—and I'm not alone here—that the material was put in writing in late monarchic times, and that it reflects the realities of late monarchic times (the seventh century, possibly also the eighth century B.C.), and that there is earlier material which found its way as memories into these texts.

That is why I don't think that you can put me either with this group or with that group. And the center camp is a big camp. You guys—and here I'm talking to you too, Hershel—you have always tried to eliminate the center camp, or you have ignored the center camp, or you have twisted the ideas of the center camp. But the center camp will prevail. There are many scholars in the center camp—in this university, in America, in Europe, in biblical studies, in archaeology, in history. Why eliminate it? Why describe me as minimalist? With all due respect to the minimalists, I'm not arguing for a date of the text in the Hellenistic period. I'm not arguing for a text that reflects the tenth century B.C. either. So, I'm not offended. I just want my views to be properly portrayed. Please try to respect this modest wish of mine.

HS: *Thank you, Israel.*

CHAPTER FIVE

FACE TO FACE
Biblical Minimalists Meet their Challengers

Clockwise from top left: William G. Dever, Kyle McCarter, Thomas Thompson, Niels Peter Lemche

One of the most controversial issues in modern biblical studies is the increasingly assertive contention that the Bible is essentially useless as a historical source, even for the period of the Israelite

"Face to Face: Biblical Minimalists Meet their Challengers" appeared in BAR, July/August 1997.

United Monarchy (tenth century B.C.E.). David and Solomon, it is claimed, are mythological, not historical. The Bible, according to this school of thought, can tell us only about the period in which it was written; naturally, these scholars contend that it was written late—in the Persian period (fourth century B.C.E.) or even in the Hellenistic period (third–second centuries B.C.E.).

To discuss these issues, **BAR** *brought together two of the most prominent scholars who take this position—Niels Peter Lemche and Thomas Thompson, both of the University of Copenhagen (Thompson recently retired)—and two internationally known scholars who hold, to a greater or lesser extent, differing views. They are archaeologist William Dever [now professor emeritus] of the University of Arizona, and biblical scholar P. Kyle McCarter of the Johns Hopkins University in Baltimore.*

Shanks: *Niels and Thomas, you have been called "Biblical Minimalists," but Philip Davies, one of your group, has called that "a sneering epithet."* What can we call you?*

Thompson: I always thought we were maximalists.

Lemche: We're maximalists because we try to get as much historical information out of the sources as we can. We're historians, after all. The only difference is the amount of information we think we can get out. We try to get as much out of it as possible, but we don't think it's very much.

Shanks: *Is there a name that we can call your school that would be acceptable?*

Thompson: I don't think that there's a real sharp distinction in the work that we do as a group. Our position in terms of understanding interpretation of archaeology historically is not very far from Bill Dever's—

*See Philip R. Davies, "'House of David' Built on Sand," **BAR**, July/August 1994.

Dever: Oh yes it is!
Thompson:—until we get into Iron II [the Israelite Monarchy (1000–586 B.C.E.)]. Then we get sharp distinctions and differences.

Shanks: *Is there a name that we can call your school that you wouldn't object to?*

Thompson: Yes, call us historical scholars or biblical scholars.
Dever: You use "revisionists" as a term.
Thompson: No, I have never used "revisionists."
Dever: You have in your *JBL* [*Journal of Biblical Literature*] article.*
Thompson: I can't remember that. I don't mind "revisionist," but it doesn't seem to signify anything.

Bill, are we dealing with the question of how we identify ourselves, or how you identify us? I know how you identify us. You've been calling me names for about four years now.
Dever: Sir, I have here from the Internet some of this electronic gossip. I'm not the name-caller. You guys have labeled me a fundamentalist and God knows what.

Shanks: *Niels, you said that the difference between you and other schools of biblical historians is that you find less in the Bible. And that's why, without meaning to be sneering, many people do refer to you as biblical minimalists.*

Thompson: We find a great deal in the Bible, it's just that we don't find the Bible to be a historical record.
Dever: Well, what do you find? What's left, in other words? Is there any history at all, and if there isn't, what's left in the Bible that's worth digging for?
Thompson: I think that we have a great deal, in terms of intellectual history, in terms of literary history, in terms of theology, in terms of the self-identity of peoples in Palestine in the second, first century B.C.E.

*Thomas L. Thompson, "A Neo-Albrightean School in History and Biblical Scholarship?" *Journal of Biblical Literature* 114, no. 4 (Winter 1995), pp. 683–698.

Dever: What's left before the second century B.C.E.? We all know that the texts were edited in that period. The real question is how much history is behind the history?

Thompson: No.

Dever: It isn't?

Thompson: No.

Shanks: *What is the question, Tom?*

Thompson: The question, as far as the biblical material is concerned, is what do the texts signify? What do they mean? How do we read the texts, and how do we understand them? The question of history is a secondary question.

Shanks: *I think our readers are interested in history. Is there any history in there before the second and first centuries B.C.E.?*

Lemche: The problem is that there's no coherent history as such except in the form of literature. Biblical literature presents you with a picture, an image of the past, as any historical reconstruction would do. But not very much can come in from the past, as we see it, from this biblical literature. That's for certain. Well, then, what's the Bible useful for as a historical source? For understanding the mental history of the people from the time in which it was composed.

Dever: Are we talking about when the text was edited or when it was composed? We all agree it was edited late.

Lemche: We don't think that there was really a vast distance between editing and composition. You're talking about a rather old-fashioned idea [biblical source criticism], about the ways biblical literature arose. It seems that you're advocating a kind of archaeology of the text, where you dig into the text to lay bare the strata of the text. It's as if you are saying that you are going to try to get behind and behind and down and down. What we are saying is that this is a kind of house of cards, and if you take away one of the cards the whole building tumbles down. It's much better to say, "We have here a piece of literature, reflecting the time in which it was finished."

Shanks: *Is it your view that the biblical author simply made it up, wrote fiction at this late date?*

Lemche: He didn't know what the word fiction meant. It's a modern term.

Shanks: *Well, did he have sources?*

Lemche: Yes, of course he had sources, of course there were traditions. The problem is whether you can get through that screen, back behind it. It's a kind of treasure hunting for historical information. Sometimes there may be some, sometimes not.

The biblical writer placed the text in a so-called historical framework. Take Pithom and Raamses [built by Israelite slaves in Egypt, according to Exodus 1:11]. Pithom was founded by Pharaoh Neco in the late seventh century B.C.E. So it's out of place in the Bible.

Dever: We don't disagree about that.

Lemche: We have a number of historical recollections here, but the biblical writer did not know where to place them.

Dever: I agree.

Lemche: What this means is that he was not really writing history. He was making it up. He didn't know the genre of history writing. Antiquity simply did not know that genre. That's a modern genre. That means there are traditions; the tradents [creators and carriers of a tradition] were creating mythologies. It has nothing to do with history.

Dever: I agree. But the Exodus and the conquest [of the promised land] are a bad case. I agree with you that [the Book of] Joshua has little to do with any historical events. If you guys think I—or the Israeli archaeologists—am looking for the Israelite conquest archaeologically, you're wrong. We've given that up. We've given up the Patriarchs. That's a dead issue. But the rise of the Israelite state is not a dead issue, and that's a better test case. I agree on the late editing of the documents. I agree that there is no connected history in Joshua, but maybe we should look at the Book of Judges. That fits a lot better with the facts on the ground as we now know them.

Lemche: No. One thing is missing in Judges—the Egyptians.

Dever: They weren't germane to the story.

Lemche: Judges really reflects what we call a heroic society, heroic in the Greek sense. It's a kind of history you find in Norse tradition, among the Vikings, my forefathers. We love those stories, but we don't believe them to be true.

Dever: We archaeologists are not trying to prove these early stories to be historical. We get accused of it, but we're not doing it.

Thompson: We don't deny that there's early material in the Bible. But we do think it's small, only fragmentary material.

One of the things we're beginning to investigate is the relationship between the biblical tradition and the Qumran materials [the Dead Sea Scrolls]. In the biblical scrolls [from Qumran], we find the process of biblical formation is still going on. I see the process of the formation of the biblical text as a kind of discussion about tradition. If you compare Genesis, for example, with Jubilees [a book of the apocrypha, sometimes called the rewritten Bible] or 1 Chronicles [which re-records genealogies and some descriptive material in Genesis], you can see that they're taking different positions about traditions that each has collected in its own way. In the Ishmael and Esau genealogies, for example, some elements and some traditions—a very, very small amount—can be dated to the Assyrian period, the seventh and sixth centuries B.C.E.

The biblical books were formed, I would say, in the Persian period [fifth and fourth centuries B.C.E.] or later, when an Israel is possible, at least an Israel of the sort that we have in the Bible is possible.

McCarter: It's true that in the Qumran materials, in the second, first century B.C.E. and first century C.E., we see biblical texts that are still to some extent in the process of being edited. The texts that the rabbis later chose existed in final form thereafter, but there were also alternative texts. That gives us a window on the editorial process that we all agree went on. I think the point of disagreement is that what we see at Qumran—the editing of texts—had been going on for several centuries. That we first see it at Qumran doesn't mean that that process started then or was new then. It had been going on for centuries.

Dever: If you guys say there is something earlier than the second century [B.C.E.] or the sixth century [B.C.E.], I'd like to know what it is. You say there are little bits, but which bits? What is left that can be pre-Exilic [prior to the Babylonian Exile in 586 B.C.E.] in the text tradition, as you understand it, that is historical?

Thompson: The king lists for one. Also a number of names, such as Amuru [Amorite] and Kinanim [Canaanite] and Peleset [Philistine] and Israel and Apiru. Certainly a number of the place names are old. There is a lot of commentary about traditions that are understood to be old; we just haven't yet been able to trace them. But if you want to deal with text archaeology, that's the kind of question you have to ask. I don't want to. But the material is there. I don't see why you find this terribly surprising. Both Niels Peter and I have mentioned these things in our writings.

Dever: Then I don't see why you find it terribly surprising that I take this outline—that's what we're talking about, an outline of some historical events that predate the Exile—and when archaeological facts seem to converge [with that outline], we say they converge. You say there is an outline there; I am saying archaeology can fill in some details. Many times it can't. Tom, you guys seem to think I'm trying to prove the Bible. I'm only looking at convergences where they exist.

Thompson: One point on which we disagree is the outline; we do not see it as early.

Dever: Well, we have king lists.

Thompson: I don't see the Bible as originating stories or traditions but rather as a discussion about traditions, as a collection of traditions.

McCarter: Both Tom [Thompson] and Bill [Dever] have expressed skepticism about what you call the archaeology of the text, the idea of excavating the text for early information. That is a very old enterprise, but I don't think it is discredited even today. Bill doesn't do it, but Bill is an archaeologist. And Tom and Niels Peter [Lemche] are skeptical of it. But I still embrace it. You can still do source-critical analysis to identify earlier strata in a text. I don't mind the archaeological language there. We can find older material within the text. The final form of the text is not the only text to which we can relate. Scholarship has been developing methods for doing this for a number of centuries. These methods are often difficult to apply, but they're valid methods.

Lemche: But you can't really find a time line between the different strata. As Johannes Pedersen [a Danish linguist and biblical scholar] said more than 60 years ago, it's ridiculous to say that the Yahwist [the J strand of Pentateuchal source criticism] should belong to the tenth century [B.C.E.] and the Elohist [the E strand] to the ninth century.* There may be a difference in vocabulary, but in general it's the same language. If you accept the different redactions, the last redaction will redact to the language of the former sources. The whole idea becomes more and more absurd.

Dever: Scholars have been looking for a *Sitz im Leben*, a living context, for the biblical text. I have argued that the best you can do is to find a literary context. But archaeology could provide an independent witness. Take the description of the Solomonic Temple (1 Kings 6). We can show that the text will fit in the tenth and ninth century, but it won't fit anywhere else. Doesn't that suggest that parts of the text may be of genuine antiquity? That's really all I'm trying to do.

Thompson: Methodologically, there's no problem with that. But if we then jump and say now we've found Solomon's Temple, then I would raise a red flag.

*According to the documentary hypothesis, the Pentateuch was composed at different stages in Israel's history by four (or more) different authors/editors, indicated by the letters J (Yahwist or, in German, Jahwist), E (Elohist), P (Priestly code) and D (Deuteronomist).

Dever: If you look at the history of biblical scholarship, almost every school of critical biblical scholarship, there is a parallel in the history of archaeology. The two have taken parallel courses. Tom, here's where the anger between you and me comes to the surface too easily, and I apologize if it does: We are trying to do the same thing, but we're badly misunderstanding each other. We need to get rid of the polemics and get to the issues. We do agree on a lot of things. I'm not nearly as radical as you guys make me out, and you're probably not as negative as I think you are. Here's something on which we might agree: Archaeology can provide a different kind of context. It's not just a context of literary transmission.

Thompson: Absolutely.

Dever: Now, let's go back to Solomon because that's where we really begin to get in trouble. We would agree on a lot of things about the Patriarchal era and the so-called Conquest era, but when we come to the Monarchy, I think, that's where the differences between us become plain, don't you?

Thompson: If you want to focus on where we have disagreements, I think that's quite correct.

Dever: While we're on Solomon, I resent the fact that on the Internet, you or somebody else is accusing me of going to Gezer [where Dever directed excavations] to find the Solomonic gate. Now that is absolutely ridiculous. Our arguments have always been on straight archaeological lines: ceramic evidence, stratigraphy, historical points that can be fixed—like Shishak's reign (c. 935–914 B.C.E.). [Shishak, or Sheshonq, was an Egyptian pharaoh of the XXII Dynasty who conquered numerous cities in Palestine. His campaign is referenced in 1 Kings 14:25 and 2 Chronicles 12:1–12.—**Ed.**] To say that we went to Gezer looking for the Solomonic gate is really slanderous. Maybe you didn't write this.

Thompson: I did write something similar to that. I talked about what we went to Gezer for. [Thompson dug at Gezer under William Dever's direction in 1967.]

Dever: You knew that we were not looking for the—

Thompson: I knew that we were looking for Solomon's gate.

Monarchy at Work? The Evidence of Three Gates

King Solomon, according to the Bible, built the walls of "Hazor, Megiddo [and] Gezer" (1 Kings 10:15). Monumental six-chambered gates very similar in design have been uncovered at Hazor, Megiddo and Gezer. Until recently, archaeologists generally agreed that all of these gates date to the tenth century B.C.E.—to about the time of Solomon (c. 965–928 B.C.E.). Now, however, there are differing opinions. Megiddo excavators David Ussishkin and Israel Finkelstein, for example, have proposed that Megiddo's gate was built by the dynasty established by King Omri (882–871 B.C.E.) of the northern kingdom of Israel; while the current excavator of Hazor, Amnon Ben-Tor, emphatically dates Hazor's gate to the tenth century.

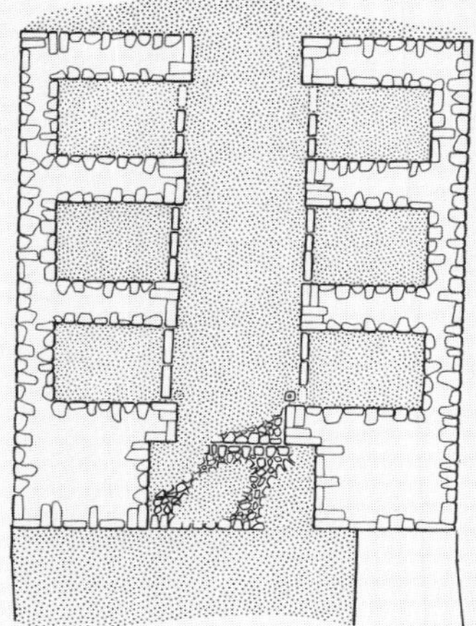

Drawing of the Megiddo gate

William Dever, excavator of Gezer, offers two pieces of evidence for a tenth-century date for the Gezer gate. First, the pottery from Gezer dating to the time of the gate and earlier is all hand-burnished—that is, polished by hand with a smooth pebble or bone, producing irregular criss-cross patterns. Hand-burnished pottery is characteristic of the tenth century. Gezer's destruction levels dating later than the gate, however, contain pottery polished on a wheel, which leaves an even pattern of concentric circles. Wheel-burnished pottery is characteristic of the ninth century. Dever thus concludes that the Gezer gate dates to the tenth century—though the evidence does not say it was built by Solomon.

Second, Dever suggests that the Gezer gate was destroyed by the late-tenth-century B.C.E. Egyptian pharaoh Sheshonq I during his military campaign in Palestine. After returning to Egypt, Sheshonq, called Shishak in the Bible, carved a victory stela on a wall of a temple of Amun at Karnak. The Bible records that Shishak "took the fortified cities of Judah" (2 Chronicles 12:4). Sheshonq's own lists claim that he penetrated even further north—conquering, among other cities, Gibeon, Megiddo and

The Gezer gate

Beth-Shean. So it is likely, Dever suggests, that the Gezer destruction—and others—occurred during this invasion.

The Hazor gate

Does it matter whether these gates date to the tenth century? According to the biblical minimalists, there is no archaeological evidence of a tenth-century B.C.E. Israelite state. From this lack of evidence, they conclude that the Bible's account of the United Monarchy is mere fiction; the stories of David and Solomon's "empire" were fabricated centuries later to dignify Israel's past. But if all or some of these almost-identical monumental gates were erected in the tenth century, then there likely existed a central administrative apparatus capable of organizing and financing such a building project—that is, something like a tenth-century state.

Dever: Well, that's something I didn't know. That's what I mean by slander. Do not impute motives to other people when you don't know what they're doing.

Thompson: I'm talking about what you told me and what we did together. And that's what I've written.

Dever: Dear sir, if you have not read what I've written about biblical archaeology for these last 30 years...

Thompson: I have.

Dever: You know very well that I have been the most outspoken foe of that kind of simple-minded biblicism. I've been the most outspoken, and I have paid for it dearly. To say that our archaeological strategy comes out of the Bible is really nonsense. Tom, I don't care in the least whether Solomon ever existed. I'm probably more of a disbeliever than you. I don't really care about the tradition. I don't believe any of the myths. But as a historian, an archaeologist, I believe the date of the construction of the six-chambered gate [at Gezer] is a historical and archaeological matter [see "Monarchy at Work? The Evidence of Three Gates"]. If the Bible had never been

written, I still would need to date that gate.
Thompson: I was reconstructing a piece of the history of scholarship. You, who were very, very central to that piece of the history of scholarship, deny what I say.
Dever: You were reconstructing this from your memory. I only ask you to go back and read what I was writing in the '60s.
Thompson: That's quite fair.
Dever: Don't hold me responsible for a memory you have of what you thought I was doing 30 years ago.
Thompson: I don't.

Shanks: *One of the things that really stuns our readers and stuns a lot of scholars is the perception that your Copenhagen group concludes that there was no ancient Israel despite the Merneptah Stele [which dates to the late 13th century B.C.E. and mentions Israel; see "The Merneptah Stele: Israel Enters History"] and that there was no United Kingdom led by David and Solomon. Is that really your position?*

Thompson: On the first part, no that is not our position. We do not deny that there was an ancient Israel; in fact, we talk about it a good deal. We don't deny the existence of the Merneptah Stele; we try to explain it and understand it in terms of the history of the period. We do deny the existence, at least I do, of a united monarchy [under David and Solomon] in the tenth century [B.C.E.]—for a number of reasons. First, I see a difference in the history and origin and formation of the peoples of the northern hill [country], that is, the hills of Ephraim and Manasseh, on the one hand, and the settlement of Judah, on the other. I see a difference in the settlement patterns. In the northern hill country we have settlement from about 1200 to about 900 B.C.E. Judah has almost no settlement at this time. It begins to be settled around 850 to 800. Jerusalem is not settled at all until about 900. We don't have a tenth-century Jerusalem.*

*The existence and nature of tenth-century B.C.E. Jerusalem is much debated. See Nadav Na'aman, "Cow Town or Royal Capital?" **BAR**, July/August 1997.

The Merneptah Stele: Israel Enters History

After defeating a coalition of Libyan tribesmen and Sea Peoples, in about 1208 B.C.E., the Egyptian pharaoh Merneptah commissioned a series of victory hymns to be carved on a 7.5-foot-high, black granite stele at Thebes. The stele depicts Merneptah receiving a scimitar from Amun, the god of Thebes. The hieroglyphic text recounts the pharaoh's earlier campaigns in Canaan, among other places "The Canaan is plundered with every hardship. / Ashkelon is taken, Gezer captured, / [and] Yano'am reduced to nothing. / Israel is laid waste, his seed is no more." This is the earliest known reference to Israel; thus the stele is also known as the Israel Stele.

Ashkelon, Gezer and Yano'am (this city has not been identified) are marked in the text with a determinative (an unpronounced sign indicating the category to which a word belongs) telling us that they are city-states; "Israel" is marked with a determinative indicating that it is a people.

The Merneptah Stele strongly indicates that a people calling itself "Israel"—a people the pharaoh thought important enough to boast of conquering—had emerged in Canaan by the late 13th century B.C.E., which is consistent with the biblical chronology. The debate that continues to divide scholars today is: Did this people gradually transform itself into an organized monarchy over the next 200 years, as the Bible also records?

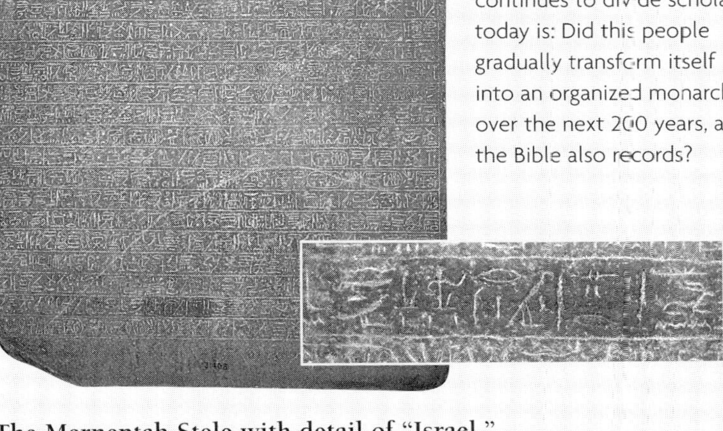

The Merneptah Stele with detail of "Israel."

Then we have the fortification of towns. This takes place around 950 B.C.E. with the high chronology, or around 900 B.C.E. with [Israel] Finkelstein's new low chronology [see Chapter Four, "A 'Centrist' at the Center of Controversy: An Interview with Israel Finkelstein"]. This includes the fortification of Megiddo, Gezer, Beersheba and Lachish. This is terribly important because it means Lachish is fortified before Jerusalem exists. Then we have the development of kingdom paraphernalia, such as seals and inscriptions in 850, 800 [B.C.E.]. The last point is that Jerusalem becomes a really major town only after the destruction of Lachish in 701 B.C.E.

Now I put this all together. Without a significant population in Judea, without a city of Jerusalem, it's very, very difficult to talk about a united monarchy [under David and Solomon in the tenth century B.C.E.]. That would be my general argument for saying that I don't see where there's room for a united monarchy within history.

Dever: I need to respond to that. First of all, your argument about the tenth century in Jerusalem, as you know very well, is altogether an argument from silence.

Thompson: Absolutely. I said we have no knowledge of any Jerusalem. We work only with evidence, Bill.

Dever: Furthermore, your argument about the population of Judah is incorrect. Based on recent surveys by Avi Ofer and Nadav Na'aman, it's simply wrong to say that Judah doesn't have a significant population before 701.

Thompson: Oh, I estimate about 2,000.

Dever: In a recent article you said, I'm quoting you, "There were only a few dozen people in Judah." I will bring you the quotation.

Thompson: Please do.

Dever: I shall. I don't misquote. And if you look at any of the studies of demography that the Israelis have done, then you know that that's quite wrong.

Thompson: The figure of 2,200 is cited from Finkelstein's most recent article.*

Dever: You said a few dozen. Many of your facts are wrong, Tom, because you do not control the archaeological data.

No Israeli archaeologist has bothered to answer you—Tom, I'm sorry to say this—because none takes you seriously. Not a single one. They have not answered you because you get your facts wrong, Tom. You need to check with archaeologists.

Lemche: That's nonsense. We have to get in here because of an attack—

Dever: When a man denies he's written what he's written, I do not trust him any longer.

Shanks: *Do you agree that there's nothing from the tenth century in Jerusalem?*

Dever: There's a fair amount of tenth-century stuff, but no monumental architecture.**

Lemche: Last year at a conference in Jerusalem on exactly this period, David Ussishkin [now professor emeritus of archaeology at Tel Aviv University] said to me, "It's not only an argument from silence. There's not a single sherd [piece of pottery] from the tenth century." Ussishkin is a very conservative scholar. I know him quite well. He really wants to retain the Davidic monarchy. Not a single sherd, not a single one belongs to the tenth century.

Dever: When Ussishkin says not a single sherd belongs to the tenth century, that's because he dates all of it to the ninth century [according to the "low chronology"]. I grew up with this generation of archaeologists. They're my best friends. I know these guys, and I know what they think. And I can tell you that not a single one of the other Israeli archaeologists agrees with this low chronology, except Israel Finkelstein.

*Israel Finkelstein, "The Archaeology of the United Monarchy: An Alternative View," *Levant* 28 (1996).

But see Eilat Mazar, "Did I Find King David's Palace?" **BAR, January/February 2006.

IS IT A FAKE? According to almost all scholars, "The House of David" (BYTDWD, *Beth David*) is inscribed on this Aramaic stela from Tel Dan, in northern Galilee. In 1993 excavator Avraham Biran found the stela's large right-hand fragment in secondary use in an eighth-century B.C.E. wall; Biran later recovered two additional fragments and attempted to fit them into place.

Apparently set up by the king of Damascus, the Tel Dan Stela boasts of victories, in Biran's reconstruction, over "[Jeho]ram son of Ahab, King of Israel" and "[Ahaz]iah son of [Jehoram, ki]ng of the House of David." The biblical rulers Jehoram (851–842 B.C.E.), of the northern kingdom of Israel, and Ahaziah (843–842 B.C.E.), of the southern kingdom of Judah, were contemporaries, supporting a mid-ninth-century B.C.E. date for the stela. The reference to the "House [or dynasty] of David" suggests that Judahite kings traced their descent back to an actual David, who is traditionally believed to have lived a century earlier.

In the accompanying interview, Niels Peter Lemche questions the ninth-century B.C.E. date of the stela; he also suggests, without providing any evidence, that it might be a fake.

McCarter: This business with tenth- or ninth-century ceramics will work itself out. It has to be permitted to do that, but I wouldn't want to anticipate either side of it at this point.

Thompson: When I talked about there not being anything in

Jerusalem, I wasn't referring to Finkelstein and I wasn't referring to Ussishkin. I was talking about Margreet Steiner's publications of the Kenyon excavations. She's publishing [British archaeologist Kathleen Kenyon's reports] with the Copenhagen international seminar, of which I'm the editor.*

Dever: You can't say there's nothing there in the tenth century. You can only say in her publication there's not.

Thompson: I'm not talking about the metaphysical existence of the reality of the past. I'm talking about the basis of evidence. And if we don't have evidence, we don't have any history—and both of us agree on that, so let's not bicker about it.

Dever: Well, you cannot use silence as an argument that there was no state of Judah with its capital in Jerusalem.

Thompson: I'm only saying that we can't put it into history.

Dever: What is your evidence that Judah was not a state before the eighth century?

Thompson: I said we don't have any evidence for it. That means we can't put it into our history. I didn't say it didn't exist.

McCarter: We do have some evidence. We have the evidence of a tradition. Judah has a traditional founder, as many states do. The question is, "Is David, the traditional founder, a historical figure, or is he a legendary figure?"

Thompson: I agree.

McCarter: But we do have the tradition. It's not that we have no evidence. People do different things with that. I think some of us think the most economical explanation of the tradition is that David was a historical figure. I think that's the simplest answer. He doesn't look like a shadowy, legendary founder to me. I see lots of those in the ancient Near East. David doesn't seem to me to be one of them.

*Margreet L. Steiner et al., *Excavations by Kathleen M. Kenyon in Jerusalem, 1961–1967, Volume III* (Sheffield: Sheffield Academic Press, 2001). Steiner also discussed her ideas in "It's Not There: Archaeology Proves a Negative," **BAR,** July/August 1998.

Shanks: *What about the new Beth David [House of David] inscription from Tel Dan? [The now famous Tel Dan stela was discovered by the late Avraham Biran at Tel Dan in 1993.]*

Lemche: You could try to make an analysis of the stone and the cutting of the stone to see whether it's a modern fake or an ancient one.

Dever: Oh geez, come on fellas. I've handled it. Have you?

Lemche: I was just talking to some of the specialists who examined it. I've also talked to the person who found the inscription, I mean the person who *found* it—

Dever: This is slanderous to suggest!

Lemche: No, it's not. The inscription was found at least in secondary use. It was found near the gate. I know this from firsthand evidence because I had a discussion last summer at a seminar at Megiddo with the person who found it. He said, no doubt it had been there for some time, but he couldn't say for how long. Whether it was five years, six years, 2,000 years, he couldn't say. All the pictures of it printed in the *Israel Exploration Journal* are fakes. They have much better pictures, this fellow said to me, where you can see it sitting in the wall. Avraham Biran was so fond of this inscription he wanted to give a nice picture where you could see the inscription. But he did not publish the original picture where you could see it sitting in the wall, but could not read it.

Dever: Niels Peter, you're too good a scholar to indulge in this sort of thing. I have seen the published pictures of it *in situ*.

Lemche: You haven't seen it.

Dever: I *have*. I was there shortly after it was found. I've known Biran for 40 years. The woman who found it, Gila Cook, I hired at Hebrew Union College. I have handled the inscription. I know what I'm talking about. There's no way. All of this was covered by debris until he started digging. True, it was found in secondary use. Nobody ever argued that it was in primary position. It was reused in the wall. But there is no way in the world anybody could have dug down there, found that wall five years before

FOR REAL? Archaeologists had long suggested that Tel Miqne was biblical Ekron, one of the Philistines' five capital cities, though until recently they had no proof. In 1996, excavators Trude Dothan and Seymour Gitin found a temple inscription bearing the name "Ekron" and mentioning two of Ekron's kings: Achish and Padi (Achish's father). In seventh-century B.C.E. Assyrian annals, Achish, called Ikausu, is mentioned as king of Ekron. Padi is mentioned in the Assyrian king Sennacherib's account of his 701 B.C.E. military campaign in the Levant, during which he captured Ekron.

In the accompanying interview, however, Niels Peter Lemche questions the authenticity of the inscription. The two kings mentioned in the inscription, Achish and Padi, are both mentioned in Assyrian sources, he notes; this is too much of a coincidence not to inspire doubt. For this reason, Lemche charges that the Ekron inscription may be a forgery.

Biran came along and planted it. It's impossible.

Lemche: We have another example. Something may be wrong down there at the moment: The new inscription from Ekron, which mentions Ekron. [The Ekron royal inscription, which gives the name of the ancient Philistine city, was discovered in 1996 by Ekron excavators Trude Dothan and Seymour Gitin.] The only two [personal] names mentioned in the Ekron inscription we know from Assyrian sources. I mean if we had known one of them, and the second was unknown to us...

McCarter: Wait a minute, explain...

Lemche: The Ekron inscription is more or less in the style of the *Beth David* inscription. It mentions two kings of Ekron. And only two. Both of them are known from Assyrian sources. It would be nice if we knew one of the kings and the second one was unknown to us. If we know both of them, it reminds me too much of Oscar Wilde: "To lose one of your parents is a mishap. To lose both of them is really carelessness." I mean, one example is OK, but two examples are one too many.

Shanks: *In other words, you're suggesting that it too might be a fake?*

Lemche: Yes. If that's shown to be true, then you have people going around faking inscriptions.

McCarter: What would be the motivation for the forgery?

Lemche: Oh, you know, a card-playing trick. I've already experienced that sort of thing, people making inscriptions. They are salting excavations with the funniest things, simply to tease and to try their colleagues. You put in an Egyptian scarab, for instance, to see whether the archaeologists will be able to recognize that it is out of place, or you may even fake an inscription. They're always doing that, simply for fun.

For instance, we have the seal impressions of Berakhyahu ben Neriyahu, supposedly impressed with the seal of Jeremiah's scribe. Benjamin Sass [associate professor of Semitic languages at Tel Aviv University], who may be the greatest expert on this, says they're fakes. He even told me who made them, of course at a dinner party, never in print. None of the bullae like the Berakhyahu seal impressions were found in an excavation. They were found in an antiquities shop on King David Street in Jerusalem. This is just an example of such fakes. It's a terrible business because outsiders will not be able to determine whether artifacts are fake or not. The Tel Dan [*Beth David*] inscription—is it a genuine inscription or is it not genuine?

Shanks: *Let me interrupt a minute here. We happen to have sitting here an expert paleographer and biblical scholar, Kyle McCarter. Can you respond to the charge that the Beth David inscription and the new Ekron inscriptions are both fakes?*

McCarter: It's not unreasonable to raise the question of whether these things are authentic. That question always has to be asked. And it's also true that unfortunately we've reached a time when there are forgers who are competent in ancient paleography. They can emulate it, they can fool us. But I think that the Tel Dan inscription is an extremely unlikely forgery. That is, it has surprising features in it; it lacks the things a forgery would have, such as the name of the king who left it, or the mention of Tel Dan. Precisely the things you're saying are present in the Ekron inscription are lacking in the Tel Dan inscription. So if that's a criterion, it tends to authenticate Tel Dan. Several people witnessed its discovery. It wasn't found by one digger alone on the site at night. It was called to the attention of others. The circumstances of its discovery are not in favor of its being a forgery. The problems that we have in reading it and understanding it also make it an unlikely forgery. The subtlety of the forger would have to be extraordinarily great.

Then there's the whole question of the motivation. I don't think there's much chance the Tel Dan inscription is a forgery.

I tend to doubt the Ekron inscription is a forgery. When we have a chance to study it, questions may arise. It's too new for us to have the confidence in it that we have in the Tel Dan inscription. I've studied the Tel Dan inscription carefully and I don't have any bad feeling about it at all and I don't think others do. The old Aramaic is impeccable. The orthography [spelling] and paleography [letter shapes] are impeccable. The Ekron discovery is new, less than a year old, and it requires study, but again I think the circumstances of its discovery are not suspicious. Many artifacts are found in this way.

Shanks: *What about the seal impressions, the bullae?*

McCarter: I think there are bullae being forged now, and we do need a scientific test. It's going to be very difficult because the impressions are stamped on small pieces of clay the size of fingernails. It's hard to imagine a non-destructive test that can settle that, but we will have one eventually—I'm already actively working on that.

The fact is that most of the bullae we have do not come from controlled excavations. Except for the City of David hoard [a collection of ancient Hebrew bullae recovered during Yigal Shiloh's excavations of the City of David], the vast majority come from the antiquities market. That underscores the need for a scientific evaluation; it also often forces us to ask the reasonable question of whether some of these are bad. But the reaction I've had from examining them very closely is that at this point I don't think there are a lot of bad ones out there. I think there will be soon.

Thompson: I'm not denying that at all, so we're not in disagreement here. I would just go further with the interpretation. I would see David as the eponymous ancestor of Judah. The whole discussion of *Beth David* in the Bible is related to that. You do have an ideology referring to David and his line and it's specifically associated with the Temple and with Yahweh. This is where I would see a good interpretation in reading *Dod* [instead of David]; the inscription contains wordplay between "David" and "Dod" that's essentially theological rather than historical.*

McCarter: David is certainly the eponymous ancestor of the

*Most Scholars read the Tel Dan inscription's critical six letters, BYTDWD, as *Beth David* ("House of David"). However, Philip R. Davies ("'House of David' Built on Sand," **BAR**, July/August 1994) argues that because no word-divider separates *Beth* and *David* (the Tel Dan inscription places dots between words), the letters form a place-name, like Bethlehem (which means House of Bread). Davies also suggests that DWD (*David*) can be read as *Dod*, meaning "beloved," "uncle" or "kettle." Thus he argues that the letters could form the place-name *Bethdod* (House of the Beloved). For critiques of Davies's reading, see Anson Rainey, "The 'House of David' and the House of the Deconstructionists," **BAR**, November/December 1994; and David Noel Freedman and Jeffrey C. Geoghegan, "'House of David' Is There!" **BAR**, March/April 1995.

House of David. That's an obvious statement and I don't disagree with it. What I disagree with is whether an eponymous ancestor can be a historical figure. He could be a legendary figure, but I think David was a historical figure. That's apparently the point of difference.

Shanks: *Let's turn to the Merneptah Stele.*

Lemche: The question is simply, "What was the Israel mentioned in the Merneptah Stele?" That's also the question regarding the Mesha Stela, which also mentions Israel. They're two separate questions. There's no reason to be surprised by the mention of Israel in the Mesha Stela if it belongs to the ninth century [B.C.E.]. We have no problems with Israel as such, with the name. We have problems with the interpretation of the name. The mention in the Mesha Stela is, of course, something you can't get around. Just not mentioning it is nonsense. In the Merneptah Stele [late 13th century B.C.E.], however, the mention of Israel must be considered in its own context and not in the biblical context. It is not so important whether you speak about proto-Israelites or about proto-Palestinians, or whatever term you would use.

Dever: You're talking about various Israels: (1) The Israel of the Merneptah Stele, (2) the Israel of the biblical account (the Mesha Stela), and (3) the archaeological Israel. I don't want to combine these Israels either. It's the archaeology of Palestine in the Iron Age (1200–586 B.C.E.) that I'm talking about. If it resembles descriptions in the biblical text, I'm willing to comment on the resemblance. I don't depend on the biblical text. I'm the first to agree that the Israel I would reconstruct in archaeological terms is certainly not the biblical Israel.

Lemche: Similarly, the David of the Bible, David the king, is not a historical figure.

Dever: Why not say, "He could be, he might not be." Are you sure he's not?

Lemche: Because [the Bible relates that] he's the king of an

empire stretching from the Euphrates to Egypt. It's a vast empire. Solomon even enlarged it. These two kings are described by the Bible as the greatest kings in their day.
Dever: In that sense, I agree they did not exist.
Lemche: The biblical David did not exist.

Shanks: *Couldn't their empire be smaller and still exist?*

Dever: I wouldn't call it an empire, I would call it a state.
Lemche: Judah, in the tenth century, is probably a territorial state of about 1,000 square kilometers [about 400 square miles]. That's all.
Dever: That's where you guys have made a mistake. You're defining statehood by size, but the anthropological literature says you cannot do that. There are many small states. All anthropologists and sociologists agree that size is not the criterion; centralization is. And archaeologically we can show centralization.
Lemche: To find this type of centralization in southern Palestine, Jerusalem is very important [implying that you can't find it there].
Dever: I want to be sure you understand me about David and Solomon. For me, as an archaeologist, it's simple. I don't have to argue whether this Solomon existed. I do have to argue that somebody built these three gates [at Gezer, Megiddo and Hazor] in a government that was highly centralized, and for me that means statehood [see "Monarchy at Work? The Evidence of Three Gates," p. 98]. In other words, it's Solomon by another name. I don't care. I'm talking about centralization and the rise of the state. And I use the term Solomon as a kind of convenient shorthand. And so therefore I would say a Solomon of some sort existed but not necessarily the Solomon of fable.
Thompson: I find myself very much agreeing with that type of description. I also think that the gates do seem to suggest some type of a state structure. I don't like the word "Solomon" because it seems to point toward Jerusalem, and that seems to point towards a biblical reconstruction of it. I don't see any need for that. I have

no problem with your reading of the archaeological material.

Dever: For me, it's an archaeological issue. If someone can prove that these gates all date to the ninth century [instead of the tenth century B.C.E.], that will not trouble me at all. I would still argue that we're dealing with a state.

Lemche: Whether you see statehood arising in Palestine in the late tenth century or the early ninth century, for normal people, this must be almost a matter of indifference. After all, it's almost 3,000 years ago. But of course it's important because if it's ninth century, then Solomon and the Bible are gone. You can't save them. Then you'll need another biblical metaphor: You could say that these gates have something to do with the House of Omri and have something to say about what we read in the Bible [concerning the dynasty established by King Omri (882–871 B.C.E.) of the northern kingdom of Israel].

If you, Bill, call it "Solomonic," as a shorthand, you bring in the connotation of Solomon as the biblical Solomon. You bring him in the side door because people's understanding of Solomon comes from the Bible, first and foremost. When you say "Solomonic," they put it immediately into this biblical context.

Dever: You know that's not what I mean. That was imprecise language on my part. But we all do that. We all, in archaeology, talk about the such-and-such palace. As an archaeologist, I am not looking for Solomon, the Solomon of the Bible. I do, however, think we will end up being able to show that state-formation processes begin in Palestine in the tenth century B.C.E. And if we can then correlate [this evidence] with some reading of the text, I'm not opposed to that. Are you? If the texts and the artifacts seem to converge, is there a problem?

McCarter: Can I try a defense of Solomon? I don't think anyone here will disagree that from a fairly early period in the list of kings of Israel and Judah, we have corroboration that they were historical kings. We have references to many of them in Assyrian records and elsewhere. These records include the names of many eighth-century [B.C.E.] Israelite kings. They take us back into the middle of the ninth century—for example, to Shalmaneser III (858–824 B.C.E.) and Ahab (871–852 B.C.E.). We also have the "House of Omri," referring to the northern kingdom [of Israel]. In short, our list of Israelite and Judahite kings, with extra-biblical corroboration, goes back almost to the time of David and Solomon. OK, you say that [the ninth century B.C.E.] may have been the time when the state arose. I agree with Bill that those gates suggest some kind of central state. If the debate is over the date of those gates, fine. If they turn out to be ninth century, that's one thing. If their customary attribution to the tenth century stands, then we have a list of kings going back to the mid-ninth century and we have an archaeologically identifiable phenomenon [the gates] that's even earlier. I don't think it's a very big leap to say, "What does that king list say, what name does it give us to correspond to that tenth-century date?" The name is Solomon. To me, that's not a very big leap. It's true that the Solomon of the biblical tradition is a Solomon whose splendor has developed in a legendary fashion, but I would still postulate a historical Solomon at about that time. I think he's responsible for the fortification of those cities.

Thompson: I have no trouble with a ninth-century state. I have no trouble with a tenth-century state. My problem is how we're reading the Bible and understanding it as expressive of history.

Dever: But I'm not doing that. My only point is this: When you do have a convergence of the archaeological reconstruction that we come up with and a history behind the history that one can seem to see, what is the problem with saying so? That's not fundamentalism. And I do resent being called a fundamentalist.

Lemche: But, of course, if you use the biblical chronology, there is a big difference whether the gates, for instance, were built in 920 instead of 940 [B.C.E.]. Then it would be Jeroboam [the first king of the northern kingdom of Israel] who built them and not Solomon. David might have been a chief who lived in the highlands in the tenth century, but this has very little to do with the biblical text.

Dever: I want to go back to the dating of the gates because so much hinges on that. Our dating of the gate at Gezer is not based on the biblical story at all. It is based entirely on the hand-burnished pottery that is characteristic of the tenth century. It is found below certain destruction layers; above the destruction layers is wheel-burnished pottery. At Megiddo, they have the same sequence. The Shishak destruction [of about 930 B.C.E.] therefore becomes the pointed issue. Our argument has been very simple. After the phase of the gate, which has only hand-burnished pottery, there is a massive destruction. You can go there and still see it today. If you study the topography of the sites on the Shishak list, there's no question that Shishak came this way. So if you have a Shishak destruction at Gezer which can be dated around 930 B.C.E. plus or minus five years, and you have one at Megiddo, and you have one now at Beth-Shean, and in all those cases you have stratigraphy and ceramic typology that fit the picture, then I am prepared to date the hand-burnished pottery and the gates to the tenth century. But it has nothing to do with Solomon.

Lemche: I think too much [importance] has been placed on those gates. The gates in themselves are not evidence of a centralized state, but only of a centralized idea about architecture; it says the same person was moving around building gates. It was Kyle [McCarter] who used the gates as evidence of statehood. That's not enough. A state requires a whole setup-organization, the appearance of towns.

Dever: We don't rely just on the gates; it's a whole complex. It's pottery, it's tomb styles, it's house styles, it's gates, it's fortifications. When you put it together, I think you can make a very good case for a tenth-century state. But if Solomon hadn't lived, we would have to invent a Solomon by another name to account for the archaeological evidence.

Shanks: *Let's talk a little about the existence of ancient Israel in the late 13th or early 12th century B.C.E. based on the Merneptah Stele.*

I take it that even your group, Tom, would agree that there was something called ancient Israel at that time, based on the reference to Israel in the Merneptah Stele. But you say that it wasn't the Israel that's referred to in the Bible. Do you want to tell us why, and how you come to that conclusion?

Thompson: The Merneptah Stele has a very clear reference to the name "Israel" in Palestine at the end of the 13th century B.C.E. [see "The Merneptah Stele: Israel Enters History," p. 101]. It is the same name that we find later used for a state in the central hill country of Palestine. And it is the name that we find in the Bible later. What I do is compare that with comparable kinds of names. There are four others that are analogous. One is the name Canaan, another is Peleshet or Philistine, also the name Amuru or Amorite, and possibly Apiru referring to Hebrew.* What I find in all these other four names is that the name itself has a continuity. But what the name signifies varies from period to period. We have an Israel at the end of the 13th century, and we have an Israel in the ninth-seventh centuries (that's the first time we come up with the inscriptions). Can we connect the Israel of the Merneptah Stele with the later Israel? What I'm saying is, we don't have a connection. I'm not saying that it doesn't exist, but that we haven't found it.

Dever: But there is a connection, Tom. There is a connection in material culture. It's very simple to show this. You would agree that there is a state of Israel in the ninth century.

Thompson: Yes.

Dever: I can show you that the pottery, the house types, the fortifications, the metals, the burial customs, everything else goes from the ninth back into the tenth, from the tenth back into the 11th, from the 11th back into the 12th. My argument is simply this: In the material culture, we can see a continuity. If the ninth-century material is Israelite, then the 12th- and 11th-century

*But see Anson Rainey, "Shasu or Habiru: Who Were the Early Israelites?" **BAR**, November/December 2008.

material is what I call proto-Israelite.

McCarter: I'm not quite sure what we mean when we talk about continuity here. I don't think anyone thinks that the Israel of the late 13th century of the Merneptah Stele is the same Israel as the ninth-century state. We need to describe the process by which Israel became a state. Yet if continuity simply means a connection of any kind, there must be some connection. We know there was a people called Israel in the late 13th century; we know that from an Egyptian record, the Merneptah Stele. These Israelites were a population group in Canaan at that time. We know that a state later took that name. The obvious assumption, unless there's some reason to doubt it, is that Israel was a traditional name in the region that had existed for some time, at least since the 13th century, and that that name was adopted as the name of the state as it later emerged.

Thompson: I agree with you. We have a continuity in name. There's no question. I would also agree with Bill, that we have cultural continuities from at least the earliest settlements in the highlands [in the 12th century B.C.E.] through the ninth century. If we could place Merneptah's Israel in the central highlands of Palestine north of Jerusalem archaeologically, then I think we could talk about proto-Israelites. We have a name that has a long, long history in Palestine. But does this name always represent the same thing? That is our historical problem. Does the Israel of the Merneptah Stele have anything to do with the Israel of the ninth century and the Israel of the biblical periods? I don't see that we have any evidence for that. We don't have sufficient archaeological evidence for Merneptah's Israel.

Dever: Well, now, wait a minute! What would constitute archaeological evidence? If you look at topography, we know where some of the peoples are that are mentioned along with Israel in the Merneptah Stele. We know where Ashkelon is. We know where Gezer is. We know where the land of the Hurru is. We also know where the Philistines were. There's not much left for Israel except the central highlands. Now you turn to [Israel]

Finkelstein's survey data and you see the archaeological evidence, the new villages and so forth. I believe that we can call these settlements proto-Israelite.

From the archaeological side, we can confidently describe a village culture. It's not because of a single trait, like collared-rim storage jars or the four-room house. The peculiar combination of traits makes it look like something out of Late Bronze Age urban Canaan, something unique. And we now know enough about Transjordan to know that what's over there is different.

I don't care if you call it Israelite [west of the Jordan] or Edomite [in Transjordan]. Archaeologically, we can begin to distinguish the village culture of the central hill country in Palestine beginning in about 1200 B.C.E. That's the reason for my term proto-Israelite. I'm not going to call it Israel, the biblical Israel, but it is proto-Israel. And that is something, at least.

CHAPTER SIX

THE PHILISTINES—AN ARCHAEOLOGICAL ROMANCE

An Interview with Trude and Moshe Dothan—Part I

Trude and Moshe Dothan

They are the first family of Israeli archaeology. Trude and Moshe Dothan each had (Moshe has since passed away) more than five decades of experience in the field, having excavated such major

"The Philistines and the Dothans: An Archaeological Romance, Part 1" appeared in BAR, July/August 1993.

sites as Hazor, Hammath Tiberias, Nahariya, Deir el-Balah, Akko, Ashdod and Ekron. In this first installment of a two-part interview, the Dothans reminisce about how they met; share their recollections of such towering figures as William Foxwell Albright, Yigael Yadin, Roland de Vaux and Kathleen Kenyon; and describe the emergence of modern Israeli archaeology—a field of study they very much helped to shape.

Hershel Shanks: *Something is very unusual about you two. I know a few other couples who are both scholars. I know Ruth and David Amiran [the late archaeologist and the late geographer, respectively], and I know Hayim and Miriam Tadmor [the late Assyriologist and Israel Museum curator emeritus, respectively], but the two of you are the only husband-and-wife team in Israel who are both archaeologists.*

Trude Dothan: I think we were the first, but now I don't know how many couples have resulted from excavating together. We may be the only two archaeologists who are directing excavations and are professors in universities. But there are other couples, some among my students. There is nothing more romantic than being on a dig, you know. You can divorce or get married or have an affair. It can happen. But anyhow, many couples do come out of excavations.

Shanks: *How long have you been married?*

Trude: My chronology is very bad. I never remember.
Moshe Dothan: Forty-three years.

Shanks: *Was it a romance on a dig?*

Moshe: No. We met in 1946. I was in the army, first in the British army, then in the Israeli army. I spent more or less five years in both armies before I started to study at Hebrew University.
Trude: I was also in the army, but very low. I was in Jerusalem

during our War of Independence [1948].

Moshe: I was not directly her commander. She was in a special group connected with intelligence. We met each other in Jerusalem. We got married in 1950.

Shanks: *So you had a long courtship?*

Trude: There were other men in between. [Laughter] This is getting very personal.

Shanks: *I don't want to get too personal.*

Trude: It's all right. It's nice.

Shanks: *Had you both been studying archaeology?*

Trude and Moshe: Yes.

Trude: And I think Moshe read with me [William Foxwell] Albright's excavation report on Tell Beit Mirsim. It's not exactly romantic.

Moshe: We got along slowly but surely.

Trude: When I left the army and Moshe left the army, that's when we got married.

Shanks: *When was your first child born?*

Moshe: He was born in 1954.

Trude: When he was a year old, two years old, three years old, we took him to the dig at Hazor, where we were both area supervisors. He was Dennis the Menace.

Shanks: *Was Yigael Yadin the director of the dig?*

Moshe: Yes.

Shanks: *Was he a great director?*

Yigael Yadin

Moshe: Very good. We learned a lot. We also did a lot. Trude's area was one of the most important—the area of the temples. Mine included some very important stratification.
Trude: Then Moshe went on to become deputy director of the Department of Antiquities [now the Israel Antiquities Authority].

Shanks: *Do you think the fact that you've never actually dug in the same square together saved your marriage?*

Trude: [Laughter] That's a very good question. In a way, it did. People used to ask me, "How can you go to a dig—a woman with children, a family?"

It's not easy. It's almost impossible to have a family and do a dig together. In Hazor, I took Dani with me. It's not the easiest thing to have a little boy with you. The whole group there were the babysitters. Even today, Dani is kind of a legend. He would sit with us in the afternoon when we were reading the pottery. We said "EB" [Early Bronze], "MB" [Middle Bronze], "LB" [Late Bronze], "Byz" [Byzantine] as each sherd was identified. When I got back to Jerusalem, Dani's kindergarten teacher called and asked me, "What kind of song is Dani singing: EB, MB, LB, Byz?" [All laugh]
Trude: Yadin was very nice to children. He thought Dani was a very smart little boy and Dani was on very good terms with him. It was in a way fun to have Dani along, but it was not the easiest thing. I'm not sure I would recommend it. Now it's different. You have a whole entourage and you can do it more easily.

Shanks: *Some couples say that they have to leave business at work and not let it intrude into their personal lives. Can you ever leave business at work if you both come home and you're both archaeologists?*

Moshe: We seldom talk about our projects.
Trude: You see, we already disagree. [All laugh]
Moshe: Very seldom. [To Trude:] Maybe for you it is too much.
Trude: Our neighbor, a very good friend who stayed with us during the war [the Scud attacks during the 1991 Gulf War], says

that when she comes here and sees that you can cut the air...that there's a terrible fight going on and she knows we are living somewhere in the 13th century B.C. There's no ideal life and we try to talk about other things. But we do talk about archaeology

Shanks: *I remember once the two of you were in my office in Washington, and you got into an argument about the Philistines.*

Moshe: Yes. I remember, but I don't remember what it was about.
Trude: But, you see, we survived it. [All laugh]

Shanks: *Moshe, you are unusual in another way. Your archaeological interests are extremely broad. You dug in Ashdod. You excavated in Akko. You directed the excavation of a synagogue on the Sea of Galilee, at Hammath Tiberias. You go from Early Bronze to Byzantine.*

Moshe: Yes. You are right. But you are wrong in one thing. I started in Chalcolithic (c. 4000 B.C.). That was my Ph.D. dissertation—1,000 years before Early Bronze. I go more or less up to the tenth century A.D.

Shanks: *Trude, in your generation, there are some extremely distinguished women archaeologists in Israel: Ruth Amiran, Claire Epstein and, of course, you. Other women who are not field archaeologists deal with archaeological materials, like Miriam Tadmor and Ruth Hestrin. Was there a greater openness to women in those pioneer days?*

Trude: Each of these women has her own individual background. Take Claire Epstein. She did a lot on her own. She got her Ph.D. at Oxford. She is a kibbutznik. She is her own one-man expedition. By force of her total dedication, she did the one thing she wanted to do: work on bichrome ware and the Chalcolithic period. It's fantastic what she did. She is a one-man team. She really belongs to the British generation. She is unique.

Shanks: *Different from Kathleen Kenyon?*

Trude: Kenyon belonged to the establishment. There is a difference. Claire did things on her own.

Shanks: *You've had your career at the [Hebrew] University.*

Trude: But I was the only one for years and years and years. As a woman professor, there was nobody.

Shanks: *Was that because of gender discrimination?*

Trude: No. Absolutely not. Perhaps I advanced more slowly to full professor than the men in my department, but that was my fault because I had other responsibilities.

It is very difficult if you want to be totally dedicated to your profession, but you also want to build a home, you want to raise a family, you want to have children. In a way, I am not a feminist, but I believe women should get the same pay. Moshe helped me all the way. But still, when the children are small, you have to stay home. Many times the younger generation, my students, ask me what they should do. I tell them, the one thing is, don't stop. The moment you stop and think that in ten years you will come back, you're lost.

But if a woman wants to live a life that has all the facets, then she will not advance as quickly. It's not easy to be a field archaeologist and to do these other things. But there are women who do it.

In the new generation, we'll have more women archaeologists. There is far more equality now. The husbands are ready to take over and be babysitters. But this question is a very, very personal one, and I don't think you can generalize.

Shanks: *When you started in archaeology, how did the work differ from today?*

Moshe: We were few, and this is why we had to do so much. I remember in the beginning, in the mid-1950s, I had two people for excavation in the entire Department of Antiquities. Today, there are at least 100.

Shanks: *How many people would be involved in an excavation in those days?*

Moshe: Usually one, two or three professionals—at a maximum. As to workers, it depends on which dig. In a small dig—in Nahariya, for instance—I had maybe 20 people altogether, including workers. In Ashdod there were 60 or 70 people.

Shanks: *You used paid workers in the beginning, didn't you?*

Moshe: Both [paid workers and volunteers].
Trude: New immigrants from Persia and Europe worked on the digs. The government paid them because they didn't have any other work. This is really what enabled us to work on such a big scale. You had immigrants from Persia. You had immigrants from Iraq, from Europe. Nobody could talk to anybody else. It was really a melting pot.

Shanks: *Did either of you know Albright?*

Moshe: Yes, of course.

Shanks: *What were your impressions of Albright?*

Moshe: He was a fantastic man. I wouldn't say he was a genius, because a genius is something very, very special but he was very close to it. Even today, there is no one to match him at judging what is important and what is not important—in the Bible, in history and in the Near East generally. He knew so much. His methods are still used today.

William F. Albright

Shanks: *What are your recollections of Albright, Trude?*

Trude: I remember him well. We met him first in Israel when he came to the archaeological congress in Beer-Sheva. He spoke Hebrew. We were amazed. To go out with him was really fantastic. He knew every piece of land. He was very interested in sharing information. He would let you know when you were wrong, which is also great. Now people frequently point out in articles that he often changed his mind. Well, it is great to know how to change your mind.

Shanks: *[William] Dever has criticized Albright for being too biblical. Do you see any trends in the relationship of archaeologists to the Bible?*

Trude: There are people who are afraid of saying they are biblical archaeologists. I can't say that I am a biblical archaeologist, but I definitely turn to the Bible. I think it's wonderful that we have the possibility of putting the material into a framework and relating it to the Bible. We don't have to take the Bible at face value. I am the handmaiden of biblical scholars. I see myself first of all as an archaeologist. But definitely I am not detached from the background. If you use the Bible properly as a source, and you don't follow it blindly, why should you be so worried about it?

What I'm doing is *Mediterranean* archaeology *in* the biblical period. I go out of Israel to the whole Mediterranean. So I can say that I am a Mediterranean archaeologist with a background in the land of the Bible, or whatever you call Israel. It's all semantics. I think you need every source you can get. We are very fortunate that we have the Bible in this period. That is why we are different from archaeologists who don't have this background.

Shanks: *Moshe, do you sense that in younger archaeologists, either in America or in Israel, that they are happier when an interpretation goes against the Bible than when it supports the biblical text?*

Moshe: Whether for or against, they must relate to the Bible. I place much more emphasis on the biblical connotations than Trude. You have to be very careful before concluding that something is different from what the Bible says. You have to look first to see if there is some interpretation of the written words that fits what you find. The Bible is really almost our only source. If it weren't for the Bible, there are so many places we wouldn't even be able to identify. There is so much we wouldn't be able to understand. Of course, not everything written in the Bible—in historical geography, for instance—is correct. Names change. People make mistakes, and so on. But, after all, this is really our only important source. I'm not talking as a Zionist. I'm talking only as a biblical archaeologist. What would we know about the Philistines if it weren't for the Bible?

Trude: I agree with what Moshe said. Who's afraid of biblical archaeology? But there is this trend away from it. I think it swings, and it will swing back. In the end, I feel it will find its right place. For an American archaeologist, it's dangerous to go to Greece with Homer in one hand and a spade in the other. You shouldn't get carried away by it, but, of course, Homer is in the back of the mind of the Greek archaeologist.

Shanks: *Today, Israeli archaeologists dominate the scene in Israel. There are some Americans and a few from other countries, but mostly they are Israelis. In the past, the foreign schools were much more significant, especially the British and the French schools. They were both giants—Père Roland de Vaux of the French school and Kathleen Kenyon of the British school. Let's talk first about de Vaux.*

Father Roland de Vaux

Trude: He was fascinating. He was one of the most charming men I ever met. I first met him when I was a student. He came to visit our excavation. I had no idea who he was. But here I saw this very good-looking man in a white robe. When we went to eat, he pulled my chair out, put my chair in. I was not used to these Frenchmen. I had never been treated like that; the *sabras* [native-born Israelis] in Israel are not exactly perfect gentlemen. Then he told jokes. He had a fantastic sense of humor. I don't know if it's true, but it was said he was a member of the *Comédie Française* [France's national theater troupe]. Later, he had a terrible accident when he fell from a horse. He was quite disfigured.

After the Six-Day War [in June 1967], we flew to the United States with him; we had such fun. He had a beard and he wore a dark jacket. He told us that the last time he flew it was on a Friday and since he looked like a priest they wouldn't give him meat. This time, too, it was a Friday. But this time they thought he was a rabbi, so they brought him kosher food. It was so funny. He was a man of culture, very liberal, a wonderful scholar. His book on Israelite institutions is really a great book.* I used it just the other day.

His excavation at Tell el-Far'ah (North), unfortunately, was never published; he only published in fragments and sections.

Shanks: *There has been no final publication of his excavation at Qumran, either.*

Kathleen Kenyon

Trude: True.

Shanks: *What about Kathleen Kenyon?*

Moshe: She was completely different.
Trude: As a student I went to London to the Institute of Archaeology, the British school. In the basement, I was going through [Sir Flinders] Petrie's material from Tell el-Far'ah (South). I was really afraid of her.

Shanks: *She was a big woman, wasn't she?*

*Roland de Vaux, *Ancient Israel—Its life and Institutions* (London: Darton, Longman and Todd, 1961).

Trude: Yes. At the agora in Greece, we had met some American women archaeologists—kind of tough women—and I thought, "Should I become an archaeologist if you have to be like this?" I was really worried. Then I was told, "Wait till you meet Kathleen Kenyon. Then you will really worry."

I met her that time in England and I must say she was very nice, but I wouldn't go up to her after a lecture and ask her questions.

Later, after the Six-Day War, I thought that now that Jerusalem was open we would be able to talk to Kenyon. We would exchange ideas and laugh. I was really extremely naive. The last thing Kenyon wanted was for Israelis to be part of Jerusalem. She really represented the end of the empire, the grande dame. We were natives. More than that, we made it impossible for her to go into the Old City, as she loved to do, as the great English matron who was in charge of their life.

Shanks: *Why was it impossible for her to go into the Old City?*

Trude: She could go, but not with the same status. With the Arabs on her excavation, she was the grande dame. She was their friend, but from above. She liked that kind of relationship. With us, it was totally different.

Once she went with Yadin on a tour of Megiddo. A group went on a bus. She told us this story later. When she got out, the driver approached her and said, "Ah, Miss Kenyon, I'm so glad to meet you. I have read all your books." And he started asking her about the stratigraphy of Megiddo. Then he took her in the bus all around Megiddo and showed her all the problems of strata 5A and 6B. She couldn't get over that—that he was a bus driver.

The last time I met her was very sad. It was in Tübingen [Germany], a big meeting to celebrate the 500th anniversary of the university. They invited people from all over—England, Germany, France, Canada, Israel. They gave Kenyon an honorary doctorate. She got up and gave a lecture on Jerusalem. That was after our Israeli excavations in Jerusalem. She behaved as if nothing had happened. It was terrible. It was really pathetic. We sat there and we didn't know what to do. A.D. Tushingham* also spoke as if nothing had happened after Kenyon. And that was one of the problems. Kenyon did not relate to other excavations.

The last time I saw her, it was a year before she died. She had on a very shiny party dress and was chain-smoking. She was a fascinating person. It was very sad that she couldn't admit that maybe something happened to change things. It was too painful for her to do it.

In a way it is very sad because Kenyon dug very meticulously in very difficult circumstances. She did pioneering work in Jericho. You can disagree with her conclusions. The pathetic thing is that she was extremely careful. She dug deep sections. But in Jerusalem, she dug only fragments and tried to build up the whole picture from those fragments—and then she was proved wrong. That is the sad part of it. She lived long enough to know that there were later excavations, but she could not relate to them. That is really the tragedy. She just couldn't take it. She couldn't face the changeover with Israel coming in, and then she couldn't take the changes that came with the new Israeli excavations.

Shanks: *She was well known as an anti-Zionist.*

Trude: She didn't love Israel.

Shanks: *Do you think that affected her interpretations?*

Trude: I don't know.
Moshe: Whenever there was the possibility, she tried to...
Trude: ...minimize.
Moshe: ...minimize the number of Israelites, and so on. If it was possible to interpret something negatively or to say there were

*Tushingham was principal author of volume 1 of the final report on Kenyon's *Excavations in Jerusalem* 1961–1967 (Toronto: Royal Ontario Museum, 1985) and was also chief archaeologist of the Royal Ontario Museum.

fewer people or that something was not important, she would do it. Perhaps it worked unconsciously, but it worked. This was especially so with her last work in Jerusalem.

Shanks: *What was [Hebrew University professor Benjamin] Mazar like in the early days?*

Benjamin Mazar

Trude: Mazar hasn't changed. He even looks the same—only an older version [Mazar passed away in September 1995—**Ed.**]. Mazar has been very important for me—and for many of us. I always wanted to be an archaeologist. I was attracted by the adventure of it. My father was involved with a lot of archaeologists and used to go on trips with them.

At first I studied with [E.L.] Sukenik [Yigael Yadin's father], who didn't teach us much. He was not very interested in his students. And then there was [L.A.] Mayer. I enjoyed his classes because I always liked art. So I enjoyed his classes because we studied mostly manuscripts and illuminations. But the one who really taught us archaeology was Mazar even though he didn't teach archaeology. He taught historical geography, but we went with him on surveys. I was never really a student of Mazar's, but I became part of the Mazar group. It was really a very special group. There were [Hayim] Tadmor, [Avraham] Malamat and at that time there were many more, but quite a number of his outstanding students were killed in the War of independence [in 1947–1948]. Mazar really created interest, and he had the knowledge. He brought things alive. He was a great teacher. He was interested in his students, and he really discussed things with us. You know, he takes you by the arm and shakes you. Then he asks you about this and that, and then he tells you what he thinks. He really brought things alive on these surveys and outings we had with him. This was, for me, terribly important. At that time, digging was not part of the curriculum. I ran away from the university to dig with Mazar at Beth Yerah; I was almost thrown out of the university because of that. After that, I went with him to Ein Gedi while I was still in the army. And then I went to Tell Qasile with him. It was really Mazar who was teaching archaeology.

Shanks: *He was never a great field archaeologist?*

Trude: He had this thing which is terribly important—the vision. He would take with him people who could do it—like Munya Dunayevsky, an architect who died; Munya was a great stratigrapher. But Mazar's intuition was unbelievable. He knew what he was looking for. In those days it was a very, very small team—Miriam Tadmor, myself, Moshe came for a time. Every afternoon we would go out, and the way Mazar brought things to life was unbelievable. He was not interested at all in the details. But he did bring everything together. He had the ability to organize. This is a great part of archaeology. You have to be an organizer if you want to direct a dig. He had this ability, besides being a historian and geographer and an archaeologist. He would not go and dig himself, but he would take the team and, in a way, show us what to look for. This was very, very important.

It's sad because his excavations have really not been published enough. That is one of the problems. But he was a great teacher.

Shanks: *I thought about that just yesterday when I was at the excavation of the southern wall of the Temple Mount. We'll never know the details of what was excavated there.**

Trude: I think it was very well recorded. They had very good

*Mazar's excavations along the southern wall of the Temple Mount have since been published by his granddaughter, archaeologist Eilat Mazar. See Eilat Mazar, *The Temple Mount Excavations in Jerusalem 1968–1978 Directed by Benjamin Mazar, Final Reports,* Qedem 43, 47 (Jerusalem: Institute of Archaeology, the Hebrew University of Jerusalem, 2003, 2007).

architects and a very good recording system. I hope that it will be published. There is no doubt a problem there. Many other big excavations have this problem. We know that.

Shanks: *What is the problem? Moshe, you have been involved in big excavations.*

Moshe: You must know Mazar really well to judge him. No one went on digs with Sukenik, who was the head of the department. [Nahman] Avigad went, but he was Sukenik's assistant. But students didn't go on digs. And here you have a man [Mazar] who was not an archaeologist—who was teaching history and historical geography—and he makes the digs and he takes the students and gives them all this, all the background for archaeology. If it weren't for Mazar, nobody would have done it. Mazar was not educated as an archaeologist. Now the question of writing all these reports, you need people of ability to write the reports. If it were history, Mazar could do it immediately but for archaeology, he needs help. I am sure in a few years the problem [of the Jerusalem excavation report] will come before a committee of the Antiquities Authority and a solution will be found.

Trude: You ask a hard question and I think it's very difficult to answer. Pioneers like Mazar did an enormous amount. You can't judge them. It's very sad that things have not been published. In Yadin's case, most of his excavations are being published after his death.

Moshe: If Mazar had someone who could help—like Avigad who helped Mazar in Beth Shearim...

Trude: It is a difficult question. And it's not only Jerusalem. It's an overall problem with excavations that have not been published. It's very easy to blame the people who were carried away with digging, who had busy periods—like Mazar, when he was president of the [Hebrew] University. But he instigated many things that happened in archaeology.

There is this problem, however, of not publishing. No doubt, this is weighing on him. I do hope that he will still be able to get it done with the help of people around him. This is terribly important. It's not easy to dig, but it's very hard to publish. We must find an easier way to do it than the way it is done now. What we should do is dig and publish immediately a preliminary report, but it's easier said than done. We are all carried away by digging.

Shanks: *Do you think the profession has really faced the problem of publication? It harries every archaeologist. There's almost no archaeologist who isn't found wanting on the score of publication.*

Trude: We should have a meeting on how to publish. We were thinking about that for next year—to get all of us together and find a way. There is no one standard. Every dig is different. Every excavator is different. We all want to put everything into the report. Maybe that's the wrong way. We don't know where to stop, to say that's it. But it's a very serious problem.

Shanks: *Moshe, you haven't dug in Ashdod for how many years?*

Moshe: Since 1972. I am now almost finished with the final report. I have published four volumes and have now finished volumes five and six. There will be one more—volume seven, the last one. I have a few other sites. Nahariya is very important. I have the material.* I hope in three years the most important things will be ready for publication.

But I haven't left a single excavation without some report—sometimes only 20 pages, sometimes 10 pages. I hope in a few years everything that is worthwhile will be published.

Shanks: *You have another volume to do on Hammath Tiberias?*

Moshe: Yes, that manuscript is already finished.**

*Volume five of the Ashdod final report appeared in 1993 and volume six was published in 2005. Portions of Nahariya are currently being prepared for publication by Sharon Zuckerman of the Hebrew University in Jerusalem.

**Moshe Dothan and Barbara Johnson, *Hammath Tiberias II—Early Synagogues* (Jerusalem: Israel Exploration Society, 2000).

Shanks: *Do you think that archaeologists should start new digs without publishing their old digs? Do you think there should be a limit on that?*

Moshe: Of course there should be. Now we can put limits on it. But when I was in the Department of Antiquities, we had only two or three people and many excavations. I excavated places with three or four people that needed 20 or 25 people. I did it myself with few volunteers. These were mostly rescue excavations. This was how most of the excavations were started. For example, take Hammath Tiberias. I had just finished working with Mazar and [Avraham] Biran at Ein Gev and the next day I had to go to excavate Hammath Tiberias.

Shanks: *Why was Hammath Tiberias a rescue operation?*

Moshe: Because the people who had the hot baths wanted to enlarge them. They had started to work.

Special police had to be called in. They asked me to excavate it because they needed this place. The people who owned the hot baths even financed the dig.

Shanks: *But they never got their site, did they? [All laugh] [It remains an archaeological park.]*

Moshe: No.
Trude: There is no justice. [All laugh]
Moshe: But I was able to save part of the city wall and the gate to Hammath Tiberias. This is how we worked. Immediately afterwards I had to start in Ashdod. When I got there, part of it was already gone.

Shanks: *Where did it go?*

Moshe: People were taking it as a material for fill. Today it is much better, you can't even compare. Now you work and you publish; there are enough people. Today, it is completely different.

Shanks: *How has excavating changed in your digging experience?*

Trude: Now, whether in a big dig or in a small dig, it's far more complex and far more interdisciplinary. That's good. But, on the other hand, you should not be overawed by the sciences. We archaeologists are still on the border of the humanities. Take a dig that I am involved in now—Ekron, which is a very well-planned dig. It is a joint Israeli and American dig. My colleague Sy [Seymour] Gitin plans very carefully and he does a wonderful job. We get all the scientists together. This is a standard thing to do. The big problem really is how to utilize the material, how to publish it and how not to be overwhelmed by it. In Deir el-Balah [an excavation Trude Dothan directed in the Gaza Strip], we have appendixes and appendixes [in the published report*] from all these interdisciplinary colleagues—written very nicely.

But then the question is how to get the overall picture. Techniques are important. If you are a good archaeologist you use these techniques; you hold your team together; you know what your aim is; you record well. It's important to have a good system, but there is nothing more important than to have the eye—to see, to be in close contact in the field. It's also important to really know what the important things are and what the secondary things are. Otherwise, you'll be overwhelmed. You want to know how people lived, what arms they used, what sanctuaries they worshiped in. It's like an enormous jigsaw puzzle.

*Trude Dothan, *Excavations at the Cemetery of Deir el-Balah*. Qedem 10 (Jerusalem: Institute of Archaeology, the Hebrew University of Jerusalem, 1979).

THE PHILISTINES—AN ARCHAEOLOGICAL ROMANCE

An Interview with Trude and Moshe Dothan—Part II

In the concluding installment from their interview, Trude and Moshe Dothan talk in depth about their own research, focusing in particular on the legacy of the Philistines and other Sea Peoples.

Hershel Shanks: *If you two had a nickname, it would be "Mr. and Mrs. Philistine." You have worked a great deal of your professional lives on the Philistines. You have just written a book about the Philistines [*People of the Sea *(New York: Macmillan, 1992)]. Do you think the Philistines have been treated unfairly in history?*

Trude Dothan: If you call someone a Philistine, it is not exactly a compliment.

We are trying to show that a Philistine is definitely not somebody who has no culture, because archaeology shows the contrary. In the period when the Philistines were in Canaan—in Philistine proper, living beside Israel—Philistine material culture—its architecture, its arts—really ranks the highest, above the Israelites and above the Canaanites.

"The Philistines and the Dothans: An Archaeological Romance, Part 2" appeared in BAR, September/October 1993.

Shanks: *Have you grown fond of the Philistines? Do you feel that you know the Philistines and that they're friends?*

Moshe Dothan: I like them. Incidentally, we have not only the Philistines; there are also other Sea Peoples who are very interesting. We don't know too much about these other Sea Peoples because the Bible is not interested in them. The Bible is interested only in those people who are near Judah.

But there was an enormous movement of people in the 13th and 12th centuries [B.C.], covering not only this country but other countries as well.

Shanks: *You have excavated sites and produced finds reflecting a particular civilization, but you never found an inscription in a Philistine site that says they are Philistine. Yet you label this pottery and other artifacts and architecture as Philistine. How do you know it is Philistine?*

Trude: One of the goals of every archaeologist is to find the written word. To find an archive of the Philistines would be wonderful. We joke about it. Moshe has found the only inscription or written signs that may relate to a Philistine language. We haven't found any written evidence [of the Philistine language] at Ekron yet.* Neither has Larry Stager [professor of archaeology at Harvard University] at Ashkelon.** Larry and the two of us talk about who is going to be the first to find a Philistine archive, but it will not be so easy. We are in a period where the written word is still rare; we are in the dark ages.

*In 1996 at the site of Ekron, however, Trude and Seymour Gitin did uncover a Philistine royal inscription written in a West Semitic language and script dating to the seventh century B.C. The inscription gives the names of five Philistine kings and identifies Ekron as the name of the ancient city. See photo and caption on p. 107, and Seymour Gitin, "Excavating Ekron," **BAR**, November/December 2005.

**But for more recent discoveries at Ashkelon related to this issue, see Lawrence E. Stager and F.M. Cross, "Cyro-Minoan Inscriptions Found in Philistine Ashkelon," *Israel Exploration Journal* 56.4 (2006), pp. 129–159.

HALLMARK OF A NEW CIVILIZATION. The distinctive Philistine pottery is one sign of the arrival of the Sea Peoples along the Canaanite coast. These pitchers and bowls from Ashdod attest to the high level of culture attained by the much-maligned Philistines. Known as bichrome ware because they were decorated with two colors—red and black—this pottery displays typical Philistine designs: ducks and other birds, fish, checkerboard patterns and spirals.

Shanks: *Coming back to the question: You find a beautiful bichrome juglet with lovely paintings with birds and ducks with their heads turned backwards, and you tell me its Philistine. How do you know its Philistine?*

Trude: We don't try to take just one component. The pottery is a kind of hallmark. It's the most visible. It comes in the largest quantities. And from the pottery we can see the Aegean background of the culture. It's like an enormous puzzle. There are many other things. In Egypt, at Medinet Habu, we have the depiction of the Philistines, the Sikila, of the Danuna, of the Shardana. There were many Sea Peoples, not just one, and we have them identified at Medinet Habu. Then we have chronology: the time of Ramesses III (1175 B.C.). Then we have the Bible. We have the biblical stories. We have the names of the Philistine cities. We have the boundaries of Philistia proper.

Shanks: *But I come back to the question: How do you know it's Philistine?*

Trude: The chronological framework fits. The geographical framework fits. It fits with the Egyptian records. The Aegean background fits. We have excavated sites where we have Canaanite cities with their culture ending and a new culture coming in. This new people comes in, settles there, builds towns with new and different plans. It's not just one thing—like pottery. There is a different type of cult building. We have a very rich, new ethnic element coming in, settling, building a new city—in Ashdod, in Ekron. They built a far larger city than the earlier Canaanite cities of the 13th century [B.C.]. From the very beginning, the new cities are well planned. They bring a new architecture. They have hearths in their houses, just like the hearths at Pylos and Mycenae [in Greece].

Shanks: *In the central courtyard?*

Trude: Yes. The hearth was the focal point of the palaces in the Aegean world. It was unknown in Canaan. The new people in Canaan didn't bring the blueprint of the whole settlement, but they brought an architectural idea. This is a new feature in Canaan. I won't go into all the small things that go with it. The important thing is that Philistia fits into the biblical framework. It fits into what we know from Egyptian sources.

Shanks: *You really know Philistia from the biblical description. Isn't that true?*

Trude: Yes, that's true.

Shanks: *And when you dig there you find a distinctive civilization?*

Trude: Yes. From the Bible, we know Ashdod, which kept its name [to modern times]. Ashkelon also kept its name. Ekron did not. But it can be identified with Tel Miqne. Gaza kept its name, but it has not been excavated. So three cities of the Philistine pentapolis kept their names.

We are in a period of coexistence of cultures. We have the Israelite settlements. We have a continuation of the Canaanite population. Egypt is still strong in this period. In Philistia proper, you get this very, very distinct entity. Then they expand.

Shanks: *I would like to make a comparison and then ask a question: At about the same time as you have the reference to the Philistines in Egypt at Medinet Habu, you have a reference to another people called the Israelites. It is on the Merneptah Stele in Egypt [see "The Merneptah Stele: Israel Enters History," p. 101].*

Trude: The Merneptah Stele is even earlier.

Shanks: *The Merneptah Stele is 1208 [B.C.]? When is the Medinet Habu inscription?*

Trude: The first half of the 12th century.

Shanks: *About 1175 [B.C.]?*

Trude: But the Sea Peoples had already been around for a long time. The inscription mentions the final victory of the Egyptians over the Sea Peoples.

Shanks: *So we are really talking about the same time. In the Bible we have a description of where the Philistines settled in Canaan. We also have a description of where the Israelites settled in the central hill country of Canaan—which fits with the mention of Israel in the Merneptah Stele. In the central hill country, we also find a kind of distinctive pottery (the collar-rim jar) and architecture (the four-room house). The question I want to ask is this: Everyone seems to accept without question the existence of the Philistines, that this culture which you excavate in Philistia, and which you call Philistine, is Philistine. Yet there seems to be so much question about the Israelites in the adjacent hill country. Why?*

Trude: I really don't want to tread on a very difficult problem, which, I must say, I can't answer. The problem is different with the Israelites. Take the material culture. What used to be called

Israelite pottery—the collar-rim jar—we now find in Jordan too. So from pottery, I would say be very cautious. You can say more on the basis of the pattern of settlement. The new hill country settlements are in a kind of vacuum area. The new settlements are small. The architecture of the buildings is, again, however, a big problem. It is found not only in the central hill country. So it is the pattern of settlement, it is the time period, it is the area where the new settlements are, more than the material culture we find in these settlements, that tells us who the people were.

Shanks: *Do you have any question about whether the new settlements in the central hill country of Canaan that were contemporaneous with the settlements in Philistia are Israelite settlements?*

Trude: I really must say that there is nothing more difficult than the problem of ethnicity.

Shanks: *You have no problem with Philistine ethnicity, yet you have a problem with the Israelites?*

Trude: I didn't say I have. I think there is a time around the 12th century that you have a coexistence of cultures. Some have a more distinctive material culture than others. I do think the Israelite settlements are well-defined. But they are well-defined more by the way they are dispersed, by the character of the whole settlement—by their initial paucity, by their being small and in areas that had not been previously settled—than by the pottery and architecture. So there are other hallmarks for identifying Israelite settlements than for identifying Philistine cities.

But it's the same question: How do you define a new ethnic element? And it's not clean-cut. In a Philistine city, the Canaanite population was not thrown out. It definitely continued. We find a continuation of local Canaanite traditions as well as new elements. This is also true in the central hill country with the Israelites. If you look, for example, at the cooking pots and the coarse ware, these continue. In Philistia, I think it was only the elite society that is very different, but there is no doubt there is also the continuation of Canaanite material culture. The same is true in the Israelite settlements. There is definitely a continuation of local traditions in the pottery although not in much more. The same is true in the cities in Canaan that were Egyptian, like Beth-Shean or Lachish or in Esh-Shari'a. There you have the continuation of the Egyptian impact. Whether for a longer or short period, you have different entities coexisting.

In Philistia, it is very striking because the newcomers brought with them a very rich, distinctive, flourishing culture. The Israelite settlements in the hill country are more enigmatic, more difficult. Your question is a good one and it is relevant. We are searching for ways to identify new ethnic groups archaeologically, to understand archaeologically the phenomenon of a new group of settlers—whether it's a slow development or a quick one, whether populations coexist or are destroyed, and so on.

Shanks: *There is a kind of symmetry between the two peoples coming in about the same time. But the issue of "coming in" is a little different in each case. There is no question that the Philistines, who were one of the Sea Peoples, "came in" to Canaan from outside; yet, in the case of the Israelites, although the Bible pictures them as "coming in" from outside, there is a great deal of controversy as to whether they really did "come in" from outside or whether they were local refugees from Canaanite cities.* Why is there that difference between the Philistines and Israelites?*

Trude: Archaeologically, I think these are parallel phenomena. With the Philistines there is the same kind of argument, although maybe less vehement than about the Israelites. We tend now in archaeology not to see things in such a clean-cut way—you know, these are the Israelites; these are the Philistines. We try to think in a larger framework, as part of a more general phenomenon, and questions arise. It's no longer clear that the Israelites "came in" and conquered, and so on. Many scholars now see it as a social development, as a

* For a more recent treatment of this issue, see Anson Rainey, "Inside, Outside: Where did the Early Israelites Comes From?" **BAR**, November/December 2008.

pattern of development. It is not one thing or two things, but several. And it is a slow development. For the Philistines, it's more drastic. You can see the change more easily archaeologically.

Shanks: *Moshe, you mentioned a number of other Sea Peoples. They are not referred to in the Bible, are they?*

Moshe: No, they are not mentioned in the Bible, but they are mentioned in Egyptian sources.

Shanks: *Along with the Philistines?*

Moshe: Along with the Philistines. They are very interesting. I am sure that some of them settled in Canaan.

Shanks: *According to the Egyptian inscriptions?*

Moshe: No, they don't say where they settled. We don't know what happened to all these people whom the Egyptians were fighting. They have to be somewhere. We are lucky that we have the Bible, and the Bible tells us about the Philistines. I stress this again and again. The Bible is really the source for so much of our knowledge. Of course, the Bible doesn't answer all our questions. But we have the stories about the Philistines, about Samson and so on. They are not just stories; they have some background. And the Bible tells where these people lived. In exactly those places, we find this culture we call Philistine. This can't be any other culture.

Shanks: *Since the Bible does not mention any Sea Peoples except the Philistines, how do you know, for example, that a site was occupied by one of the other Sea Peoples? Why don't you identify it as Philistine also? And what are these other sites settled by other Sea Peoples?*

Moshe: The majority of the Sea Peoples who settled in this country in the late 13th and early part of the 12th century were Philistines. We know this from the Egyptian records. After some very prolonged fighting, Ramesses III settled them here. There are some years for which we don't have any evidence as to what was going on in Egypt.

We know only that it was a very bad time for the Egyptians. Something happened for perhaps 10 or 20 years and then most of the Egyptian rulers were gone from this country. Somebody came in. They have to be the Sea People. In the Bible, I think Philistine is a generic term for more than one tribe of Sea Peoples.

Shanks: *I understand that at Tell Qasile, for example, which is within the city limits of Tel Aviv today, it was not the Philistines but another Sea People. Similarly at Dor, farther north on the coast, another Sea People settled there. Is that correct?*

Moshe: Yes.

Shanks: *Who were the other Sea Peoples at these sites?*

Moshe: There are at least two we are certain of. One is called the Sikila and the other is the Shardana. The Sikila settled north of the Philistines in the middle part of the Canaanite coast. The Shardana were still further north. We have this from Egyptian records, of course. I believe there may be one more tribe of Sea Peoples here—the Danuna or Danaoi, also mentioned in Egyptian sources.

Shanks: *Is there a connection between the Israelite tribe of Dan and the Sea People known as the Danuna?*

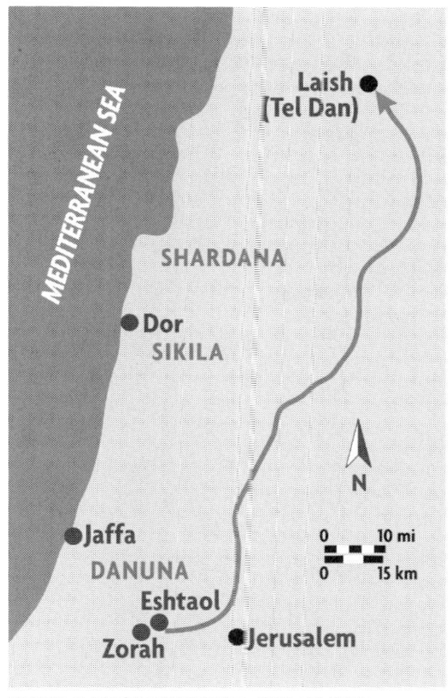

THE MIGRATION OF DAN. Moshe Dothan, following the suggestion of Yigael Yadin, believes that the Israelite tribe of Dan and a Sea Peoples tribe named the Danuna or Danaoi were related. The seafaring Israelite Danites, unable to establish themselves on the coast near Jaffa (their original tribal allotment), migrated north to Laish. With echoes of their seafaring past, the Song of Deborah (Judges 5) castigates the tribe for having failed to answer her call to do battle against an alliance of Canaanite kings "And Dan, why did he abide by the ships?" (Judges 5:17).

Moshe: Yes. They meet somewhere on the coast near Jaffa in the area of the territory allotted to the tribe of Dan in the Bible. The two people somehow mix. I don't know the origin of the tribe of Dan. But the Danuna was an old tribe in the western Mediterranean; afterward they appear in many places. I am sure that some of them somehow mixed with the tribe of Dan.

Shanks: *Do you think that when the Sea People tribe of Danuna settled in Canaan that they then mixed with the Israelites who took the name of Dan from the name Danuna? Is that how it worked?*

Moshe: We don't know exactly how it happened, but it is very interesting that the Danuna appear somewhere near Jaffa, precisely where, according to biblical tradition, the Israelite Danites were supposed to settle.

Shanks: *Were the Israelites already there?*

Moshe: This is the question. We still don't have the evidence that would connect the two. But it is too close for there not to have been some connection. For some reason the Danites left the place allotted to them and then go up to northern Dan. This is told in the Bible (Judges 18:11–12,27–29). At the same time we have the Danaoi mentioned in all kinds of sources, including Egyptian sources. I am really following in the footsteps of Yigael Yadin here.

Shanks: *I can understand where the Danuna or Danaoi came from. They were a Greek Aegean element. But what is the Israelite source of the Danites?*

Moshe: I don't know how it was written, what the source of the story is. But suddenly part of the Israelite tribe of Dan leaves its allotted territory and goes north. They may be the Danaoi who were more closely connected with the Israelites. All the other Danaoi stay somehow in Danuna, if you like—that is, in the original tribal allotment of Dan.

Shanks: *How did the element of the Israelites who mixed with the Danaoi get to the area of Jaffa?*

Moshe: According to the Bible, they were very near the coast, only a few miles from the coast. Maybe they were in Jaffa under Egyptian rule. The names are so close; but we don't have the last piece of evidence that ties it all up.

Shanks: *Who was at Dor?*

Moshe: The Sikila were at Dor. The Shardana were farther north.

Shanks: *How do you know this?*

Moshe: The Egyptians list them in this order.

Shanks: *You assume that the Egyptians put the names in geographical order. The Egyptian records don't actually say which Sea People are where, do they?*

Moshe: No, they don't say, but it seems so. The Shardana are always in the north because they are always mentioned after the others. The Sikila are mentioned in the Egyptian tale of Wen-Amon as being in Dor.

Shanks: *The Wen-Amon story dates from when?*

Moshe: We think it dates from the 12th century.

Shanks: *And Wen-Amon speaks of being in Dor and seeing the Sikila in Dor?*

Moshe: Yes. The Sikila are the easiest to pinpoint because of the Wen-Amon story.

There is one more element, the Greek Wanax.

Wanax is a kind of king or head of the tribe. It is also a generic name for the king or head of a community or of tribes. It appears in hundreds of ancient Greek inscriptions—in Linear B and later in regular Greek. I believe Wanax is related to the

HISTORIC CONFRONTATION. This artistic rendering of the reliefs from Ramesses III's mortuary temple at Medinet Habu near Luxor shows the Egyptians repulsing the Sea Peoples naval advance towards Egypt. The depicted battle likely occurred about 1177 B.C.E. Large numbers of these Sea Peoples, including the biblical Philistines, ultimately settled along the narrow coastal plain of Canaan.

Anakim referred to in the Bible as a people who are in the southern part of Canaan before the Philistines. The trouble is that it is not so easy to transform the Greek *omega* and make it an *'ayin* in Hebrew in this period. Otherwise I would jump on the connection immediately.

Shanks: *Are you saying the biblical Anakim may have been one of the Sea Peoples?*

Moshe: In the end they were. Originally, they were in the Peloponnese in Greece. I think when the Greek peoples dispersed and went to all kinds of places, part of them came to Canaan. These Greeks were already settled here when the Philistines came. They came a little before the Philistines. In Ashdod, they may be our stratum 13.

Shanks: *Is that the monochrome stratum?*

Moshe: Yes.

Shanks: *How do you associate that with the Anakim?*

Moshe: In the Bible, it says the Anakim were in Ashdod before the Philistines (Joshua 11:21–22).

Shanks: *You think there may have been another Sea People here before the Philistines?*

Moshe: I don't say 100 percent, but I think it was something like this. The Anakim were in other places, but Ashdod may have been their most important site.

Shanks: *Why do you think all of these different Sea Peoples, who were really Greeks, as far as we know—their culture is clearly related to the culture found contemporaneously in the Aegean area—why did they all go to Egypt and the eastern Mediterranean littoral?*

Moshe: We really don't know. So many books and so many articles have been written about what really happened in the Peloponnese at this time. But these people started to leave their own country or countries and look for someplace else to live. We don't know why. Perhaps there were wars or maybe famine. The Shardana, for example, gave their name to Sardinia. The Sikila gave their name to Sicily. We know this from later traditions—from the eighth or ninth century B.C.—but, of course it all goes back much earlier.

Shanks: *So they didn't go only to the eastern Mediterranean?*

Moshe: Not at all.

Shanks: *The whole world was in great turmoil at this time. The Hittite empire was collapsing, Egyptian hegemony was losing its hold. Isn't that correct?*

Moshe: Yes. It started at the end of the 13th century [B.C.]. We don't exactly know when Sardinia and Sicily got their names, but it seems it was quite, quite early. Archaeologists in Sardinia and Sicily are finding evidence of this, but we can't yet pinpoint the time.

Our most important source, really, is the Egyptians. The

Egyptians called them the Sea Peoples. That's how we got their name. They say they are coming by thousands with enormous troops. Many more nations are mentioned than those we have already referred to, nations that are otherwise completely unknown. No place is given for them, so we don't know where to look. But this was an enormous movement.

Shanks: *Are you saying that there was one cause for all this upheaval all over the Mediterranean?*

Moshe: Perhaps there were some inner causes in certain countries. But don't forget that some enormous towns like Ugarit were destroyed.

Shanks: *That's in modern-day Syria?*

Moshe: Yes, but this destruction occurred all along the Syrian coast, from what is today Turkey.

Shanks: *Isn't it hard to believe that thousands, or tens of thousands of people, would come out of this turmoil in the Aegean and be able to destroy much of the world?*

After all, there were sophisticated civilizations in Egypt and in Ugarit, for example. How could these people destroy these civilizations? It is at least as difficult to imagine such a destruction by the Sea Peoples as to imagine the destruction of Canaanite cities by the Israelites.

Moshe: The Sea Peoples didn't destroy the Egyptians.

Shanks: *But how could these Sea People come from the Aegean and take over and destabilize other civilizations?*

Moshe: They didn't take over Egypt.

Shanks: *They destroyed Ugarit.*

Moshe: Yes.

Shanks: *Let's take the case of Ugarit. It was a fantastic civilization.*

And here you have these Sea Peoples who are apparently leaving because of famine or war and yet somehow they were able to organize a military armada on land and sea and fight the Egyptians even if they lost, and destroy Ugarit. I'd like to know how they did it. And then I'd also like to know, if they could do it, why can't we as easily imagine the Israelites coming in and successfully fighting the Canaanites. Trude, maybe you could provide part of the answer.

Trude: I don't know the answer to this. I don't know how the Sea Peoples did it. It's one of the cardinal questions. It used to be very clear that the Sea Peoples came and destroyed. That was always the explanation. Now I don't think it's so clear. Now the trend is very different. Many scholars are working on the problem—on the end of the Hittite empire in Anatolia, the end of Ugarit, the destruction of cities in Canaan, the end of the Mycenaean palace culture in Greece. They don't see it anymore as attributable to the Sea Peoples. That's not the main cause. The coming of the Sea Peoples is an outcome. Now, the explanation is more often famine, or drought or things like that.

But of course, this too is an easy way out. You have to be very careful. I don't think that the Sea Peoples came with an armada and did it all. The situation is different in different places. Ugarit was destroyed. No doubt about it. Egypt is another story. Here there was a very short interregnum of destabilization between the XIXth and XXth dynasties—only 10 or 15 years. But Egypt was very strong. In Philistia [Canaan], the picture is again different. Here we do have a continuation of a previous culture with the Philistines settling down.

Moshe: But they destroyed it first.

Trude: They destroyed it, but then they settled it. The cities were definitely destroyed.

It's not a simple picture. These are very complex things. You talk about the end of the Hittite empire. That is another story. The Hittitologists have so many different ideas as to what happened. Cyprus is another story.

Shanks: *Were there destructions on Cyprus?*

Trude: Yes, but then there is a rebuilding. The 12th century was one of the most flourishing periods in Cyprus. It may have begun in the 13th century, but it definitely comes again from the Aegean world.

We have a very similar phenomenon with the settlement of the Philistines in Canaan.

There is, it is true, an end of a period, the end of maritime trade, the end of the great maritime cultures of the Late Bronze Age, the powers of the 14th century and 13th century. In Iron Age I (1200–1000 B.C.), we no longer find a maritime connection between the Greek world and the Orient.

Shanks: *There was a kind of disintegration?*

Trude: Definitely.

Shanks: *So you do have a disintegration, for whatever cause, and these Sea Peoples go around the world and in effect take over or insert themselves into other cultures, other civilizations. Its a complex process. In some cases there are destructions.*

But if the Sea Peoples are fleeing, if they are running from a difficult situation, they are not in a position to organize. How could they impose themselves on peoples who didn't want them? How could they conquer the cities that were destroyed? Yet they appear to have done it. Now, what I want to ask you is this: The situation of the Sea Peoples sounds to a lay person a lot like the biblical description of the conquest of Canaan, where you have these runaway slaves as it were, people who weren't of high culture, yet who were able to infiltrate and conquer and in some cases, according to the biblical text dispossess other peoples and to settle there. The descriptions in the Bible are all very realistic in their geopolitical aspects. Militarily the Bible is very careful to describe it in a way that is strategically very clever and makes sense in terms of the topography. There is a tendency to completely reject this in the case of the biblical Israelites, yet we accept it in the case of the Sea Peoples.

And we even say we have archaeological confirmation of this in the case of the Sea Peoples. Can you explain this, Trude?

Trude: Again, you ask a difficult question. I won't even venture to answer it. I can only say that as an archaeologist, I'm definitely modest about it. I don't think I can solve all the problems: Why the Hittite empire fell; why there is no continuation there; why there is this dark age; why Ugarit wasn't rebuilt; et cetera.

The whole Mediterranean was in an upheaval, no doubt about that. There is definitely an end of trade. This is terribly important. Some places recover very quickly, others [do] not. In Canaan, we have the phenomenon you talked about with the Israelites and the Philistines. I think this has to be studied and restudied. It has been done, but we see how different the conclusions are.

You ask, "How did these Sea Peoples wander in these ships, meandering through the seas?" I don't think those who fled were the lowly people. Whoever managed to go on the ships were not only the sailors, but the elite who brought their culture with them. In Philistia they built large, well organized cities

Shanks: *Was there a cultural break in Greece itself?*

Trude: There you had the culture of the Mycenaean palaces. This ends. But then you have a continuation of life in these palaces. In Tiryns, for example, there is a revival, similar to what we have in Philistia. But the social structure is then very different in Greece. No longer is there a Wanax or king. It's a different social set-up.

Shanks: *Do we have any idea what caused the upheaval in Greece?*

Trude: Well, it needn't be the coming of the barbarians or the Dorians, as used to be said. So now we can say that it's the result of social change. Or you can speak about drought, or about climatic change or wars. Again, it's the same question.

This is something that is very hard to answer archaeologically. Something happened. But interpretations of what happened will be very different. On the other hand, archaeology can show that there is a new barbarian pottery in Greece.

Earlier you asked if archaeology is the handmaiden of history. I think we really need to take historians and linguists and archaeologists and sociologists and people who can talk about drought and climates—and all work together. In a way, this is what it is all about. We have to have this interdisciplinary approach.

Shanks: *One thing seems clear in Philistia, that there was a monochrome phase in the pottery and then a bichrome phase. Am I correct?*

Trude: Yes.

Shanks: *Moshe associates the monochrome, the earlier phase, with the Anakim?*

Moshe: It's a suggestion.

Shanks: *Is this monochrome phase at all Sea People sites?*

Moshe: This monochrome phase appears in all sites that are being or have been excavated with modern methods. We don't know about sites excavated 100 years ago. We don't have enough evidence.

Shanks: *If the monochrome phase appears in all these sites preceding the bichrome phase, Moshe, do you associate the monochrome phase with an earlier Sea People before the Philistines at all these sites?*

Moshe: This is my suggestion. But it doesn't have to be the same at all sites. In the Bible, it says that there were people called Anakim in Ashdod and afterwards we have only Philistines in Ashdod. I think that I have the right at least to suggest it.

The Bible says there was an earlier people in Ashdod. In the biblical period—the 13th, 12th century or 11th century—people knew about it. Perhaps they even saw it with their own eyes. So, if we find, as we do at Ashdod, one early group with monochrome pottery, and a second group with bichrome pottery and with a different town plan, I would say that we have to correlate this with the

Bible and conclude that the monochrome is connected with the first people mentioned in the Bible, the Anakim, and the bichrome ware is connected with the second people, the Philistines.

Shanks: *How do you explain the elimination of the Anakim?*

Moshe: They were just assimilated because they were cousins of the Philistines.

Shanks: *So the Philistines are a little like the Russian immigrants who are now coming to Israel?*

Moshe: Exactly. The name Wanax is not completely the same as Anakim but I do have good evidence of the relation from my friend, Mrs. [Anna] Morpugo [Davies, of Somerville College, Oxford]. She is the best in this pre-Greek grammar and philology. She says it is 50 percent.

Shanks: *What is your view of this problem, Trude?*

Trude: First of all, what Moshe said relates to Ashdod. The only city of the Philistine pentapolis that the Bible says has Anakim is Ashdod. It's an idea, but it has to be proven. It's a philological problem connected to archaeology, so it's very legitimate. On the other hand, there are differences in the cities of the pentapolis. For me, it is not important. It's one group of the Sea Peoples. I can call them early Philistines. For me, the first phase of settlement, the monochrome phase, is the Philistines—in Ekron, in Ashdod and in Ashkelon. It's definitely part of the same picture. And it will be the same if these are the Wanax, or Aegean or Achaean or whatever. But I don't go as far as that yet.

Shanks: *I'd like to ask you about the relationship between the Philistines and the Israelites. In a site like Lachish, which is perhaps 20 miles away from Philistia or less, you don't find any Philistine ware. What does this tell us about the relationship between the Philistines and the Israelites?*

Trude: [Laughter] This is a discussion that David Ussishkin [the excavator of Lachish] and I always have. First of all, there are I think a few Philistine sherds from Lachish. Second, Lachish was not settled at that time. There was a gap after Ramesses III.

Shanks: *So you do think that when there was simultaneous settlement there would be trade?*

Trude: Yes, definitely. But Lachish has this gap in settlement. This we know. Between stratum 6 and stratum 5 something happened. The second half of the 12th century is not there. The 11th century is problematic.

Shanks: *What does archaeology tell us about relations between the Philistines and Israelites?*

Trude: In the early periods?

Shanks: *Yes, in this monochrome and bichrome period of the Philistines. Are there Israelite sites where we find some evidence of relations with the Philistines?*

What about the small settlements in the central hill country that are supposedly Israelite? We have no Philistine pottery there, do we?

Trude: A sherd was found at Izbet Sartah. I believe.

Shanks: *Can we conclude that in this early period, the Israelites and the Philistines led lives very isolated from one another?*

Moshe: There were not too many Israelites living in the southern part of the country. This is where the Philistines were strong.

Shanks: *We know where the Philistines were strong. We know where the Israelites were living. What I am asking is whether there was any relationship, commercial or otherwise, between the two peoples?*

Moshe: Very little. There was perhaps a kind of coexistence at a place like Afula, near Megiddo, where I found both Israelite and Philistine pottery. So there was some coexistence. It could happen.

Shanks: *But not in the central hill country. I don't know of a single Philistine sherd found in the hill country. Do you, Trude?*

Trude: No. You asked the right question. But I think one has to look at the quantities—not one sherd or two, here or there. Dan, incidentally, has some very interesting Philistine pottery. So should we connect this with the Danuna?

Shanks: *In Philistia or in the areas settled by the Sea Peoples, do we have any indication that the Israelites traded with them? For example, do we find any collar-rim jars at Sea Peoples sites?*

Moshe: Never along the coast.

Shanks: *So it seems from the archaeological evidence from the early period, the Israelites and the Philistines were very isolated from one another?*

Moshe: Apart, yes.
Trude: In the initial phase, yes. But by now everybody more or less agrees that the collar-rim jar is not the hallmark of the Israelites. It is found so widely that we have to be very careful about that.

Shanks: *Isn't it true that most of the collar-rim jars—the heaviest concentration of them—are found in the area that the Bible ascribes to the Israelites?*

Trude: Yes it is, but it is also found quite widely elsewhere.
Moshe: The collar-rim jar was needed more in the hills for water.

Shanks: *Are you saying the collar-rim jar cannot be used as an element in identifying the site as Israelite?*

Moshe: It may help but its presence is due mainly to the economic factor. In the hill country, they needed it. But if some non-Israelite tribe lived in the hill country they would also be using it.

Shanks: *We have established that there is very little evidence of Philistine culture or trade coming into the areas that were occupied by* *the Israelites. Can we also say that there is very little from the Israelites coming into the Philistine areas at this early stage?*

Moshe: I would say extremely little.

Shanks: *Moshe, we haven't found a Philistine archive yet, but what little writing that has been found at a Philistine site was found by you at Ashdod. Is that correct?*

Moshe: I have two pieces but they are not yet read. Somebody in the United States tried.

Shanks: *Who was that?*

Moshe: Robert Stieglitz [professor of Hebrew and archaeology at Rutgers University]. He's not sure of his reading. I am even less sure of his reading.

Shanks: *So, we haven't really found any Philistine writing yet?*

Moshe: No. Not from the early period. Later they probably used the Hebrew or Phoenician alphabet, but nothing earlier than the eighth century B.C.

Shanks: *What do you think about the Philistine control of metal in early Israelite times? Did they really have this monopoly on metal, and was this the reason that they were such a threat to the Israelites?*

Trude: This has been a kind of myth, one of those holy cows. It's supposedly based on the Bible (1 Samuel 13:9–21). But in the Bible you don't have the word "iron." The Hebrew word is *barzel*. Jane Waldbaum has shown very beautifully that *barzel* is not iron. The Philistines had a monopoly on metal working but not on iron. The Philistines brought with them the knowledge of how to work iron. That is what the biblical sentence is referring to, but iron is not mentioned. Only metal working is mentioned. At Ekron, we have found a large number of iron objects. But they are mostly elite, artistic objects—knives with ivory handles found in the shrine on the *bamah* [offering platform]. In the initial phase of Philistine settlement at Ekron, iron objects were found near a decapitated puppy burial. But iron is not yet part of everyday usage in the 12th and 11th century B.C. The same kind of iron knives were found in the Philistine temple at Tell Qasile. They have parallels in Cyprus and Greece. But it's not yet in everyday life. It's not like the tenth or ninth or seventh century when you have iron plows and things like that. Earlier iron was used for religious objects, like these ivory knives found on the *bamah*.

Shanks: *Toward the late 11th century a clear conflict developed between the Israelites and the Philistines. There was an important battle somewhere between Aphek and Ebenezer.*

Trude: Yes.

Shanks: *The Israelites lost the battle. The ark was captured by the Philistines. Did the Philistine expertise in metal working play any part in that battle?*

Trude: I don't think that archaeology can answer that, but we can say that these Philistine cities were strong. But we haven't found the tombs of the warriors. Emily Vermoule [professor of classics at Harvard University] asked me, "Where are the tombs of the heroes?" That's where the fantastic finds would be, if there are any—in the burials. We haven't found them—not in Ashdod or Ashkelon or at Ekron. This makes it a little difficult to give a complete picture. But we know the organization of the city plans, we know the buildings, we know that economically they were flourishing. So the military force must have been elite. But we haven't found any weapons at Ekron or at Ashkelon. It would be nice to find them.

Shanks: *Do either of you want to add anything that I haven't asked about?*

Moshe: As time goes on, we see that more and more of the facts mentioned in the Bible can be used in reconstructing what we find in our excavations. The truth is that everybody, even people who are against the Bible, go first to the Bible to see if something there supports what they find. Many biblical texts have been vindicated. When the Bible gives us a sentence or even a word, we have to use it.

Shanks: *Trude, do you want to add anything?*

Trude: I am an archaeologist, a dirt archaeologist. But without having a framework I would just have to call what I find a pot. It would be anonymous. I think we are very fortunate that we have these biblical records, but we take them cautiously. We don't go with the Bible in one hand and the spade in the other, but it definitely must be used.

Why is this country so important archaeologically? It's not because we have such grandiose finds. It's important only because it speaks to us. It's part of our heritage. It feels great that you can, in a way, read about your finds in the Bible. If you find an inscription, it talks to you straight. It bridges the centuries. I think that this is really a great feeling, but you have to do it cautiously. You can't go about it blindly. I'm not a biblical scholar. I am a plain archaeologist. I try to use all the sources available and go to the people who know more about these things for help. And then I try to integrate it all.

Shanks: *Thank you both very much.*

CHAPTER SEVEN

AGAINST THE TIDE

An Interview with Maverick Scholar Cyrus Gordon

Cyrus Gordon through the years

Cyrus Gordon was a scholar of enormous range. His bibliography of more than 35 books and 350 articles can be divided into over 20 categories, focusing largely on linguistics and social history.

"Against the Tide: An Interview with Maverick Scholar Cyrus Gordon" appeared in BAR, November/December 2000.

Among them are Aramaic-Syriac-Mandaic studies, art and archaeology of the Near East, Assyriology, Biblical studies, Egypto-Semitic studies, Minoan, and Phoenician and Hebrew inscriptions.

Gordon's views, however, have gained varying degrees of acceptance in the academic world. His Ugaritic Grammar *(Pontificium Institutum Biblicum, 1940) is universally hailed as a major contribution, making Canaanite religious literature accessible for the first time. His emphasis on the connections between the Greek world and the Hebrew world was initially met with great skepticism when Gordon first proposed it nearly 45 years ago. Today it is commonplace to acknowledge such connections.*

On the other hand, his decipherment of Linear A, which as he says in the following interview he regards as his greatest scholarly achievement, is extremely controversial and is accepted mostly only by his former students. Likewise, his continued belief in the authenticity of North American inscriptions (such as the Bat Creek inscription from Tennessee) that would place Semites in the western hemisphere in about 800 B.C.E. has very few adherents in the scholarly world.

What remains certain, however, is that Cyrus Gordon occupied his own unique scholarly niche. Throughout his long career, he was, as he described himself, "a disturber of the pax academica.*" In this interview, Gordon discusses his unique personal and academic story and fires back at those who have criticized his ideas.*

Hershel Shanks: *You were born in 1908, 92 years ago. If my calculations are correct, that's only 18 years after the first scientific excavation in Palestine by Sir William Matthew Flinders Petrie in 1890 at Tell el-Hesi.*

Cyrus Gordon: Yes. Petrie really established scientific archaeology in that excavation, by combining ceramic typology and stratigraphy. He worked out the typology with wavy ledge handles. [Such handles are placed near the broadest section of a vessel. Ledge-handle vessels can be picked up by placing one's fingers underneath the handles.—**Ed.**] Petrie put these handles in sequence. Over time, they would change in size—growing or shrinking. So you find one stratum in which the handles were bigger and later strata in which they ended up smaller. [That is, the stratigraphy establishes the typical sequence of handle sizes over time.—**Ed.**] The idea of stratigraphy he got from that character who excavated Troy—Heinrich Schliemann.

SIR WILLIAM MATTHEW FLINDERS PETRIE (1853–1942) revolutionized archaeology when, in 1890 during a dig at Tell el-Hesi in southern Israel, he combined typology and stratigraphy.

HS: *Did you know Petrie?*

CG: Yes, but not well. I used to meet him at tea parties at the American School of Oriental Research in Jerusalem [now the W.F. Albright Institute of Archaeolcgical Research]. I was there—between there and Iraq—from 1931 to 1935.

HS: *So he was already an old man?*

CG: Younger than I am now. He was married to Lady Hilda. Although she was on the threshold of old age, she was still a beauty. She retained the charms of youth even in her old age.

I also went to see Petrie at Tell el-Ajjul, which he thought was ancient Gaza. He was wrong, but he found more gold in that one year than archaeologists have found in the past hundred years in every site combined.

HS: *How do you account for that? Archaeologists today aren't able to* *find such magnificent things very often.*

CG: Petrie explained it perfectly. He said that idiots—the other archaeologists—would go to the places where the prophets lived. Now, if you want to know about Amos, it's in the Bible. You don't dig for it. And also the high standards of morality and ethics in the Bible don't go with high standards of living with a lot of gold sitting around. We know, for example, that the Philistines came from the West with a tradition of miniature work in gold. In the Bible, when the Philistines wanted to appease the God of Israel, they made five golden hemorrhoids, or tumors, and five golden mice (1 Samuel 6:4–5) because a plague of mice had afflicted them.* They wanted to appease the gods they had offended. The Hebrews were concerned with God and the Ten Commandments and with what was right; you don't go there for gold. Petrie said, if these idiots had only had more sense, they could have found these things, but they always went to the wrong places and for the wrong reasons. He was a very shrewd guy. I got along very well with him. He published a report with time-exposed photographs every year after his excavation. That's not the usual thing. He had a lady's hatbox, and he put a hatpin through it and took time exposures, very long-time-exposures. This was the beginning of photography in archaeology.

HS: *You got your Ph.D. from the University of Pennsylvania in 1930 at the age of 22, didn't you?*

CG: Actually, two weeks before my 22nd birthday.

HS: *Were you raised in Philadelphia?*

CG: Yes. We lived in a very fine brownstone house at the corner of Broad and Mifflin, but my parents sent me to public school.

*For a different interpretation of this passage based on archaeological evidence, see Aren M. Maeir, "Did Captured Ark Afflict Philistines with E.D.?" **BAR**, May/June 2008.

My fellow students in public school were African-American and Neapolitan and Sicilian Italians, who were gearing up—although they didn't realize it—for the prohibition age. They would grow up to be bootleggers.

CYRUS ON CYRUS. Cyrus Herzl Gordon, while on military assignment in Fars (Persia), visited the tomb of his namesake Cyrus the Great, who allowed the Jews to return to Palestine in the sixth century B.C.E. The Persian king was, therefore, according to Gordon, the founder of ancient Zionism; Gordon's father, an ardent political Zionist, chose to name his son for that famous king and for Theodor Herzl, the founder of modern Zionism.

The kind of family that I came from knew what to do with a book, knew what to do with a text. Someone with some funds was not what was respected. What was respected was learning. You see, not all Jews are the same. A Litvak [a Lithuanian Jew] worked on texts. If you have two sons, and one is a conformist, good kid, gets good marks in school, he's a gentleman and all that, but if he's in business, you can't expect too much of him. However, if you have a son who can't earn a nickel, but he's a brilliant scholar and knows how to analyze a text, that's what would bring respect in our community. That's the way I was brought up. Nothing was said about it. You don't have to say anything. It's in the atmosphere.

My father was a physician, but at night he would come home and work on his books. He read a whole series of books on the history of medicine.

HS: *What did he do to educate you?*

CG: I learned from a *malamed* [a children's tutor]: A *malamed* is a guy who couldn't make it in scholarship. If you're a high-class guy in the community, you're in the yeshiva [studying Talmud], but you don't teach children. So the *malamed* had a bad reputation, and they were often sadistic, taking it out on the kids. My father hired a man, a very sweet man, Mr. Abelson, who had a wife and two daughters. He was my teacher; I could ask him questions. One of the questions I asked him was where babies came from. He said they come out of ladies. I was five years old. At the supper table my parents asked me what I had learned. So I told them. My mother was very Victorian; she went to school in the 1890s in New York. She nearly hit the ceiling. She said to my father, "You discharge him at once. He's teaching our child immorality." My father, who was much more worldly, said, "Look, he's got a wife and two kids to support; he needs this money. I'll tell him not to discuss things like that anymore." So that established peace in the family.

HS: *Your first name is Cyrus, and your middle name is Herzl. Herzl, of course, is the father of modern Zionism. Were your parents Zionists?*

CG: Yes, Cyrus [the Great, the Persian successor to the Babylonians] sent the Jews back to Palestine to rebuild the Temple [in the sixth century B.C.E., ending the Babylonian Exile; see Ezra 1:1–3; 2 Chronicles 36:22–23]. Theodor Herzl came to the fore in the Dreyfus case.* During the Dreyfus case my father became an ardent Zionist, not just a theoretical Zionist or an idealistic Zionist, but a conscious political Zionist. Herzl

*In 1894, Alfred Dreyfus, a Jewish captain in the French army, was convicted of treason and sentenced to life imprisonment on Devil's Island. His conviction was motivated by anti-Semitism, which was then rampant in the French military. Ultimately it was shown that Dreyfus's conviction was based on forged documents. In 1906 a French court exonerated him, and he was reinstated in the army.

was an Austrian journalist and a theater critic. Very respected. He realized that you have to have a country to represent you. You can't just be a stranger in every land. So my father took the name of the founder of ancient Zionism, Cyrus, and the founder of modern Zionism, Herzl, and that's why I'm called Cyrus Herzl Gordon. My father was very active in the Zionist movement. He organized Zionist clubs in Philadelphia and across the river in Camden.

HS: *When you got your doctorate, had you ever participated in an archaeological excavation?*

CG: No, I never wanted to be an archaeologist! But my mentor at Penn, James A. Montgomery, told me that I could get a fellowship to go out on digs with [William Foxwell] Albright and others, and I should do this. "You have to have field work," he said. "This is where the new discoveries come from." So I got the fellowship, and they renewed it for four years. Montgomery, who was president of the American Schools of Oriental Research, got me fixed up so I would work in Iraq during the winters, and in the summers I would work in Palestine.

HS: *How did you get to Palestine?*

CG: I came by ship. It left from Philadelphia, then it went to New York, and then it stopped at Boston, and then it went to the Azores, and then to Lisbon. It was a wonderful experience. You got this gradual change. Then we went through the Straits of Gibraltar, to Marseilles, and then to a couple of Italian cities, and then to Athens, and then to Istanbul, and then we went on to Haifa, which was a military harbor. Then we went to Jaffa. In Jaffa there were two very big rocks. If the seas were quiet, you got off the boat in rowboats with your baggage. If it was stormy, everyone had to wait until the storm subsided. The boats were all manned by Arabs, most of whom could not read. The people they ferried were mostly Jews. The older ones came to die there and the younger ones to build up the land. I wanted to get to the American School in Jerusalem, so I asked my boatman how to do this—in classical Arabic. He didn't understand a word. Then I asked him in classical Hebrew. He didn't know that. I tried English. Not a word. Then he says to me, *"Efsher redst du zhargon?"* (Do you perhaps speak Yiddish [literally, jargon]?) This was the international language. I told him I knew German. We didn't speak Yiddish at home, but I was able to talk to him in German.

HS: *How long did that trip take, from Philadelphia to Jaffa?*

CG: A month.

HS: *How did you get from Jaffa to the American School in Jerusalem?*

CG: I took a seat in a cab. I took a front seat, but the trouble is, they sold two front seats, and the guy with the other front seat was holding a goat.

I spent just a few days at the American School. And then I went to dig at Tell Beit Mirsim under Albright and also at Beth-Zur under Ovid Sellers [professor of Old Testament at McCormick Theological Seminary in Chicago]. Sellers was a wonderful guy, but, although he was the director, Albright made all the decisions as to where to dig and how to dig.

HS: *And what did you do?*

CG: I worked on the mound; I learned ceramic chronology from Albright. Some of the time I spent in the work tent, where I kept the record of all the finds, of all the scarabs and coins.

HS: *Did Albright or Sellers do any actual digging with their own hands?*

CG: No.

HS: *And you did not either?*

CG: No, we thought this was beneath our dignity. You didn't have educated people soiling their hands until the Israelis were running the place [after 1948].

HS: *Who did the actual digging?*

CG: All local Arabs. And we used Egyptian taskmasters. To get the workers to bring you the finds, you had to give them *bak-sheesh* [bribes]. They brought you the finds, and you would buy it from them with a chit [voucher], and on payday they would collect. Now, we didn't give them too much *baksheesh,* because if we did, they would bring things from outside and say they had found it on the dig. You had to give them enough *baksheesh,* but not too much.

HS: *I don't understand.*

CG: Suppose I gave them five dollars for something that on the open market was worth 50 cents. They would then get such things not from the mound but from the market. I had to learn how to do these things.

HS: *Was there no American supervising them, watching them?*

CG: I was supervising them, and other people were too. If they gave me a Seleucid or Ptolemaic coin, I knew this could be found there, but if they gave me a Turkish [Ottoman] coin, I knew that it came from the outside. If they did that, I fired them. I wouldn't tell them why. I would just fire them. And then they'd tell the other workers, "These Americans are magicians; they knew that I was lying."

HS: *How did you control for stratigraphy?*

CG: The Egyptian taskmasters were very good at implementing our instructions. They cracked whips. They used to beat the workers. I couldn't imagine an American beating the workers, but the Egyptians did.

HS: *Why were they beating them?*

CG: That's the only kind of communication they understood. You didn't have working men's rights, human rights, things like that.

HS: *Were there Egyptians with whips at Tell Beit Mirsim?*

CG: All over. You couldn't have a Palestinian whipping people of his own tribe. The Egyptians did it. They wouldn't eat with the Palestinians. They mustn't have any intimacy. I think the Egyptians were dignified about it and efficient. They were mostly Coptic Christians.

HS: *Did they actually hit the workers with their whips?*

CG: Of course they did. Look, you couldn't tell the Egyptians how to make the Palestinians work. You couldn't do that.

HS: *Was there any effort to dig layer by layer?*

CG: Look, you dig. And when you come to hardened earth, this is because this was a floor. So you tell them, don't dig through the floor. Just clear away laterally. And then when you clear away laterally, you run into what's left of walls. So both the walls and the surface of floors tell you where to stop and clear a level. Then, when you've cleared a level and removed the objects of value, you're ready for the next level, and after you've taken photographs of everything, you destroy the floor and dig down further. The Egyptians, the taskmasters, knew it. And the men, by the way, the common laborers, were very intelligent about it. They understood.

HS: *Did you dig in squares?*

CG: No. But we knew we couldn't dig the whole mound. So we'd take a 20-meter square and just dig in that area.

HS: *How did you decide where to dig?*

CG: If you want to get the big buildings—the palaces, the governor's house—you go to the highest point on the mound. At the foot of the mound, you'll have a city wall if there was a city wall.

HS: *What was your impression of Albright?*

CG: He was revered. Albright was looked upon as a genius. But he built himself up.

HS: *In what way?*

CG: I'll give you one example. It's how I got into Egyptology. Albright was giving a course in Egyptian—I think in Jerusalem. And only one student had signed up. I felt he'd be happy that I joined; it's nicer to have two students than one. He kicked me out of the class. I asked him why. "You know too many languages already." He kicked me out because I knew too much already. Did you ever hear of anything like that? Coming from a man of that position and stature?

Later, I got a job teaching Assyriology at Dropsie [a college for Hebrew studies in Philadelphia]. When I arrived I was told I was to teach Assyriology and Egyptology. I didn't know Egyptian. But whenever people did this to me, I never disillusioned them. I tried to live up to their illusions. So I taught a course in Egyptian. I taught semester after semester. And I never read the same literary text. I always changed things; I either read Middle Egyptian, Late Egyptian or Coptic. At the end of the ten and a half years I was there, I was known as the most distinguished of the Coptologists outside of the University of Chicago and a man at the University of Michigan.

This, by the way, is characteristic of me. When I was to write my doctoral thesis, [James] Montgomery said to me, "It takes a Jewish scholar to read rabbinic texts—the Babylonian Talmud, the Jerusalem Talmud. You're a Jewish scholar. You can do this. I want you to write on the rabbinic exegesis of the Vulgate of Proverbs." Now, I could have said, "Look, I may be Jewish, but I wasn't born with a knowledge of the Jerusalem Talmud." I mean, this isn't something that is part of the baggage of being

Jewish. But I didn't say that. My first instinct was to live up to his illusions.

HS: *How many ancient languages do you know?*

CG: I would say there are upwards of 20. Somewhere along the line, I was told that you should always go back to the sources, and if the sources meant the original language and the original script, then you simply do it. My students—there are about 60 of them in tenured positions in about 20 different fields—were all raised this way.

HS: *How many modern languages do you know?*

CG: French and German were required. But I also passed sight-reading exams in Portuguese, Italian, Dutch, Danish and Norwegian; Swedish I knew before.

HS: *What about Yiddish?*

CG: No. There was a reason for that. My father wouldn't send me to a congregation with an Eastern European tradition because it wasn't American enough. I went to the congregation of Mikveh Israel [which followed the Spanish and Portuguese tradition]. That congregation was founded in 1740. They recently celebrated their 250th anniversary. This was the congregation of Haym Solomon, who gave his whole fortune to George Washington for use in the Revolution. When the war was over, the United States didn't have a treasury to return what they owed to Haym Solomon, so by an act of Congress, long after he was dead, they voted money to his heirs to pay him back.

This congregation was a flag-waving congregation. I was raised there. The most prominent families among the Jews of Philadelphia belonged. You didn't get any Yiddish there.

HS: *Didn't your parents speak Yiddish?*

CG: Only to keep secrets from the children.

HS: *Where did you go after Tell Beit Mirsim and Beth-Zur?*

CG: After Tell Beit Mirsim and Beth-Zur, I was given my instructions to go to the dig at the American School in Baghdad.

HS: *How did you get from Jerusalem to Baghdad?*

CG: In a 1920 Rolls Royce across the desert. We went over desert trails. We came to the area of Baghdad where the Tigris and Euphrates come very close together. From there I took a train to Mosul. Mosul is just opposite Nineveh [one of the capital cities of the Assyrian empire].

HS: *Where did you excavate in Iraq?*

CG: In two places near Nineveh—Tell Billa and Tepe Gawra. Fred [Ephraim A.] Speiser was the director of both of these digs. But after a year he went back to America to run things from headquarters [at the University of Pennsylvania]. Speiser wanted to undo me completely, ruin me.

HS: *Why?*

CG: I'm not a psychiatrist. The best I can figure, I think he sensed in me a person who could not be trusted to abide by the consensus. I mean, how can you trust a guy who says that you have to look at original sources and if the consensus doesn't fit in and your new facts are right, then you don't accept the consensus? That's the best I can make of it.

Speiser was bright, Albright was certainly bright. And the two of them hated each other, which was fortunate for me, because my business until I got tenure was simply survival. Speiser wanted Albright to fire me. So Albright made a deal with Speiser. He [Albright] would take me as his assistant at Johns Hopkins [University in Baltimore], and I'd stay there for three years. And Speiser could keep a nobody as his stooge at the dig while he remained in Philadelphia.

You know, academia is not a pretty place. I guess you've discovered that, haven't you?

HS: *So you were fired?*

CG: No, they did something else. They gave me a great honor. They named me the first Albert T. Clay Fellow without a salary. So here I was going back to America, and I was given this very great honor. But I never acknowledged it. I felt that what they considered an honor was simply a first-class burial.

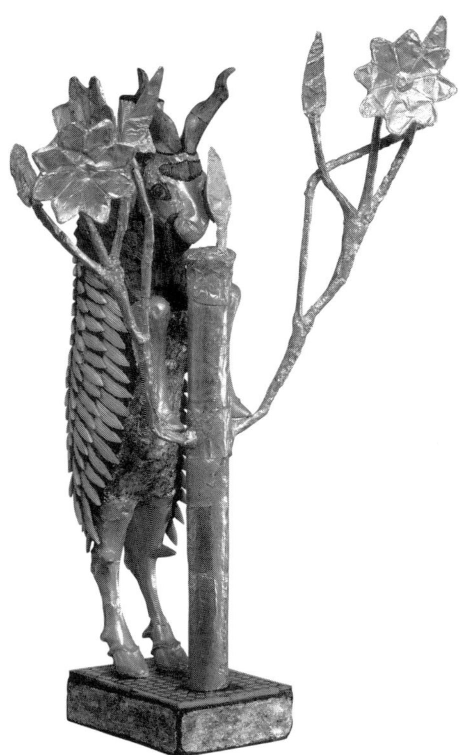

A GOAT IN THE THICKET? When Sir Leonard Woolley found this artifact at Ur, he identified it with the ram in the story of the binding of Isaac (Genesis 22:13). In fact, Wooley's animal is a goat.

HS: *How did you get back into archaeology?*

CG: I continued to teach archaeology. I had photographs of all the seal impressions [of the seals] in the Baghdad Museum, and also I made frequent refresher visits. I had Albright behind me at the time. Albright was a big shot. So I would go back to see things, and I would keep up with their publications of what was going on in the field. And in 1935 I worked with [Sir Leonard] Woolley at Ur.

HS: *What did you do at Ur?*

CG: My job was to read the [cuneiform] tablets. Woolley had no Sumerologist [on his team]. I was it.

HS: *Did you have anything to*

do with the actual excavation?

CG: No, except that I spent part of every day with Woolley walking around to see what was being dug.

HS: *What were your impressions of Woolley?*

CG: A marvelous field man. And he had another ability. He knew how to get money from pious widows who were well-heeled. He did it by proving the Bible. Now how do you prove the Bible? Do you remember the goat grazing off a tree, made of gold, that he found [at Ur; see photo opposite]?

HS: *Yes.*

CG: What he did was identify this with the ram of the *Akedah*. [The binding of Isaac. A ram caught in a thicket became the substitute sacrifice for Isaac (Genesis 22:13).—**Ed.**] That won't stand up at all. But nonetheless, for the public it was all right, and for the widows it was all right. And he got the money from the widows.

HS: *Why won't it hold up?*

CG: Well, a ram is not the same as a goat.

HS: *And that's a goat, is it?*

CG: Yes, it's a goat. A ram doesn't browse like a goat. A goat grazes, browses, it does everything.

HS: *You wrote a book called* The Common Background of Greek and Hebrew Civilization *(W.W. Norton, 1965). For a long time that idea was rejected; it was considered meshuga [crazy].*

CG: It was against everything that was holy: The Greeks were rational; the Hebrews were religious. Greeks were artistic; the Hebrews were against art and against idolatry. [This was the standard view.] I was reading the texts, both the Greek and Hebrew, and I saw that this wasn't so.

HS: *Now everybody accepts that.*

CG: Of course.

HS: *How did it finally come to be accepted?*

CG: The opposition died off.

HS: *You mean physically died off or your arguments finally won out?*

CG: No, no, no, no, no. They died. The arguments were never there on their side, [the arguments were] on my side.

HS: *Give me an example.*

CG: There is a relationship, for example, between the tribe of Dan and the Danaans—Greeks. [See Moshe Dothan's discussion of this issue in Chapter Six, "The Philistines—An Archaeological Romance, Part II."] The tribe of Dan came in with the Philistines. The Philistines pushed the Danites into the sterile hills and took over the fertile plains for themselves. So the Danites had to find a better home for themselves. They sent spies to find a nice quiet place up north, at Laish, and they seized it and renamed it Dan (Judges 18). The Philistines worshiped gods other than Yahweh [the God of the Hebrews], for example, Dagon. But Dagon is every bit as Semitic as Yahweh.

I believe the language of the Philistines [when they arrived in Canaan] was Semitic. I like to say that when Samson was courting Delilah [a Philistine], he never took an interpreter along. Scripture records cases where an interpreter was used. They translated between Joseph and his brothers in Egypt, where Joseph was supposed to be an Egyptian (Genesis 42:23). But Samson and Delilah both spoke Semitic. The Philistines are supposed to be Indo-Europeans. But this is only dogma. True, they didn't practice circumcision, but circumcision emanates from Egypt, from Africa. And none of the other Semites except the

Hebrews practiced circumcision. There was no circumcision among the Babylonians, for example.

HS: *Larry Stager [of Harvard University and director of excavations at Ashkelon] says that if we ever find some Philistine inscriptions, they'll be Greek. Do you agree with that?*

CG: No, no.

HS: *What's your view?*

CG: There's simply no basis for it.

HS: *Well, they came from the Aegean, didn't they?*

CG: Look, Noah's son Shem is the ancestor of the Semites. Japheth [another son of Noah] is connected with the Greeks. Now look at Genesis 9:27: "May God enlarge Japheth, and let him dwell in the tents of Shem." The Greeks will dwell in the tents of the Semites. In other words, the area was Semitic before it became Indo-European. Or to put the matter differently, the area was a Linear A area before it became a Linear B area. When the Philistines came to Canaan, they were already speaking what we would call Hebrew. You remember Abimelech, king of Gerar? Gerar is one of the old Philistinian cities (Genesis 26:1). There is no more Semitic name than Abimelech—a Philistine king.

HS: *You mentioned Linear A and Linear B. Can you tell me what Linear B is?*

CG: Linear B is Greek. Tablets in it were found in a whole variety of places in the coastal areas of Greece. For instance, in the palace of Nestor [at Pylos, in the western Peloponnese]. It had to be deciphered. That was a great accomplishment [by Michael Ventris]. It's not written in regular Greek. This opened up the possibility of deciphering Linear A [the earlier script], and that's what I did. The signs that are used have the same phonetic value in both systems. It's like Hungarian and English; both are writ-

Is Linear A Semitic?

By Gary A. Rendsburg

As Cyrus Gordon describes in the accompanying interview, one of the most controversial aspects of his long academic career was his work on Minoan Linear A, an ancient script found on the island of Crete.

The modern rediscovery of ancient Crete was in great measure the work of Sir Arthur Evans, an English author and adventurer who came to archaeology in middle age. Starting in 1894 and for several decades thereafter, Evans excavated at various sites on Crete and there discovered the great Bronze Age civilization that he called Minoan, after the legendary king Minos, described by Homer, Herodotus and other Greek writers as the ruler of Crete in the period prior to the Trojan War. Among Evans's many important finds on Crete were several hundred clay tablets inscribed in two different, yet very similar, scripts. Evans called the older of the two scripts Linear A and the more recent one Linear B. Due to the number of signs in Linear A and Linear B, scholars assumed—correctly, as it turned out—that the two scripts were syllabaries and not alphabets—that is, each sign represented a syllable rather than a single letter.

Linear B was deciphered in the 1950s by the young and brilliant Michael Ventris (an architect by training), with the collaboration of John Chadwick (a professional philologian). Ventris and Chadwick showed that Linear B was Greek—not the classical Greek of the Iron Age (from 1200 B.C.E. onward), but an earlier variety from the Late Bronze Age (1550–1200 B.C.E.), which they called Mycenaean Greek. They presented their work in *Documents in Mycenaean Greek* (Cambridge University Press, 1956), a volume that was enthusiastically received and that opened many new avenues in the study of ancient Greek language and culture.

Gordon obtained his copy of *Documents in Mycenaean Greek* in December 1956 and immediately set out to decipher Linear A. His method was to apply the values of the Linear B signs, as determined by Ventris and Chadwick, to the Linear A texts.

Actually, Ventris and Chadwick had begun to do the same thing and had come to realize that the words in Linear A were not Greek but rather reflected some other language. Among the words that Ventris and Chadwick recognized on Linear A tablets were names for four kinds of vessels: *qa-pa, su-pu, ka-ro-pa* and *su-pa-ra*. They knew that these were words for vessels because they were followed by the pictograph for "pot". They also deduced that the word for "total" in Linear A was *ku-ro* because this word was used repeatedly at the end of administrative tablets.

Gordon immediately identified the words followed by the pot pictograph as names of vessels in such Semitic languages as Hebrew, Akkadian and Ugaritic. Gordon equated *qa-pa* with Hebrew and Ugaritic *kp* and Akkadian *kappu; su-pu* with Hebrew and Ugaritic *sp; ka-ro-pa* with Akkadian *karpu* and Ugaritic *krpn* (the predecessor, incidentally, of "carafe"); and *su-pa-ra* with Hebrew and Ugaritic *spl* (the Linear A and B scripts do not distinguish l and r). The word for "total," *ku-ro,* was obviously Semitic *kull* (again, with no distinction between l and r in the script).

Gordon continued to search for further connections between Linear A and Semitic. A startling example was the presence of the word *ya-ne* on a wine pithos (storage jar) from Knossos, on Crete, clearly the Minoan form of the West Semitic word for "wine," as in Hebrew *yayin* and Ugaritic *yn.*

Gordon published a series of articles in the late 1950s and early 1960s arguing that the Minoan language was Semitic, with its closest relatives in the West Semitic branch. His work on the subject culminated in the monograph *Evidence for the Minoan Language* (Ventnor Publisher, 1966).

Gordon's view of Linear A led him to a very significant—but much disputed—conclusion: The Minoans, the creators of the high civilization of ancient Crete, were Semites. In fact, this would be in keeping with the ancient Greek tradition that Minos was brought to Crete by Zeus from Phoenicia. Gordon further believes that the Minoans played a key role in the interaction between Greek and Hebrew civilizations, a subject that has formed a major area of research during his career.

I hasten to add that most scholars have not accepted Gordon's interpretation of Minoan Linear A as Semitic. Some believe that the material is Anatolian (a branch of Indo-European that includes Hittite, Luwian et al.), while other scholars believe the question cannot be answered given the limited evidence. But the data we have just reviewed are, in my opinion, plain and straightforward. The most telling objection to Gordon's work is the view that the Minoans could not have been Semites simply because it could not be so. The prevailing attitude, that the Semites were landlubbers, associated more with the desert than with the sea, helped to foster this disbelief. But such closed-mindedness is the antithesis of scholarship, especially as practiced by Cyrus Gordon throughout his remarkable career. He taught his students, of which I am one, to follow the evidence wherever it should lead. And if the above sampling of words from Minoan Linear A points in the direction of Semitic, then such is the path that one should follow.

ten in the Latin alphabet, but they're different languages. If you know one, however, you can pronounce the other.

HS: *Is Linear A Greek?*

CG: No, Linear A is Semitic.

HS: *That's a very controversial statement, isn't it? [See "Is Linear A Semitic?" p. 178.]*

CG: Look, I read this [text], and I give the basis of the explanation and everything else. It's in black and white and documented, so you can check on everything.

HS: *But it's still very much a controversial matter, isn't it?*

CG: Look, a lot of things can be controversial. But we have facts to deal with. Controversy is made by individuals arbitrarily.

HS: *But why is it controversial? Michael Ventris's decipherment of Linear B is not controversial.*

CG: It was for a while. I'll tell you why. The Greek scholars were relieved when it [Linear B] turned out to be Greek, because many scholars had said that it's not Greek. When I come along and say that Linear A—the oldest language found on European soil of which we have any hope of pronouncing and translating—is Semitic, this they don't want. And as far as the Semitists go, you take them away from Hebrew script and they're lost.

HS: *I think your student Gary Rendsburg [now chair of the Department of Jewish Studies at Rutgers University] pointed out that it's only your students who agree with you.*

CG: They're the only ones who've been trained in the damned thing [Linear A]! They're the only ones who read all the languages, not just some of them.

HS: *You have no doubt.*

CG: I have no doubt whatever. But you have to see it yourself, then you'll see why there's no doubt.

HS: *You have written that as a result of your decipherment of Linear A, other scholars have been derisive.*

CG: Well, what else can you do if you don't have any factual arguments?

HS: *You went on to say, "decades of rebuff, denial and outright scorn followed."*

CG: Right. Hershel, I have the thing documented with actual readings, and the evidence. And the evidence, by the way, is in several different scripts, confirming that it's there.

HS: *Where does this attitude come from? Where does this derision, this scorn—these are strong words—where does this come from?*

CG: It makes no difference whether you go to this campus or that campus; if you have a classics department, this is the attitude. You see, [this decipherment] takes it out of their hands. I show them this, but they are not capable of handling it. If you're not capable of handling a thing, then you resort to denial.

HS: *And the Semitists?*

CG: There's a wine jar found at Knossos [on Crete] with three other jars. On all three of them the ideogram for wine appears. In other words, you read it as "wine" in English, and *vin* in French. It's an ideogram. But the fourth one reads *yanna*—apparently a place. *Yanna* I recognize immediately; it has to be Semitic *yayin* ["wine"].

HS: *Are the ideograms in Linear A?*

CG: Yes. Linear A. The ideograms for wine are the same in Linear A and Linear B. This is an ideogram, so you pronounce it in whatever language the text happens to be. There is a place called Yanna, so you write it with the ideogram for "wine" and the suffix *na* syllabically after it.

HS: *Initially you thought that Linear A was East Semitic, and then you later changed your mind and decided it was West Semitic.*

CG: Yes. This is because the same words occur in both East Semitic and West Semitic.

HS: *You changed your mind?*

CG: It's just because I didn't know the same words occurred in West Semitic. But the thing is, I've answered all these things, and it's all arranged in a rational way.

HS: *On another subject, do you still maintain that the Semites came to the western hemisphere—the United States and South America—in 800 B.C.E.?*

CG: No doubt about it. You have a very big inscription near Albuquerque. And then an expedition of the Smithsonian, at Bat Creek in Tennessee, found the same script.*

HS: *So you still maintain that the Bat Creek inscription is authentic?*

CG: No question about it.

HS: *The scholarly consensus today is that it is not authentic.*

CG: The evidence is overwhelming, just overwhelming. And what's more, another one was found near Newark, Ohio.

HS: *What about the Parahaiba inscription from Brazil?***

CG: Parahaiba is another thing. I was right in seeing relationships with other inscriptions, but I was not right in dealing with something that I didn't know anything about: This is the work of a secret society. It's not modern, and it's not ancient. It's in between. It's like the Masonic documents, which are not from Solomon's time, but they weren't created yesterday either; they

*For another view, see P. Kyle McCarter, "Let's Be Serious About the Bat Creek Stone," **BAR**, July/August 1993. See also J. Huston McCulloch, "The Bat Creek Inscription: Did Judean Refugees Escape to Tennessee?" **BAR**, July/August 1993.

Frank M. Cross, "Phoenicians in Brazil?" **BAR, January/February 1979.

were created some hundreds of years ago. So I didn't have the requisite experience with secret societies.

HS: *The authentic inscriptions then are only in the United States—the Bat Creek inscription and the others? You recognize that almost no scholar agrees with you on that.*

CG: But they don't know a thing about it. They simply don't know.

HS: *That's true even of your own students.*

CG: Well, that's where they have jobs.

HS: *Why do you say that?*

CG: For instance, if they have a job in a Christian seminary that is very conservative in most ways, they may have pressures put on them, consciously or subconsciously, I don't know.

HS: *What do you regard as your greatest scholarly accomplishment?*

CG: Linear A. No question in my mind.

HS: *How about your Ugaritic grammar?*

CG: Well, for Ugaritic, we have a great body of texts. It is taught at every great university in the world, and in seminaries. It [my grammar text] has gone through five editions and reprintings. But I feel that the most significant thing I've done is the Linear A [decipherment].

HS: *Why is it so important that Linear A is Semitic?*

CG: Because this explains the contacts between the most ancient Greeks and the most ancient Hebrew literature. In other words, you had this common language that was used all through the [Eastern Mediterranean] area. The area was Semitic speaking before the Semites were driven out. It was Linear A before it was Linear B; this explains why there is the common background.

HS: *You've also seen correspondences and cultural connections between Homer and the Bible.*

CG: Oh yes, certainly. When [the Israelites] of Jabesh-gilead retrieved the bodies of Saul and Jonathan, they burned the bodies and they fasted (see 1 Samuel 31:11–13). This is a Homeric funeral for people who die on the field of battle. It doesn't matter whether it actually happened. That, we can't prove. But what we can prove is that the same custom prevailed, that they didn't burn the bodies of those who died[during peace time] at home, but only those who lost their lives on the battlefield.

HS: *Thank you very much. You've been very enlightening.*

CHAPTER EIGHT

THE STAR OF ISRAELI ARCHAEOLOGY

An Interview with Yigael Yadin

Yigael Yadin

This interview took place only two years before Yadin passed away. He had recently returned to full time archaeology after one of the many discursions, this one into Israeli politics, that had marked his amazing life.

In 1948, Yadin had commanded the Haganah, Israel's pre-

"BAR Interviews Yigael Yadin" appeared in BAR, January/February 1983.

state army, in that country's War of Independence. From 1977 to 1981, he served as Israel's Deputy Prime Minister. Before and after his time in office, he lived a life of the mind as an archaeologist, biblical scholar and historian. But he also got his hands dirty as a field archaeologist, having led a number of important expeditions—including Masada, Herod's wilderness palace-fortress where Jewish fighters made their last stand in the First Revolt against Rome; and at Hazor, a site Yadin believed was captured by Joshua. Yadin also figured prominently in Israel's acquisition of the Dead Sea Scrolls. In 1983, he published a three-volume edition of the Temple Scroll, the latest to be found and the longest of the Dead Sea Scrolls.

Hershel Shanks: *Professor Yadin, one of the things that we hear about most frequently from our readers, and which is somewhat puzzling to them, involves the relationship of archaeology to the historical accuracy of the Bible. We know that archaeology is not supposed to prove the truth of the Bible. Most of our readers are more sophisticated than that. But sometimes they get the feeling that archaeologists are too quick to accept archaeological evidence and find that it contradicts the Bible, too quick to conclude that therefore the Bible is inaccurate. Our readers often point out how uncertain archaeological evidence really is; how often archaeologists argue from silence, from the absence of evidence; and how often there are explanations other than that the Bible is wrong. After all, we know very little of the full archaeological picture. Most of it still lies underground. And even if it were all uncovered, there would still be enormous gaps in our knowledge of the ancient world. I wonder if you feel that archaeologists are sometimes too quick to reject the Bible in favor of limited archaeological evidence?*

Yigael Yadin: I think your question is really a basic one. Our knowledge of the Bible as a historical document is not yet complete. It's limited. And with all the advances in the archaeological discipline, including field archaeology with all that goes with it, it is far from providing 100 percent answers to many questions people would like to know about the Bible.

My definition of archaeology sounds a bit sophisticated—and incidentally I didn't invent it. It was written by someone a hundred years ago. I don't remember who wrote it, but I follow it, and that is that archaeology is the science that examines the mind of man to the extent it is reflected in material or has been expressed in material.

If the thoughts of Jeremiah or Isaiah were not written down, let's say they were known only orally, or if the writings were lost, archaeology can never recover what was in their minds. It's beyond archaeology's realm.

On the other hand, if Jeremiah says that as a result of the onslaught of the Babylonians, only Lachish and Azekah remained undestroyed until the time that he was uttering his words (Jeremiah 34:7), here of course is a field day (double meaning) for archaeology. Because here I think archaeology can say, "Yes, Lachish and Azekah really were destroyed in 586 [B.C.]." We can say, "Yes, they were in the end destroyed by the Babylonians." And if we excavate, as we have, an adjacent fort, let's say 50 miles from there, we are in trouble again. Although it may seem very easy, we cannot prove that some fort, say Eglon, was destroyed five years before the other two sites. We cannot determine things so closely. If we didn't have the Bible, an archaeologist who excavated Lachish, Azekah, and, let's say, Tel Ira, would have come to the conclusion that they were all destroyed at the beginning of the sixth century. Does that disprove or prove what Jeremiah said? Jeremiah is saying that on the day that he was uttering his thoughts, only Lachish and Azekah remained [undestroyed], which means that a month before, five years before, twenty years before, the other sites had already fallen into the hands of the Edomites or Babylonians. We archaeologists cannot be so precise as to say that. But we can say for sure that these cities were destroyed at the beginning of the sixth century.

So to sum up, I think that there are certain questions that the archaeologist can answer. Sometimes if the answer contradicts what the Bible says, then we have to accept it because, after all, the Bible itself was not composed as a historical book. Some of those historians who wrote it, or compiled it, perhaps didn't know exactly what the historical facts were. But in many, many cases—and there are more of those cases than the others—archaeology, at the moment, cannot give a positive answer as to whether a historical statement in the Bible is true or not.

If there is a contradiction between a biblical assertion and the archaeological evidence, I would be extremely reluctant to say that archaeology proved that the Bible was wrong. There are some cases like that, but they are fewer than most people think.

HS: *The most well-known supposed contradiction concerns Jericho. At the time most scholars date the conquest of Canaan, there was no settlement at Jericho, according to Kathleen Kenyon, who excavated the city.*

Or take Jerusalem, the City of David. Only yesterday, at the City of David excavations, Yigal Shiloh [the late professor of biblical archaeology at the Hebrew University in Jerusalem and one-time director of the City of David excavations] showed me the evidence he found in a very, very limited area for a tenth- and 11th-century occupation of Jerusalem. Now, if Shiloh had not dug in this particular area, there would not be archaeological evidence for the existence of Jerusalem in the 10th-11th centuries. But now Shiloh has the evidence.

Kathleen Kenyon's Jericho excavations also involved opening only a very limited area, so can we really be sure that there was no city at Jericho at the time of the Israelite conquest?

YY: I think there is enough evidence, even in Kenyon's excavations—and also in the earlier excavations of [John] Garstang—to show that at Jericho there is no necessary contradiction to the Bible. We shouldn't forget that there were Jericho tombs to show that there must have been a Late Bronze 14th–13th century settlement in Jericho, even if we haven't found the settlement itself. How large it was, unfortunately, we cannot say. I think the site has been absolutely mutilated, both by nature and by earlier archaeologists. But there is evidence that there was something there [in the Late Bronze Age]. Now whether the walls fell the way the Bible describes (Joshua 6:1–21), that is another story.

HS: *That's beyond the realm of archaeology, isn't it?*

YY: That's beyond the realm of archaeology, and I think it's beyond the realm of history as well. It's a matter of faith. The ancient people believed that this was the cause. Now if you want to believe it, you believe it; if you don't believe it, don't. But the fact is that there was a city there, in my opinion, and it was conquered. There can be no doubt. Maybe it was a small city. Maybe tradition then magnified it until it became larger than it was, but there must have been a core of history there.

I belong to a school of thought that thinks tradition must be used as a source for history, of course with caution. People don't invent certain things. For example, you can't deny that the Israelites were once in Egypt. What nation would invent such a crazy story, that they were slaves in Egypt and they left that country and came to this country, and then make that the kernel of all their history? There is a historical core. Even if you want to minimize it, there is a core of truth there. Maybe it did not happen exactly as it is recorded, down to the last detail. But there is a historical core.

So, what I'm trying to say is, in the case of Jericho, for example, I entirely agree that one has to be very careful. They didn't find a Late Bronze Age wall. But when Kathleen Kenyon excavated Jericho, in fact even when the Germans excavated there, and then later, Garstang excavated, they found a Middle Bronze wall (2000–1550 B.C.) absolutely intact. Now, if the Middle Bronze wall was intact when the archaeologists found it in the 20th century, then it was surely intact in the Late Bronze Age. We archaeologists sometimes make a terrible mistake. We think that when a new king begins to reign, then a new level must be found in the city; when he dies, the city must die as well. When a new period comes, there must be a new city wall. But this isn't true. Look, today, even today, you can see old city walls that have survived for 300, 400, 500 years. And I believe that the Middle Bronze city wall at Jericho was used in the Late Bronze Age.

I would go further; in fact I believe that most of the Canaanite cities in Canaan at the time of the conquest were rather weakly fortified. Not only in Jericho—in other cities too that the Bible claims were conquered, and in other cities that [Pharaoh] Ramesses II claims he conquered, and that [Pharaoh] Seti I claims he conquered. We acknowledge these Pharaonic conquests of Ramesses II and Seti I as accurately reported because there are reliefs and there are inscriptions as proof. Some scholars do not rely on the Bible (as you know, there is so much skepticism regarding its historical accuracy). When we come to these cities conquered by the Egyptians, however, and we excavate, we don't find any formidable new walls that Ramesses destroyed and that supposedly were built by the people of the 14th–13th centuries. We find walls that were built in an earlier period.

One of the reasons scholars are reluctant to believe that there is a kernel of truth in the Jericho story is that they say that there is no evidence from the Late Bronze Age at Jericho. But this is not true. There is evidence, even according to Kenyon. She had to admit that in one spot she did find one house. All right, if you find one house, there may be more. Secondly, that they didn't find a city wall from the Late Bronze Age is not evidence. The Middle Bronze Age city wall could easily have been reused in the Late Bronze Age.

HS: *You mentioned that there are some cases in which archaeology does contradict the Bible. Now you say Jericho isn't one of them. What is one of them?*

YY: Well, I'll tell you what. When I say contradict, I still qualify it a little bit, and I'll tell you why. Apparently there is a contradiction. But even this may not be true. Take the story of the second city occupied by the Israelites, the one after Jericho; that is Ai (Joshua 8:1–29). Ai was excavated rather thoroughly by the late Judith Marquet-Krause and by Joseph Callaway. Neither found any evidence for a Late Bronze Age city. Of course there still can be room for doubt. It's a huge site, and it's still possible that in one quarter, evidence of a Late Bronze Age city will be found. If I were in court, I would say it's still possible that in one area there may be a Late Bronze Age city. But from the evidence we have today, and there has been quite an extensive excavation, no Late Bronze Age city, not one Late Bronze Age sherd has been found at Ai. Now, if we believe that Joshua conquered Jericho in the 13th century, in the Late Bronze Age—and we do have evidence for this—and Ai was the second city occupied a few weeks or months after Jericho, and we can't find evidence of a city at Ai, then there is here an apparent contradiction.

***HS:** Are there no other possibilities? For example, that we've incorrectly identified the city that Joshua conquered.*

YY: That's why I qualified my statement a bit. We identify this tell, et-Tel as it is in fact named which means literally the ruin—Ai also means the ruin—we identify this site as the biblical Ai. There have been many surveys in this area and no other candidate for biblical Ai has been found. But still I do qualify my finding of an apparent contradiction. Maybe we were looking all the time for a huge mound strongly fortified, as it is described in the Bible. The Bible has crystallized in writing what the biblical writer imagined the city to be. But it may have been a much smaller place. That's why I do qualify my statement.

Let's sum it up. If we take the biblical stories concerning the two cities you mentioned, Jericho and Ai, if we take these stories literally, and if people would like to know whether archaeology can say whether the trumpets caused the walls to fall or not, I say it is beyond archaeology anyhow. This is a matter of belief. I don't believe it was the trumpets that caused it, but some people may believe it. This is not a matter of argument for us now—it has nothing to do with archaeology. But as a historical question, I think we have a problem. In the case of Jericho, I would say most probably archaeology does not contradict the biblical story. In the case of Ai, I would say that at present our knowledge, our archeological knowledge, does contradict the Bible. But still I qualify it as I indicated.

HS: *You said that you don't believe the trumpets mentioned in the Bible caused the walls to fall down. Does that reflect your view of the Bible, your personal relationship to it as a matter of fact?*

YY: Well, I think the Bible is composed of many, many elements, absolutely different from one another. For example, let's take the first few chapters of Genesis. You cannot put the first few chapters of Genesis in the same category as the books of Kings. The books of Kings are based on the annals of the kings in which, more or less yearly, a scribe recorded the main events. If you believe that God created the world in seven days, or six days rather, to be more accurate, then you believe in that; if you don't believe, you don't believe. I, as a man who knows enough about geology, about the history of this planet, think that the way it is described there—I leave God out of the story for the moment—is contradicted by science. The early Genesis stories are more in the nature of mythology. They crystallized perhaps a certain knowledge. I think basically the stages of creation are perhaps correct as they are described in Genesis, stages that were telescoped in the tradition, in the faith, into short periods rather than much longer. Of course, people can say that the days referred to in the Bible meant actually millions of years and the years were billions of years. I don't want to go into that. But I can't put the first few chapters of Genesis in the same category as the books of Samuel or Kings. And therefore I cannot speak of the Bible as a whole, as it relates to archaeology or faith or belief.

HS: *But even in the historical sections the Bible reflects a presence of God, a God acting in history. And even if you accept the historicity of the conquest of Jericho, you've indicated that you don't accept the miraculous aspects of the trumpets causing the walls to fall down.*

YY: When we study history, I think it's very important not to project what we think onto what people thought at the time. Today there are millions of people who believe that events happened exactly as described in the Bible and I'm sure that in those days when the Israelites managed to conquer cities, and when their grandchildren saw that they, a desert people, were able to become masters of a land that had been owned by giants and had been fortified, the Israelites were absolutely convinced that it was not only their act of valor but it was mainly God's wish and with God's help that they were able to do this. Therefore, whatever they wrote is not a bluff. They really believed it. Now you can say that this doesn't prove that God actually helped them, but it does prove one thing: it proves what motivated them, what moved them to do what they did; it was that belief. We have to understand that; otherwise we can't understand why they built these temples and in fact why they behaved as they did. Whatever I think today is my own private view which I am free to believe. I don't even have to tell anybody what I believe. It is not important. If, however, as a scholar, I have evidence that shows that something didn't happen the way the Bible says, then it is my duty of course to present it. I gave you one example in which there are difficulties. There are also other difficulties that the editors and the compilers of the Bible knew about. They themselves knew that there were contradictions within the Bible.

But it is absolutely untrue that archaeology disproves the Bible.

On the contrary, I think archaeology proves it, that is, that the great events—for example the conquest of Canaan by the children of Israel, which was a major event in the history of the people—cannot be thrown away and be explained by all sorts of sociological theories, as is sometimes attempted. First, archaeology proves that there was a conquest at that period, and second, the tradition is so strongly imbedded in the Bible, I don't believe that it was invented.

I am reminded of the story about whether it was Joshua who conquered Canaan. Who would invent Joshua? It's like the discussion about whether there was a Shakespeare; whether it was Shakespeare or somebody else by the name of Shakespeare. Was it Joshua or somebody else who was called Joshua? Why suddenly invent a Joshua? Now maybe he did less than is ascribed to him. But to deny completely the fact that there was a hero by the name of Joshua who led the tribes at a certain period and that they managed to conquer the land is, I think, to deny archaeology and the Bible at the same time.

HS: *You mentioned that you would leave God out for the moment.*

YY: Well, I don't think God has anything to do with archaeology.

HS: *You've been an archaeologist almost all your life.*

YY: That's true.

HS: *Has that affected the way you think about God or feel about God?*

YY: No, it hasn't. Incidentally, I didn't tell you what I believed before I was an archaeologist.

HS: *And you haven't told me what you believe now.*

YY: I said it did not affect my beliefs. It did not affect my thinking about whether there is a God or not. This has nothing to do with archaeology.

HS: *Has your career in archaeology affected your appreciation of the Bible?*

YY: Oh, yes.

HS: *Has it deepened your respect or made it more questionable?*

YY: Well, let's put it this way. My reaction to the Bible is very, very complex and subjective. I must be very, very careful to answer your questions as an archaeologist. After all, as a Jew, as an Israeli, I was brought up from childhood on the Bible as the history of my people, as the mandate for my being in this particular country. I still believe the Bible really records the main, the salient events in the history of my ancestors. If someone attacks the Bible, saying that it is not historical (I'm not talking about the early part of Genesis but the historical books), that it is nonsense and fiction, then I say that archaeology has increased my belief that basically the historical parts of the Bible are true. No doubt of that. But if I say, okay, I'm not a Jew at the moment, I'm not an Israeli, I am only an archaeologist, I would still say yes, on the whole, archaeology has increased by belief in the historical parts of the Bible. In fact, I am amazed. I am amazed because the more we discover, the more we dig, we see—how shall we put it?—there is always a grain of truth and I minimize it, in any event the Bible actually describes. It is true that if you understand the Bible literally, there are apparent contradictions. But if you look at the more general sweep, it is accurate. I think archaeology has actually given me, if you ask me subjectively, a greater respect for the Bible.

You know the same kinds of questions are involved in other ancient documents. I wouldn't put the Bible in the same category, but the same kinds of questions are involved. Take Josephus, for example [a first-century A.D. Jewish historian]. Before archaeological excavations, it was the vogue among historians—very serious historians—to argue that Josephus in many places relates sheer nonsense, that he is not historical, that he exaggerates, and so forth. But the more we dig in Jerusalem and at

Masada and at Herodium and in [Herodian] Jericho, the greater respect we—both archaeologists and historians—have for the accuracy of Josephus. He is one of the greatest historians. Of course he had his own prejudices. But show me any historian without them. Josephus is accurate not only for his own period but for previous periods as well, for example, the Hellenistic period (332–37 B.C.). Josephus had theories; of course he made mistakes in his theories—so we think—but basically as historian, he is much, much more respected as a result of archaeology.

Take Homer as another example. He was always considered and still is, but less so, like the Bible, as a kind of fiction writer recording myths and legends of a heroic period that is not really history. A whole feud went on in classical studies exactly as we have in biblical studies between those who said that whatever is in Homer is nonsense and fiction that has no historical validity and the others who said the opposite. Slowly but surely, archaeology showed that basically the whole idea—the destruction of Troy and the Mycenaean might, and so on and so forth—was true. Of course Homer is a later recording of events that took place several hundred years before they were written down. I have a book here by Professor [Hilda Lockhart] Lorimer, which I cherish, *Homer and the Monuments* (Macmillan, 1950). Lorimer is one of the most serious classical scholars, and what she does is to show that all the excavations at Greek sites have proved that Homer actually was right, even in details, when he described the shield of Ajax, or the shape of an arch, or an arrow or whatever.

To sum up, tradition is a very powerful historical instrument, provided we know how to understand it. We must not simply swallow it lock, stock and barrel, on the one hand, and we must not throw the baby out with the bath water by saying the whole thing is nonsense. If we can sharpen our tools for understanding the recorded tradition, then, together with archaeology and other sources, we can understand much better what is described in the Bible.

HS: *Is there a subject, an academic discipline of biblical archaeology? As you know, some scholars believe that it's not a real academic discipline, but simply a historical description of what certain scholars in the past have done and they believe that the term should be abandoned.*

YY: Well, of course, as the editor of *Biblical Archaeology Review*, you are touching on something very important to your readers. You're touching a very vexing problem. I know, of course, about the views you refer to.

I think those who object to the term biblical archaeology have absolutely misused it and therefore created confusion. You put in the mouths of those who object to the term a very mild description of their objections. Some of those who object say that biblical archaeology is "coffee table archaeology," for example. The truth of the matter is that unfortunately we are working in a country—let's say Palestine, it's the land of the Bible we're talking about—which for a 2,000-year period (3000 B.C. to 1000 B.C.) left no substantial inscriptions or writings to enable us to understand what we excavate, unlike Egypt and Babylon which have left substantial inscriptions on monuments and written documents.

Now I wouldn't like to be an archaeologist who is only a technician in dissections. Of course it's important to know how to excavate, just as it is vital for a pathologist to know how to make a dissection. But if this is all he knows, then he'll never be a doctor; he'll never contribute to the understanding of the human body. So what are we to do. From 3000 B.C. to at least 1000 B.C., we have so little written material because our forefathers [unlike Babylonians] did not write much on clay; and papyrus, because of the humidity, did not stay well preserved. We don't have Egypt's dry weather which preserved not only the pyramids but also papyrus. So our forefathers are silent in this respect. So today we can dig. We can know exactly the pottery, the fortifications, and stratification and relative chronology of sites and so on. And we shall be able to reconstruct a fair picture of the culture. But this is not enough. In order to understand the human mind, we have to know more. And we do have sources. We have the Bible, if we understand it correctly. We have Egyptian archaeology. We have Mesopotamian archaeology. We have philology. There are written documents from Mesopotamia and from Anatolia. Some of them are related to what happened here. Now why should we, as archaeologists who want to understand what happened in the minds of the people who lived here and built these skeletons of cities that we find, the ruins, why should we deprive ourselves of all these other sources of knowledge that I just listed?

This is biblical archaeology. I wouldn't say biblical archaeology is a discipline as you put it. I think it is a multi-discipline. Or, if you like, an art.

It is necessary to control certain disciplines in order to achieve certain knowledge. Today it is true that you cannot be a master of all the many disciplines I mentioned. But if somebody's studying archaeology today with the aim of understanding the minds of the ancient people in this part of the world and he's being taught only pottery and the technique of digging, and typology and fortifications, I would say that he is not going to be an archaeologist unless he also studies at least one or two other disciplines that will help him to understand what he is going to find, either the Bible or philology or Assyriology or history.

I really don't understand why this objection to the term biblical archaeology has arisen. Can you show me one archaeologist in Greece who has not pursued classical studies as a *sine qua non* of his education?

HS: *That's an interesting observation. I recently discussed this subject with a prominent scholar in Israel who noted that some scholars wanted to substitute Syro-Palestinian archaeology for biblical archaeology as a technical term. This scholar asked me, "Would the same people want to substitute Balko-Aegean archaeology for Greek archaeology?"*

YY: I would like to comment afterwards about Syro-Palestinian archaeology, where we delineate the supposed geographical limits of our branch of archaeology. But I still want to finish the point I was making. If someone wants to excavate Knossos [on the island of Crete] and uncover materials from the beginning of the second millennium, or Mycenae [in Greece] from the third millennium, he would never be given a license, he would not even dare to go to Crete or Mycenae unless he first mastered classical studies, unless he knew Homer, unless he understood the literary sources. Similarly, no one would think of excavating in Mesopotamia who has not been trained in Assyriology. Perhaps one or two have not been trained, but they are the exception to the rule. Because in Mesopotamia, too, you cannot interpret bricks and pottery unless you understand and study a little about the history of the area from the written documents. This is also true about Egypt. All the great Egyptian archaeologists are Egyptologists too. In other words, it is a discipline which is more than just the technique of digging to discern the artifacts, to be able to reconstruct history based on typology. Impossible. This is only a skeleton without a soul. Biblical archaeology really is the complete thing. It's like a human being. You have a skeleton, you have flesh and you have a soul, so to say. For the periods, let's say, from the Bronze Age to the Second Jewish Commonwealth [70 A.D.], it must be biblical archaeology.

What used to be called in the good old days "field archaeology" some people now would like to call "archaeology," period. For them, archaeology is identical with field archaeology. It's a technique, they say. But the real job of the archaeologist is to understand the human mind as expressed in the material, as I said before. And that's why I think that biblical archaeology should not be discussed, vis-a-vis archaeology itself, as something different.

Of course, the prehistoric periods [the Paleolithic, Neolithic and Chalcolithic] are different. I wouldn't call that biblical archaeology in the same sense because unfortunately the prehistorical archaeologist hasn't got the Bible to provide the background. But even there, if he studies the Paleolithic period of Palestine, of the Holy Land, I would still call him a biblical archaeologist in that sense, as I would the Greek scholar, the Greek archaeologist who studies the Paleolithic period of Greece. After all, this is the land of the Bible. True, there is very little difference between the hand-axes that we find here [in Israel] and those that are found in France. But there is a difference. The difference is that they are found here. Therefore they add to the understanding of the history of the human being, of man and his history in the land of the Bible. So this is another aspect of biblical archaeology. But it's not the same as biblical archaeology in the periods in which the Bible as such is a source of information.

I would make two circles. The inner circle of biblical archaeology is the period in which the biblical historical books are sources of information. We supplement this and enrich it with all the cognate studies I mentioned before. The outer circle is the history of the land of the Bible.

Now we come to your question, "What is the land of the Bible?" I don't criticize those who use the term Syro-Palestinian. I think we should let it stand if they wish. It is a political term. But is has nothing to do with our discipline of archaeology. You can show that it is true that Syria and Palestine had a lot in common in certain periods of history. But today the term Syro-Palestinian is used by certain archaeologists in such a way that they will be able to roam about in Jordan, to roam about in Syria. You know biblical archaeology has already become taboo there. The Bible is already not to be mentioned in certain areas. In Syria, for example, I'm sure biblical archaeology is becoming a dirty word. But Syro-Palestinian is acceptable, particularly if you put Syro before Palestine, as it was phrased by the Roman conquerors and even before them. The Romans always saw Palestine as an offshoot of Syria. Well, that is wrong. It is not an offshoot.

Now where do we fix the geographical border of biblical archaeology? That is a very difficult question.

I had an argument with a gentleman who always used the term Syro-Palestinian. I told him that I cannot teach the archaeology of Palestine unless I also teach at the same time the archaeology of Anatolia, of Mesopotamia and of Egypt in certain periods. You cannot understand the archaeology of this country—particularly because it was a bridge between these other countries and was always being conquered—unless you understand what happened there as well. I called my book on warfare "The Art of Warfare in Biblical Lands." War is something between two parties. Normally, it is between one party and another who comes from the outside. How can we understand what happened here unless we know exactly how the Hittites or the Egyptians or the Mesopotamians fought? So the whole book tried to present the way the Assyrians fought, the way the Egyptians fought and so on, because how can I understand fortifications in this country unless I know what it was fortified against? This is clear.

We should project this same idea onto culture, trade, all sorts of things, which are reactions and counter-reactions to things that happen around us. Syro-Palestine is definitely not a meaningful archaeological term in my opinion. For the ninth century, the eighth century and the seventh century B.C., it is more vital to know what happened in Mesopotamia than in Syria. How can we understand the fortifications, the culture, the artifacts we find here unless we know Assyrian archaeology?

Therefore, if we're talking about biblical archaeology, obviously the land of the Bible is the center. If we're talking about Homeric archaeology or Greek archaeology, then obviously Greece is the center. You have to draw circles around the center. Some giants, like [W. F.] Albright, managed to control many disciplines. Of course in those days we knew less. Today, when knowledge is accumulating, each of us is able to control fewer disciplines. But this is only because of our shortcomings, not because the discipline doesn't need it. Therefore, we have to cooperate. I would say that a good biblical archaeologist today is composed of at least five people. Albright could do it by himself. We can't; so we are five.

For example, yesterday you and I attended a panel discussion about a statue found at Tell Fakhariyah in Syria, inscribed in both Aramaic and Assyrian. In that discussion there were two epigraphers, one Assyriologist, one specialist in Semitic languages and one historian. Even this was not enough because archaeology proper was not represented. Neither was the history of art, the history of statues and so forth. So these five people yesterday were together, in a way, one biblical archaeologist, if you like.

Because of the accumulation of knowledge, we cannot master everything. Because of that, I wouldn't like to define biblical archaeology in a limited way.

HS: *You mentioned that there is very little extant written material in Palestine. This leads me to a personal question. Are you yourself going to go back into the field?*

YY: Well, I will go back to Hazor and I think that I will find an archive there.

HS: *Why?*

YY: Well, we have some very simple evidence to begin with. For example, in the famous archive from el-Amarna [in Egypt] from the beginning of the 14th century B.C., we have letters written by kings—or rather mayors we would call them today—of cities of Palestine. These letters [written in cuneiform on clay tablets] were written here [and sent to Egypt]. From these letters we know that there were archives here. I mean those people here must have kept copies of their letters. After all, there was a correspondence. And they had a bureaucracy in those days. So if we find letters in Egypt from the king of Hazor, there must have been an archive of that particular king in Hazor. This applies similarly to quite a number of biblical cities. In Mari [in northern Mesopotamia], we found a letter written three hundred years, if not four or five hundred years, earlier, saying that they are sending an ambassador to Hazor. And ambassadors from Hazor go to Mari. Some letters found at Mari concern shipments of precious metals to Hazor and vice versa, and so on and so forth. At Hazor, a young boy—not an archaeologist—found a little broken piece of a tablet which contained a dictionary, a Sumero-Akkadian dictionary; this find shows there was a scribe at Hazor. This dictionary must have been made by a scribe for other scribes. So I think up to now we have simply been unlucky in many of the cities where we have dug in Israel. You know, we excavate on a huge mound, and if you don't hit the archive, you don't even know it's there. Even in Ebla [in Syria where a significant third-millennium archive was found] they had fantastic luck. They could have dug for another 50 years and not hit that one particular spot.

Personally, I still hope that I will be able to contribute to negating the statement I made at the beginning, that Palestine has no inscribed writings for two millennia. I still want to go back to Hazor. I worked there for five years (1955–1958, 1968), in the biggest excavation up to that time. That excavation was in fact the cradle and the school of Israeli archaeologists. It shaped the whole method of those Israeli archaeologists who were with us at the time. Now they are archaeologists in their own right.

I believe I know at least where the palace of Hazor was. That much I am sure of. I will bet that I know where the king's palace was, just as I bet when I last dug there that I knew where the water tunnel was. (And I found the water tunnel.)

It is not just that I am a soothsayer. My belief about the palace is based on deductions, observations there at the site. We found a corner of a huge building, of such proportions that it could only be a palace.* And these tablets I mentioned, the two fragments of tablets that were found by visitors, came from the debris not far from that spot.

Unfortunately, we hit only the corner. We went down 14 or 13 strata from the top, working our way for four years. And then we came to the corner. What I want to do now is to go down systematically, because every layer above it is important, although I only want to find the archive. I want to go down in the area between the two arms of the corner. And I know where it is.

I have two difficulties, which I would like to share with your readers. One is very simple. I have to go down first through a great many other layers. Nothing would deter me from doing that carefully and systematically, stratum by stratum. Each stratum might bring surprises of its own. I don't know what might be uncovered. I have to go through Ahab's period again, then Solomon's period and so on.

The second difficulty is a real dilemma. In the area where I think the palace is I have already found very important monuments which I left on the site as they were excavated. These include the famous pillared building of Hazor from the time of King Ahab [second quarter of the ninth century B.C.]. There is also a very beautiful private house or mansion or villa, named in my book Yael's House after the student who served as the area supervisor there. I left these buildings standing at that time because they were so rare. In order to go now to the palace where I believe the archive is, I would have to remove all this, to dig beneath. If I undertake this project, I think the Department of Antiquities [now the Israel Antiquities Authority] will give me

*The building Yadin believed to be a palace proved upon further excavation by Hebrew University archaeologist (and Yadin's one-time student) Amnon Ben-Tor to be a large temple complex. The search for the Hazor archive has continued under Ben-Tor, however, with attention now focused on a large palatial structure adjacent to the site's acropolis. It has still not been found. See Sharon Zuckerman, "Where is the Hazor Archive Buried?" **BAR**, March/April 2006.

permission to remove the existing monuments. I may perhaps first dig around the exposed buildings a little bit. But if I have to remove them, I would like to rebuild them exactly as they are a hundred yards away. It will not be a fake. Every visitor will know they are the exact buildings with their original stones, but they will stand 50 or 100 yards away. For example, in London when they found within the city a temple of Mithras where they intended to build a bank or a post office, they rebuilt the whole temple nearby.

Anyway, this is a problem for me. It is even possible that under the presently exposed buildings I will find something else I wouldn't like to remove before I reach the palace. But that's the risk.

It might take a good year, one season, just to reach the palace. I think we have a very good chance of finding the archive of Hazor—from the end of the Late Bronze period (more or less the time of Joshua), from the Amarna period (14th century B.C.) and the earlier one from the Mari period (18th–17th centuries B.C.). The archive from the Mari period might be as important as the Ebla archive and perhaps even more important because Hazor covered as big an area as Ebla and was definitely as important as Ebla. In all the Mari correspondence, Ebla is not mentioned but Hazor is. Ebla was perhaps in decline at this time. Perhaps Ebla was off the beaten track of the Mari correspondence that we have found so far.

I would like to come back to what I said earlier. Daily written material from our area, such as transactions and letters and even what the prophets wrote, has unfortunately been lost because most of it was written on papyrus. Even the Dead Sea Scrolls would have been lost were it not for the fact that they were, so to say, buried or hidden in caves in the Dead Sea area which is so dry. Otherwise, they would have been lost as most other scrolls either on papyrus or on leather have been lost everywhere else in the country. But I think there's a good chance that one day we shall have a surprise either from Hazor or from Aphek or from Lachish or from somewhere else in the country. And we will find these clay tablets from the Amarna period, even up to the eve of the conquest of Canaan.

HS: *When are you going to start at Hazor?*

YY: I don't know yet. I have to finish preparation of the English translation of my Temple Scroll book.* I must get that out. And I have other work. But I think at the moment it might be in the autumn of '83. I can't give you a firm date yet. I have to think about it very carefully. I do not want to start this dig before I push some other publications. You are one of those who are always harassing us for not publishing, and I think you are right. And I still have on my desk some publications that I must finish before I start with a new dig.

HS: *Let me mention just one of them: The publication of Hazor.*

YY: Well, Hazor, I can tell you that it's not [being ignored]. First of all, I've already published three huge volumes; very few excavations even today have been that well reported. The fourth volume of Hazor, which is the complementary text to the plates in Volume III, is being worked on. I have an assistant, and I think it is in a very advanced stage now. In the future, I can't say when, but in the near future, I hope to see light. It is already on the right track.**

HS: *So that will be it for the publication of Hazor?*

YY: Hazor, yes. But I still have the Masada material. The technical work hasn't been finished, the mending and cleaning of the material. We have so much of it. But I also want to accelerate this.

*Yigael Yadin, *The Temple Scroll: The Hidden Law of the Dead Sea Sect* (New York: Random House, 1985).

**Amnon Ben-Tor completed the publication of *Hazor IV* (Jerusalem: Israel Exploration Society, 1989) and also co-edited (with Ruhama Bonfill) *Hazor V* (Jerusalem: Israel Exploration Society, 1997), which dealt with the finds from Yadin's fifth season of excavations in 1968.

This doesn't mean that I will have to wait until it is finished to go to the [new] dig, but before I go to a new dig I want to set up the apparatus and staff to prepare these publications.* As you know, this [delay] is not only because of the scientific reasons. Maybe it's my fault. But for five years I was out of circulation, trying to do something else which maybe archaeologists in 2,000 years or 3,000 years from now will discover. [Professor Yadin served as Deputy Prime Minister of Israel from 1977 to 1981.] This of course slowed down my archaeological work a bit.

HS: *Would you tell me a little about the difference in the way of life and what it's like to be an archaeologist as compared to a politician who's a leader of his country and second in command, so to speak.*

YY: It was quite a change from an archaeologist's way of life. There is really a difference between a scholarly way of life and, as I learned, a political way of life. I always remembered, when I was being attacked and my life was not very happy, the answer your President Wilson gave when he was in trouble and being attacked and people asked him how did he find life in the White House compared to life as president of Princeton. He said, "It's nothing compared to Princeton."

My own personal view—and my political colleagues will, I am sure, try to discredit this—is that a scholar is raised to tell the truth. And not only the scholar. Every American is told the story about [George] Washington and the cherry tree and is told to tell the truth. But for the scholar, it is in his blood. I mean he cannot present data, he cannot present material, unless he is sure that he is presenting it to the best of his knowledge. In politics, unfortunately, I discovered what I should have known before, that to tell a lie—some people want to euphemize it by calling them "white lies"—is considered all right. (When a treasurer cheats on the

*The Masada excavations have since been published by a host of scholars in a series of volumes. See *Masada: The Yigael Yadin Excavations 1963–1965, Vols. I–VIII* (Jerusalem: Israel Exploration Society, 1989–2007).

budget, that is a black lie. That is a sheer lie.) But I found that very difficult. I couldn't play the game, by the rules of the game of the politician. That was, I think, my greatest weakness. I suddenly found myself in a jungle, if you like. And in the jungle, there are the rules of the jungle. If you can't play by the rules of the jungle, then you are prey for other animals.

On the other hand, I don't regret those five years. I thought the social programs of the country were in trouble, and they still are, and I managed to establish something that I think is the greatest social enterprise ever undertaken by the country and the fruits of which will be shown in the coming years.

HS: *You're referring to Project Renewal?*

YY: I'm talking about Project Renewal, which is a giant enterprise of Jewry throughout the world working with the people of Israel to really change the social structure of the slums, not only the physical structure of the slums.

I was a part of the government that signed the peace treaty with Egypt [in 1979]. I really had great moments and hours of sitting with [Anwar] Sadat and in negotiation with his government.

So all told, I am very glad. After five years as a politician, I have something to go back to. And it's good that it is in archaeology. All the things have not been discovered. They are just five years older than they were.

HS: *Do you have any advice for a student interested in archaeology as to how he or she should pursue a career in archaeology?*

YY: Yes, I think every student should do it the difficult way, the hard way and not the easy way. First of all, really master the techniques of archaeology. As everyone who starts to study medicine has to know anatomy, so a student of archaeology has to study the pottery and the stratigraphy and the technique of excavation and the typology and so on. But I would advise the student who wants to study the archaeology of this part of the world also to take a course in the history or in the literature or the philology of the country or the adjacent countries. Don't limit yourself to becoming only a technician/archaeologist. My advice would be to do both. And remember it takes seven years, at least to really become a qualified archaeologist. That is not a short time. Of course field experience is very important. It is like any practice. But don't neglect the theoretical, the historical, the philological, the background of the area in which you want to dig. I think it's vital to do this.

CHAPTER NINE

HOW THE HEBREW BIBLE AND THE CHRISTIAN OLD TESTAMENT DIFFER

An Interview with David Noel Freedman

David Noel Freedman

Ours is an age of increasing specialization, especially in biblical studies. Scholars today frequently restrict themselves to a single text (or portion of a text!), or to the history of a particular place during a narrow period of time. In refreshing contrast to this ever more frequent practice stands the towering example of David Noel Freedman. Freedman, who passed

"How the Hebrew Bible and the Christian Old Testament Differ: An Interview with David Noel Freedman" appeared in *Bible Review*, December 1993.

away at the age of 85 in April 2008, was one of the last of the great Bible generalists. The entire Bible and all of archaeology was his domain. He was General Editor of the Anchor Bible Series *and also edited the* Anchor Bible Reference Library, *which consists of volumes on broad themes beyond the confines of individual biblical books. He was General Editor of the* Anchor Bible Dictionary, *the six-volume work that serves as one of the standard reference works in the field. He served as editor of* Biblical Archaeologist *[now* Near Eastern Archaeology*] and of the* Bulletin of the American Schools of Oriental Research. *He also authored numerous Bible commentaries, books and articles.*

In this interview, Freedman discusses his colorful family history and his conversion to Christianity before turning to one of his primary concerns as a scholar: the overall organization of the Hebrew Bible. Freedman then outlines his thoughts on how—and when—the Hebrew scriptures came to take the shape they did.

Hershel Shanks: *Noel, you have an unusual background that might give you a unique perspective on Christianity and Judaism, seeing both of these two great religions from the inside. Your grandfather was a Yiddish journalist, wasn't he?*

David Noel Freedman: Yes, for the *Jewish Daily Forward* in New York City.

HS: *Where did he come from?*

DNF: Romania, a place called Botoshani, around 1900. My father was also born in Romania but he was brought to this country as an infant.

HS: *Your father was a secular Jew?*

DNF: That would be a good description.

HS: *He wrote for the Broadway stage, didn't he?*

DNF: He was a humorist and wrote for stage, screen and—the new medium at that time—radio.

HS: *He was a writer for some of the great comedians, wasn't he?*

DNF: Eddie Cantor especially, but also many others.

HS: *So you come from New York?*

DNF: I was born and raised in New York City.

HS: *I've heard a story about your father employing the young Herman Wouk.*

DNF: That's right. It was kind of a joke that we used to say that Herman's first job out of college was working for my father and my first job out of college was working for his father.

My father had a joke factory. He had to create radio programs, at the rate of as many as six a week. He employed a number of assistants: Two of them, toward the end, were Arnold Auerbach and Herman Wouk. Arnold and Herman had written two Columbia University varsity shows together, so they came prepared. The joke factory supplied materials not only for radio programs but also for a variety of stage and screen shows, for many actors and actresses. After working for my father, Arnold and Herman were hired as writers by Fred Allen, a great comedian. Arnold Auerbach then wrote several Broadway shows on his own. Herman of course later became a famous novelist.*

HS: *Was your father connected with Broadway?*

DNF: Yes, he wrote for the stage and screen as well as radio. In

*The author of *The Caine Mutiny* (1951), *Winds of War* (1971), *War and Remembrance* (1978) and *Inside, Outside* (1985).

his twenties, my father had a successful comedy on Broadway called *Mendel, Inc.* That comedy was based on short stories he wrote for *Pictorial Review,* which were later collected in a book called *Mendel Marantz.* That established my father as a humorist. On the basis of the book, he began to work for Eddie Cantor. My father actually wrote Eddie's autobiography, *My Life Is in Your Hands* (Harper & Bros., 1928), a very successful book in the late 1920s.

Much earlier my father and Irving Caesar, the well-known songwriter, wrote a musical comedy for Florenz Ziegfeld called *Betsy.* It was a real turkey, as they say. [Laughter] I remember seeing it at the age of four. I must have been one of the very few New Yorkers who did see it. It closed and there were all kinds of recriminations.

Later, my father had a number of very successful runs—the Ziegfeld Follies of 1933 starred Fanny Brice, and a new version with the same stars came out in 1936. Fanny Brice, Bert Lahr and Beatrice Lillie all starred in these shows. There was one called *Life Begins at 8:40,* another called *The Show Is On.* For several years, just before he died, my father worked on a string of extremely successful musical reviews. He was the principal writer of the sketches. These shows did not have the continuity of later musicals like *Oklahoma.* They had separate sketches, musical numbers and all kinds of things, starring different people.

HS: *I understand that in one of Herman Wouk's novels, your father appears as a fictional character.*

DNF: That's correct. Herman's most recent novel, called *Inside, Outside* (Little, Brown, 1985), is largely autobiographical. The leading character is Herman himself, but with a *nom de plume.* The same with my father. He is called Goldhandler in the book. A large part of the book is devoted to Herman's experience in the joke factory. It's a very lively and generally accurate account of what went on. My father worked at home in a three-story penthouse on the upper West Side, Central Park West. The top floor was an office; the boys would come over for supper and then work would begin.

At its peak, there were five or six fellows like Herman. Churning out these scripts was a major undertaking.

The comedians they wrote for all came from the vaudeville circuit and they had routines that, with minor changes, they could use for 20 years. Radio wiped all that out in one week! [Laughter] So each of these vaudeville comedians came to depend on someone to provide new material. This included comedians like Jack Benny, Fred Allen (who wrote his own material, but also needed help), Eddie Cantor and Fannie Brice. My father—and a few others—were able to reprocess, recycle this stuff, and produce new programs week after week. Eddie Cantor became the biggest thing in radio comedy, first on the Chase and Sanborn program and later with other sponsors. Jack Benny was sponsored by Jello.

HS: *(sings) "I love to spend each Sunday with you. As friend to friend, I'm sorry it's through."*

DNF: Sunday at 8. And a full hour. You wouldn't believe the incredible pressure—to turn out these programs week after week. Herman describes all this in his book. That's why my father preferred Broadway; the skits could be repeated for six months or a year.

Herman's father was president and chief stock-holder of the Fox Square Laundry, in the Bronx. After college, I worked there as his private secretary for three months. That is all I could take.

HS: *This early comedy had a particularly Jewish context, didn't it?*

DNF: Very much so.

HS: *You are the grandson of a Yiddish journalist and the son of a*

Jewish comedy writer who wrote humor with a largely Jewish context. What was your religious upbringing?

DNF: The truth is there was none. Both my father and mother had abandoned their religious traditions. We grew up like hundreds of thousands of other Jews in New York City without any religious connection.

HS: *Did you feel a strong ethnic connection?*

DNF: I was aware of being Jewish, but we didn't belong to any kind of Jewish community group or anything like that. It was largely atomistic—the family was very important, as were the institutions we attended (the schools primarily). Mostly I went to public schools. For a while, I went to Bentley School, where French was the only language used.

HS: *Did you have a seder in your home on Passover?*

DNF: Not in our home. Once in a while we attended a seder. We used to go up to the Catskills for vacations. Grossinger's was the major hotel, but we always went to a rival called the Flagler. I remember a Passover or two up there during spring vacation.

HS: *Did you go to synagogue on the high holy days in the fall?*

DNF: No.

HS: *I take it you did not have a bar mitzvah.*

DNF: No.

HS: *At one point you converted to Christianity. Can you tell me how that happened?*

DNF: It's a rather complicated story, and there are some things I'd prefer not to discuss.

HS: *Is there anything that you'd be willing to tell me about?*

DNF: I think I'd rather leave that.

HS: *What denomination did you become?*

DNF: Presbyterian.

HS: *Did you teach at a Presbyterian seminary?*

DNF: Yes, in two of them, for many years.

HS: *What were they?*

DNF: Western Theological Seminary in Pittsburgh, which later merged with another school to form what is now called Pittsburgh Theological Seminary. And the other was the San Francisco Theological Seminary.

HS: *Did you hold positions in the church?*

DNF: I was ordained as a minister. I served as a temporary pastor in various churches, but never as a permanent pastor. My career in the church has almost exclusively been as a teacher.

HS: *Are you still active in the church?*

DNF: No. I retired in 1984.

HS: *Did your family also convert? Your brothers and sisters?*

DNF: No, none of my relatives.

HS: *As you probably know, among your colleagues and friends you are thought of as both Jewish and Christian.*

DNF: Right. I've never made a special issue about that. I have never been observant but, if I understand correctly, the basic definition of a Jew is that your mother is Jewish. That's certainly true in my case. I have never renounced Judaism, but if it's automatic that when you profess Christianity you're no longer a Jew, then I'm no longer Jewish. But my own attitude is that you can be

Jewish and Christian at the same time.

HS: *You have spent your life in Hebrew Bible scholarship.*

DNF: Right.

HS: *That's essentially a Jewish document.*

DNF: It's also a Christian document.

HS: *Correct.*

DNF: Which is really why I picked that, because it allows me to satisfy my own concern about my identity. If I stick to the Hebrew Bible, I can be both.

HS: *You obviously study these texts from a dual perspective, from a Jewish perspective and from a Christian perspective. Are there differences in these perspectives?*

DNF: Oh, a dramatic difference. It has taken me a long time to realize that there is such a difference. But there is also a basic scholarly approach to the Hebrew Bible that is neither Christian nor Jewish, where there's a kind of common denominator, where people with different persuasions, different commitments can meet.

HS: *Can you give us an example of the different perspectives?*

DNF: Yes. The use made of the Hebrew Bible in the New Testament pretty much determines the Christian approach to the Old Testament. In the New Testament, the Hebrew Bible is regarded as a book of prophecy and prediction—the view that many Old Testament predictions are fulfilled and realized in the New Testament.

The writers of the Dead Sea Scrolls also used the Hebrew Bible as a collection of predictions and prophecies that find fulfillment in their own experience, according to their understanding. For example, take the Dead Sea Scroll known as the Commentary on Habakkuk, or Habakkuk *pesher.* The Book of Habakkuk itself is about the Chaldeans (the neo-Babylonians) who conquered the world. The prophet has a lot of things to say about them. Well, what does that mean to people 400 or 500 years later, when the Chaldeans have vanished from history? The Dead Sea Scroll people use a neat little device in the Commentary on Habakkuk and elsewhere: They assume the prophets themselves weren't entirely aware of what their words meant. But thanks to the inspired interpreter, the Teacher of Righteousness, their leader, they could now understand the real meaning of the prophet's words, which are, after all, the words of God. For the Dead Sea Scroll people, Habakkuk is really about the Kittim, not the Chaldeans. It's like the joke [William F.] Albright used to tell about what Moses and Middlebury had in common. Well, you take off "oses" and add "iddlebury" and they're the same. [Laughter] That's exactly what these [Dead Sea Scroll] people were doing; they were simply replacing the Chaldeans with the Kittim.

HS: *Who were the Kittim?*

DNF: A code name either for the Seleucid Greeks in Syria or the Ptolemaic Greeks in Egypt or possibly the Romans. They are the contemporary conquerors and invaders.

The device is easy to see: Since the Dead Sea Scroll people didn't have a prophet of their own, the next best thing was to have an inspired interpreter. They *used* prophecy that everybody accepted as authoritative and adapted it. No problem with this, except that according to these people theirs is the only, the real, interpretation. This isn't just homiletics. This describes a convergence of all the events recounted in the prophets of the past about this present eschatological moment, when everything's going to change.

As an academic exercise, that's very interesting and challenging. No problem. A few years pass, however, and that interpretation becomes obsolete, so you make another adjustment, with a different interpretation. And ultimately you give up the whole thing because the prophecy is equally applicable to this period, to that period, to another period, or inapplicable to any of them, because what the prophet says just doesn't happen. Then you banish the prophecy to a distant future.

But when you say, "This is the *only way*, this is the *real* meaning and any other interpretation is invalid," then you're creating a problem.

When this happens, I think you have to go with the text, not with the commentary. You have to understand the text in its own historical setting, just as any scholar would do with any piece of literature.

HS: *Is this the same thing that was going on in Christian texts?*

DNF: Indeed, it is. One of the most famous, or infamous, passages [in the King James Version] is the passage in Isaiah 7:14: "A virgin shall conceive and bear a child." The Gospel of Matthew (1:18–23) makes this explicit, that the prophet is talking about the birth of Jesus Christ. If you read Isaiah 7:14 in Hebrew, however, there's a problem about the meaning of the Hebrew word *almah*. Does it mean young girl or virgin? In the Greek Septuagint it is translated *parthenos*, which is virgin. Matthew was apparently relying on the Septuagint, which may have mistranslated *almah*. That's one problem. In addition, the context of Isaiah 7:14 makes it clear that the prophet is talking about his own day, something that's going to happen within a very few years and that, in fact, has already happened, so the prophecy was fulfilled. What does that have to do with Jesus Christ 700 years later? Well, that's the Christian perspective, the New Testament perspective. These people are convinced that Jesus is the messiah and therefore they comb the Old Testament for prophecies and anything that pertains or seems to pertain to this belief or illustrates it. And this is all brought into focus by the events surrounding Jesus.

The principle [of interpretation of Scripture] is the same as in the Dead Sea Scroll texts. Now obviously Jews don't have the same perspective.

HS: *What's the Jewish perspective?*

DNF: Well, that varies. After all, the methods we've just described were invented and practiced by Jews. The idea of using the Hebrew Bible in this way is a Jewish way; it's not non-Jewish.

HS: *But Jews don't seem to use this method of interpretation.*

DNF: Not anymore. They got burned by all this in two ways: One was the final collapse of all of this eschatolcgical, apocalyptic expectation. When the Romans suppressed the Second Jewish Revolt, the Bar-Kokhba Revolt (132–135 C.E.), the Jews finally abandoned this expectation of the immediate apocalyptic moment. Some thought that Bar-Kokhba was the messiah. He proved not to be. So the Jews adapted to the situation in other ways. The second factor was the incredible rise of Christianity, which in a way took their [the Jewish] scriptures and turned the Bible against them; I think this cured the Jews of this kind of speculation—until the Middle Ages when there were other messianic movements and some parts of this got revived again.

HS: *What is the alternative Jewish approach to the Hebrew Bible?*

DNF: The major concern of traditional Judaism has been the Torah and *halakhah* [Jewish religious law]. In other words, how to interpret and understand the teachings and the rules of the Bible so that people can practice them. This is an entirely different orientation.

As you know, the Bible itself is not always clear or entirely consistent. The Bible can seem to say one thing at one place and something different at another. So how do you actually practice what it teaches? Answering that is almost the whole history of rabbinic interpretation.

There is much more flexibility in Jewish interpretations of

prophecy and predictions [than in the legal sections of the Hebrew Bible] because these things aren't decided in a legal way. You're not determining practice.

Of course there's a great variety between Orthodox Judaism and Reform Judaism.

But my concern is entirely with scholarship. I'm concerned with the underlying requirements of scholarship. You have to be faithful and true to questions of language, grammar, vocabulary and you have to deal with historical and other contexts and simply try to recover the meaning of the original. This is a common endeavor everybody can get into, but they have to leave some of these prior convictions and commitments outside.

HS: *I was going to ask you about these prior convictions. Does your interpretation of the Christian approach to the Old Testament imply a literal belief in the Gospels, for example, that interpret the Hebrew Bible in this predictive stance?*

DNF: There are at least two separate questions here. One is the way in which the Old Testament is used. And certainly we can describe that.

HS: *You did a moment ago.*

DNF: This has little or nothing to do with real history or the intention of the prophet. On the other hand, the Gospels constitute a narrative and they are subject, just like the narratives of the Old Testament, to questions of historicity and evidence and reasonability. It's really the same.

I don't believe that the Old Testament was ever meant to support the narrative in the Gospels. The conviction about Jesus' messiahship and resurrection had very little to do with the Old Testament. But once these things became the basis of Christian profession, then the Old Testament was used to demonstrate or to enhance belief. When it comes to the historical question about the Gospels, I adopt a mediating position—that is, these are reliable records, close to the sources, but they are not in accordance with modern historiographic requirements or professional standards. In all ancient writings, you find elements of naiveté or credulity. Even Josephus and classical historians like Herodotus and Eusebius include a lot of material that we can't accept as rigorous historical inquiry.

HS: *I take it the biblical text can still be used for inspirational and theological purposes.*

DNF: And also for historical purposes. But we have to accept somewhat looser standards. In the legal profession, to convict the defendant of a crime, you need proof beyond a reasonable doubt. In civil cases, a preponderance of the evidence is sufficient. When dealing with the Bible or any ancient source, we have to loosen up a little; otherwise, we can't really say anything.

HS: *Your personal background is very secular. How did you become interested in the Bible, in biblical scholarship?*

DNF: That relates to my conversion and that arose out of personal experience. My concern at the seminary was to find a way to adjust to this new life. I turned out to be a little more academic than I thought I was. The Bible has a fascination all its own, partly because of its antiquity, but mainly because of its literary character. Catholics, Protestants and Jews, as you know, have different Bibles. The one thing they have in common is the Hebrew Bible. I call it the Common Bible. This Bible that's common to everybody is the foundation. I had a naive notion that the Hebrew Bible could provide a basis for not only dialogue, but also for some kind of reconciliation among religious communities.

The Hebrew Bible is the one artifact from antiquity that not only maintained its integrity but continues to have a vital, powerful effect thousands of years later.

I believe that, in its present form, the Hebrew Bible is a product of a very carefully worked-out plan to achieve symmetry, totality, even perfection. There's a deliberate effort made to pool together all the heterogeneous elements in the Jewish tradition and make a single whole. This book was intended to reflect what they believed about the perfection of God, more especially about the importance of his word. It was to reflect in written form the activity of God in the world and the link between members committed to this word. Just as God created the universe and rules the universe and directs history through the word spoken, here in the Bible is the word written. It's the equivalent of the word spoken. This makes the Bible something even more special, not just another relic from antiquity. It has a unique quality. My brother, who is a professed atheist, says the Bible is the richest source that he knows for human experience.

HS: *This has been an abiding concern of yours, to explore the overarching connections within the entire text of the Hebrew Bible. Your most recent book is called* The Unity of the Hebrew Bible *(University of Michigan Press, 1991).*

DNF: That's correct. Actually I have published another book since then with Sara Mandell, *The Relationship between Herodotus' History and Primary History* (Scholars Press, 1993). It's a comparison between the Primary History in the Bible [Genesis through Kings] and Herodotus, who is often called "the father of history." We try to show that if there's any priority here, it belongs to the Bible. Moreover, the Primary History in the Bible achieves greater unity, greater focus, is more of a history than Herodotus.

But, to return to the unity of the Hebrew Bible, I'll give you my view on that. It might help first to identify a real chasm between Jewish and Christian belief here. As is well known, the arrangement of the books is very different in Christian Bibles and Hebrew Bibles [see "The Jewish Bible and the Christian Old

Testament," p. 226]. The Christian order is based on the Old Greek Bible, the Septuagint. Originally, this was a Jewish translation, but all the copies of it that have survived—from the fourth century [C.E.] on—were preserved by Christians.

The last section of Christian Bibles, following the order in the Septuagint, contains the literary prophets, ending with the prophet Malachi. The order in the Jewish tradition is different from the order in the Christian tradition. Both begin with what I call the Primary History—the Pentateuch (the five books of Moses) plus Joshua, Judges, Samuel and Kings. The Christian tradition varies here only by the insertion of Ruth between Judges and Samuel.

In the Jewish tradition, the Primary History is followed by the literary prophets—the three major literary prophets (Isaiah, Jeremiah and Ezekiel) and the Book of the Twelve Minor Prophets. Not so in the Christian tradition. In the Christian tradition, these four books of the literary prophets plus the Book of Daniel are placed at the end. Malachi, the last prophet in the Book of the Twelve Minor Prophets, leads directly into the Gospels, which are supposed to be the fulfillment of these prophecies. For Christians, the Old Testament is a book of prophecy and prediction of the coming of the Messiah that is fulfilled in the New Testament. Basically, with the coming of Jesus Christ the predictive factors in the Old Testament are fulfilled or, if not fulfilled, are largely fulfilled with others yet to come.

Now what is the Jewish view of the Hebrew Bible? From the Jewish perspective, the Bible is divided into two halves. The first half is the story of the fall of Israel (Israel and Judah, after the kingdom divides), how they lost the land, lost their city, lost their Temple, everything. It's the fall of Israel.

HS: *Ending with the Babylonian destruction in 586 B.C.E.?*

DNF: Correct.

HS: *And beginning with creation?*

The Jewish Bible and the Christian Old Testament

The Bible that Jews and Christians share is not the same in all respects. The order of the Hebrew scriptures—what Christians often call the Old Testament—varies in Jewish and Christians Bibles. The chart below shows the differences. The Jewish Bible consists of three major sections: the *Torah,* or Pentateuch (the Five Books of Moses). *Nevi'im,* the Prophets; and *Ketuvim,* the Writings. The Prophets (*Nevi'im*) are divided into the Former Prophets, consisting of Joshua, Judges, Samuel and Kings; and the Latter Prophets (the literary prophets—Isaiah, Jeremiah, Ezekiel and the Twelve Minor Prophets).

Bible scholar David Noel Freedman calls the books of the Hebrew Bible from Genesis through Kings the Primary History. It tells the story of God's promise of the Land of Israel to the Jewish people, their conquest of that land and their subsequent loss of it.

The Christian Bible basically follows the same order as the Jewish Bible from the beginning (Genesis) through the end of the Primary History (through the Former Prophets, i.e. Kings, in Jewish tradition). The only difference up to this point is that in Christian Bibles, Ruth is inserted after Judges.

After the Primary History, however, there are major differences. The most important is that the literary prophets (the Latter Prophets in Jewish tradition) are placed at the end of the Old Testament in Christian Bibles.

Other differences are shown in the chart.

The Jewish Bible	**The Christian Old Testament**
Torah-Pentateuch	Pentateuch
Genesis	Genesis
Exodus	Exodus
Leviticus	Leviticus
Numbers	Numbers
Deuteronomy	Deuteronomy
Nevi'im-the Prophets	
Former Prophets	Historical Books
Joshua	Joshua
Judges	Judges
	Ruth
1 & 2 Samuel	1 & 2 Samuel
1 & 2 Kings	1 & 2 Kings
	1 & 2 Chronicles
	Ezra and Nehemiah
	Esther

Other Writings

Job
Psalms
Proverbs
Ecclesiastes
Song of Solomon

Latter Prophets	**Literary Prophets**
Isaiah	Isaiah
Jeremiah	Jeremiah
	Lamentations
Ezekiel	Ezekiel
	Daniel
The 12 Minor Prophets	**The 12 Minor Prophets**
Hosea	Hosea
Joel	Joel
Amos	Amos
Obadiah	Obadiah
Jonah	Jonah
Micah	Micah
Nahum	Nahum
Habakkuk	Habakkuk
Zephaniah	Zephaniah
Haggai	Haggai
Zechariah	Zechariah
Malachi	Malachi

Ketuvim-The Writings

Psalms
Proverbs
Job
Song of Songs
Ruth
Lamentations
Ecclesiastes
Esther
Daniel
Ezra and Nehemiah
1 & 2 Chronicles

DNF: Right. That's the Primary History—from creation to the destruction of the Temple—the five books of Moses (Genesis, Exodus, Leviticus, Numbers and Deuteronomy—of course they have different names in Hebrew) plus Joshua, Judges, Samuel and Kings. That's the first half. The first half is tragic. If that's all they were interested in, that would be the end. But what the Hebrew Bible is really all about—in Jewish tradition—is how they came back. That's the last half, the story of the return.

Both parts are equally important. This is really a quasi-legal brief on behalf of Israel and its claim to the land. The contention is that even though the original grant of land to them was conditional—provisional—and they failed to maintain the conditions—they didn't fulfill the requirements of the covenant and they lost the land—nevertheless, overriding this historical truth is the original commitment made by God to Abraham in Genesis 15 (and repeated elsewhere to Abraham and his descendants). There it's spelled out. God committed himself by oath to give the land to Abraham and his descendants. According to their understanding, even if they deserved to lose it and lost it, they still have this claim because the original commitment was unconditional, irrevocable—"To your offspring, I give this land" (Genesis 15:18)—and there's no way it can be reversed.

HS: *And this is the story of the second half of the Hebrew Bible?*

DNF: Yes, especially Chronicles. In Jewish Bibles today the last book is Chronicles, after Ezra-Nehemiah. This actually makes no sense, because it is in reverse chronological order. Chronicles begins with creation and takes the story up to a certain point and then Ezra-Nehemiah takes it from there. Nevertheless Chronicles is the last book.

But in the best and oldest copies of the Hebrew Bible—the Aleppo Codex around 900 C.E. and the Leningrad Codex shortly after 1000—the arrangement is different. Chronicles appears immediately after the literary prophets, and Ezra-Nehemiah is the last book of the whole Hebrew Bible. This section from Chronicles to Ezra-Nehemiah is known in Jewish tradition as the Writings (*Ketuvim*). It is the third major section of the Hebrew Bible. The first is the Torah, the Pentateuch. The second is the Prophets (*Nevi'im*), which in Jewish tradition includes the Former Prophets (Joshua, Judges, Samuel and Kings) and the Latter Prophets (the four books of literary prophets). In the Aleppo Codex and the Leningrad Codex, the Writings begin with Chronicles and end with Ezra-Nehemiah. These two historical narratives (Chronicles and Ezra-Nehemiah) form an envelope around the Writings, what we call an *inclusio*.

Chronicles begins with the word "Adam." This is clearly an echo of Genesis, obviously recapitulating the whole story. But this time it is the story, not only of how they lost the land, but also how they got it back.

HS: *How is that conveyed?*

DNF: At the end of the story—Ezra-Nehemiah—they're back in the land, the Temple has been rebuilt, they've reoccupied Jerusalem and Nehemiah has put in the last piece of the puzzle—the walls. Jerusalem is once again a walled city. This has great significance; her integrity has been restored.

The only thing missing is that they're not entirely free: they don't have their own king. But that's for the future. Because this is history and not fiction, it can't be a complete circle, because that isn't the way things really happened. That's going to happen later, however. That's the reason the Book of Daniel was added, to bring the story up to date 250 years later. The Book of Daniel is the odd man out.

But the point is that the Hebrew Bible in its totality is a quasi-legal brief for Israel's right to be on that land. The whole story is how it was promised by divine grant, how they occupied it, how they lost it and how they got it back. And finally, there is a messianic future. That remains yet to be fulfilled.

The literary prophets (Isaiah, Jeremiah, Ezekiel and the Book of the Twelve Minor Prophets) form a kind of connecting link between the Primary History, which I've already described, and the Writings. The literary prophets are called the Latter Prophets in Jewish tradition, as opposed to the Former Prophets (Joshua, Judges, Samuel and Kings), which form part of the Primary History. The Primary History ends when they lose the land and they are carried into captivity. The Latter Prophets overlap with this story. They start before the end of that story but go beyond it, with the return and the imminent rededication of the Temple at the end of First Zechariah (chapters 1–8).* In other words, that gives us the transition. And then the Writings are a heterogeneous collection, enclosed in an envelope, with Chronicles at the beginning and Ezra-Nehemiah at the very end, tying the whole thing together within this context of the promise of the land, the occupation of the land and then the loss and the resettlement.

HS: *How do you account for the fact that in Jewish tradition you have the Former Prophets and the Latter Prophets? In your division, you put the Former Prophets with your Primary History.*

DNF: There is a symmetry here, a bilateral symmetry that we see again and again. There are four Former Prophets. [Joshua, Judges, Samuel and Kings;1 and 2 Samuel and 1 and 2 Kings are each regarded as single books in Jewish tradition.] Ruth is not in the Former Prophets but in the Writings, where it is grouped with the four other Megillot (Scrolls: Song of Songs, Lamentations, Ecclesiastes and Esther). And there are four Latter Prophets (the literary prophets—Isaiah, Jeremiah, Ezekiel and the Book of the Twelve). The Book of the Twelve Minor

*Zechariah is really two books, not one. The first (chapters 1–8) was written shortly after the return from Exile. The second (chapters 9–14), sometimes called Deutero-Zechariah, differs considerably in style. It was written much later, during the Hellenistic period, but scholars do not agree on the date.

Prophets is always one book. That's an artificial way to establish symmetry.

I divide it somewhat differently. I believe that the Primary History was one unit and that the Torah was then separated from the Primary History.

HS: *The Torah being the five books of Moses?*

DNF: Right. Normal scholarship holds that the Torah came first and the Former Prophets were added to make the Primary History. I think the Torah was extracted from the whole Primary History for a reason—to create a legal constitution, a document that would be the law of the land. The Primary History is a story. The Torah is intended to be a law. In fact, neither quite fills the bill because the Primary History has a great deal of legislation in it. The Torah is laws, but it has the Book of Genesis, which isn't law. Most scholars agree that Deuteronomy goes with the Former Prophets to form the Deuteronomic History. Deuteronomy is really the introduction to the Deuteronomic History.

The only analysis that makes literary sense is that the entire Primary History is a unit. Any other division produces anomalies. For example, if you divide the first four books—Genesis, Exodus, Leviticus and Numbers, the so-called Tetrateuch—from Deuteronomy and the Deuteronomic History, you're in trouble because you end up at the end of Numbers where you're not supposed to be, in Transjordan. The Israelites haven't made it to the Promised Land, the land promised in Genesis. You're stopping in the middle because the fulfillment of Genesis, with all its promises, can only come in Joshua. It doesn't come in Numbers or Deuteronomy.

HS: *Is that why the Samaritan canon includes Joshua and that's all?*

DNF: Well, that's yet another story. In classical critical analysis we talk about the Hexateuch—the Pentateuch plus Joshua.

HS: *In Joshua they take possession of the land?*

DNF: Yes. The west bank of the Jordan, not the east bank, because the west bank is what was promised to Abraham. The conquest of the east bank, which is in Numbers, is more or less an accident. So, that can't be the literary connection.

HS: *According to common scholarly belief, the Pentateuch was canonized by Ezra and Nehemiah, or in that period when they return from the Exile (fifth century B.C.E.).*

DNF: Right.

HS: *But you are saying that they canonized more than that, that they canonized the entire Primary History?*

DNF: More than that, the whole Bible.

HS: *So it all must have been written by then.*

DNF: Yes, I think it was, all except Daniel. The way I see it is this: Ezra is the one who establishes the authority of the law in the restored community. We are told this quite dramatically: In our last image of Ezra, in Nehemiah 8:13, he is reading from the Torah to the people. I believe Ezra is responsible for the formation of the Torah out of the Primary History, which already existed. That's how the division after Deuteronomy occurred. Practically all the laws are contained in the first five books, and the law is what Ezra is trying to get the people to commit themselves to do, to live by the words of this document.

Then I believe Ezra wrote his own memoirs (the Book of Ezra) and died. The overall work, however, was done by Nehemiah; he has the last word in the Hebrew Bible. And what is it? "Remember me, oh my God, for good." Nehemiah is like King James; he's the executive (i.e., the governor) who sponsored this. He put up the money, and he's unhappy because he didn't get enough credit. His book is about putting everything together.

The words with which the Hebrew Bible (that is, Nehemiah) ends are *"Zochrah li Elohay l-tovah"* "Remember me, oh my God, for good." The two key words are *Elohay,* simply a form of *Elohim*—God, and tovah, the feminine form of *tov*—good. The dominant words in the first chapter of Genesis are *Elohim* and *tov,* "God" and "good." After every day's work, God says, "It's good." I think in Nehemiah, which according to the most reliable witnesses (the Aleppo and Leningrad codices) ends the Hebrew Bible, we have an echo of the very beginning of the Hebrew Bible. The word *Elohim* is repeated, while the pair *tov* and *tovah* form a *merismus* or totality. It's as if to say at the very end, very deliberately, "Now we are done."

HS: *When Ezra-Nehemiah put the whole thing together (except for Daniel), was the Primary History already in existence?*

DNF: Yes.

HS: *When was that done?*

DNF: Well, my answer is based on the axiom, the simpler the better. When does the Primary History end? It ends with the Exile, following the Babylonian destruction in 586 B.C.E. There's no hint in the entire Primary History of the actual return from Exile.

HS: *You think the Primary History was put together somewhere in Babylonia during the Exile?*

DNF: Definitely. What else did they have to do? And the two people who could produce an authoritative work like that—the king and the high priest—were both in exile in Babylon. They could give it the imprimatur, the stamp of authority, the prestige that was required.

I think that's what happened, because if they had the faintest notion of what was going to happen 20 years later (the return from Exile), it would have been included, just as the Chronicler includes it. For the biblical people, the return was the most important event after the destruction. I think the Primary History was written in anticipation of the return from Exile, but before it happened. The Persian king Cyrus, who conquered the Babylonians, issued an edict allowing the Jews to return to their land. Nobody predicted that. Afterward, they all claimed to have, but we know it was a total surprise.

CHAPTER TEN

ESCAPE AND RESCUE
An Interview with Geza Vermes

Geza Vermes

Despite the close historical links between Judaism and Christianity, few scholars cross the line to work in both Second Temple Judaism and early Christianity. One notable exception is Geza Vermes, professor emeritus of Jewish studies at the University of Oxford and director of the Forum for Qumran Research at the Oxford Centre for Postgraduate Hebrew

"Escape and Rescue: An Interview with Geza Vermes" appeared in *Bible Review*, June 1994.

Studies. Vermes specializes in the crucial centuries that gave birth to both Rabbinic Judaism and to Christianity. He is particularly known for his work on the Dead Sea Scrolls. Indeed, it is probably fair to say that more readers encounter the scrolls through his* The Dead Sea Scrolls in English *than through any other work, but he has published a number of important works on the historical Jesus. In this interview Professor Vermes discusses his remarkable personal story, his life's work and the Jewish context of the historical Jesus.

Hershel Shanks: *You're the first Oxford Don I've ever interviewed. What is an Oxford Don? And why aren't you called an Oxford Joe or an Oxford Sam or an Oxford Pete? Why an Oxford Don?*

Geza Vermes: Don comes from the medieval abbreviation of *dominus,* which just means "Mr."

HS: *Not "Lord"?*

GV: No. An Oxford Don is just an Oxford teacher—very often an Oxford teacher born and bred, not someone like me. A traditional Oxford Don used to be someone who had been through Oxford himself or herself, whose father and grandfather had been through the Oxford mill, and so on. The most characteristic Oxford Don I've ever met was the late Professor Sir Godfrey Driver, who was professor of Semitic philology from the end of the First World War until 1960 or so. He told me, "My father"—that was S.R. Driver, former Regius Professor of Hebrew in Oxford and canon of Christ Church—"My father and I have taught in Oxford for 90 years." Now that's a genuine Oxford Don. Godfrey Driver once told me that his first memory was of being taken up to Tom Tower, the big tower of Christ Church, by Lewis Carroll, the author of *Alice in Wonderland,* to watch the inauguration of the new Oxford town hall by the future Edward VII. Driver was born in Christ Church—his father's college—

lived in Oxford, taught in Oxford as his father before him. I can't hope to match that.

HS: *Well, you do have an extraordinary personal history that surely provides a background to your two primary scholarly interests—first, the Dead Sea Scrolls, and second, early Christianity and the life of Jesus. You don't have an English name; you speak with an accent. It's a Hungarian accent, isn't it?*

GV: I always wonder what sort of accent it is. When I hear Hungarians speaking English, they have a somewhat different accent. Mine is probably a cosmopolitan accent. But definitely not Oxford English. [Laughter]

HS: *Were you born in Hungary?*

GV: Yes, I was born in 1924 in Mako, a town in southeast Hungary. My father was a journalist.

HS: *At one time your family converted to Catholicism. Was that because of the rise of Hitler?*

GV: No, that happened before Hitler.

HS: *Was it because of anti-Semitism?*

GV: I'm pretty sure it was. It happened when I was six.

HS: *Do you have any memories of a Jewish upbringing?*

GV: My parents were not observant Jews in any way. Though my whole family was Jewish, none of them participated in Jewish communal life. This was very typical of a certain stage in the sad story of Hungarian Jewry, characterized by very strong steps towards assimilation. For example, nobody in my family spoke Yiddish, going back several generations. My great-grandmother, whom I knew—she was born in 1839—told me that they used to sing Hungarian nationalist songs during the 1848 revolution. They were Hungarian-speaking even then. I don't know how far back we would have to go to reach the Yiddish stream in the family, but it would be more than 150 years.

HS: *Did they still know they were Jewish?*

GV: Oh, yes, certainly they knew they were Jewish.

HS: *And they married other Jews?*

GV: Yes, yes, they married other Jews. I don't know the detailed reasons why my parents decided to convert. No doubt they thought it would probably help me if they joined Christianity.

HS: *What were they thinking of?*

GV: The basic anti-Semitism that was rampant in that part of the world for hundreds of years. It didn't work. They themselves were victims of the Holocaust.

HS: *Do you recall growing up as a Catholic?*

GV: From primary school onwards, I was brought up that way.

HS: *At one time, you decided to become a priest.*

GV: Yes.

HS: *How old were you?*

GV: Eighteen. My intentions were serious and honest, but, at the same time, I knew that without opting for that solution, my chances of a higher education would have been next to nothing.

HS: *If you were 18 when you decided to become a priest, that would have been 1942. By that time things were already pretty clear.*

GV: Things were pretty clear, granted. But the Nazis did not actually take over in Hungary until 1944. This was different from most other countries in Eastern Europe. Before March 1944, Hungary had a very Germanophile government, but without direct violent action against Jews in civil life. Jews were deprived of most civic rights, but their existence was not endangered until 1944.

HS: *If your parents converted when you were six, that would have been 1930. Were they regarded as Christians thereafter? If someone in the community were asked whether they were Jewish or Christian, would the answer be Christian?*

GV: I suppose so, although nearly all my father's friends were Jews. He moved entirely in Jewish circles.

HS: *How were your parents finally swept up in the Holocaust?*

GV: My father was picked up in the first stage of anti-Jewish action in May 1944. The Nazis occupied Hungary in March and set up a Quisling government. The previous government was right wing, but not Nazi. By May some sort of decree was issued whereby all Jews of any influence and all left-wing people (communists, socialists) were put into concentration camps. My father was taken then as a Jew and a liberal journalist. Gone without a trace...

HS: *And your mother?*

GV: My mother was deported with all other provincial Jews in June 1944.

HS: *Even though they were baptized?*

GV: Absolutely.

HS: *Were they taken because they were Jewish?*

GV: Oh yes. Legally, people with four Jewish grandparents counted as Jews, irrespective of their present religion—or absence of religion.

HS: *How were they identified? They had been Christians for 14 years.*

GV: In order to be recognized as non-Jewish, you had to produce certificates that your grandparents were Christian.

HS: *Where were you at this time?*

GV: I was already in a theological college.

HS: *Do you remember hearing about your parents being taken away?*

GV: I heard of my father's arrest, but later I was on the run myself.

HS: *Can you tell me about that?*

GV: Well, the college authorities wished me luck. They were unwilling, however, to bear the responsibility of hiding a Jew. They provided me with false documents. They were useless; it was so patent they were not genuine that I wouldn't have dared to use them. From the summer of 1944, I traveled in Hungary from east to west and back again. I must acknowledge, with profound gratitude, that I did this with the help of a number of priests and bishops. They helped me not just because I happened to be a baptized Jew; they would have sympathized with anyone in those circumstances. The parish priest who had baptized my parents—he became a bishop afterwards—helped me to move to Budapest, where I thought I would have the best chance of surviving. He provided me with recommendations to the theological college at the University of Budapest. I was there when the capital was occupied by the Russians in December 1944.

HS: *The Russian occupation of Budapest saved you.*

GV: Yes. But the bishop who saved me was murdered by Russian soldiers when he tried to protect a woman whom they wanted to rape.

HS: *When were you ordained a priest?*

GV: That was years later, in 1950 in Belgium. After the war, I got out of Hungary as quickly as I could. I went to Belgium and studied in Louvain. In 1950 I became a priest, associated with the Congregation of the Fathers of Zion.

HS: *What was your thinking at that time?*

GV: I wanted to be a scholar and to teach, but I had no chance in those days to do that.

HS: *Why not?*

GV: You ask me, and I ask you. I was not given an opportunity. I then moved to Paris, where I was involved in editing a journal called *Cahiers Sioniens*. All my first articles on the Dead Sea Scrolls were published there. In Paris I studied with a man who had a great influence on me academically, a Hungarian professor at the Sorbonne named Georges Vajda, a graduate of the famous Hungarian Jewish Rabbinic Seminary. He was teaching Jewish studies at the École des Hautes Études, and I was one of the very faithful members of his weekly seminar. With his help, I became a part-time researcher at the Centre National de la Recherche Scientifique in Paris. Yet I felt my life was not really where I would find myself most at home. I was wondering where to go.

I visited England a number of times, liked the atmosphere and met my future wife. I decided to turn my back on my Christian past, pull up roots from France, where I lived, and move to England. With enormous help from the late Professor [Paul] Kahle, who lived in Oxford, I obtained a lectureship at the University of Newcastle. I was most fortunate. At the time I was in England on a tourist visa, I was a stateless person and I had no money or any local connections. I spent eight years in Newcastle, from 1957 to 1965, teaching Hebrew Bible. There were not many students, so I had plenty of time to do my research. During those years I produced my first English book, *Scripture and Tradition in Judaism* (Brill, 1961). I had already written a book in French on the scrolls, which had been translated into English [*Discovery in the Judean Desert* (Desclee, 1956)]. In 1962 came *The Dead Sea Scrolls in English* (Penguin, Harmondsworth), which since then has never been out of print and has sold close to 300,000 copies.

HS: *You could have done all this without giving up your Catholicism. You didn't have to become a Jew.*

GV: Once I ceased to be formally a Christian, I knew that I was a Jew. In fact, I never was anything but a Jew with a temporary sort of outer vestment. I realized I ought to recognize my genuine identity. It happened straightaway, although it was only formalized later.

HS: *How was it formalized?*

GV: When I joined the Liberal Jewish Synagogue of Great Britain in London.

HS: *Did you have to go through a conversion process?*

GV: No. I had to make a declaration and pay a membership fee.

HS: *This reminds me of a story that's told about Charles Steinmetz, the discoverer of electromagnetism, who was a hunchback. He was walking in a garden with a friend who said that he, too, used to be a Jew, as Steinmetz was. Steinmetz replied, "Ah, yes, and I used to be a hunchback."*

GV: Yes, I suppose there is something in that, although in my case both things happened in a sort of imperceptible way. I became a Christian as a child without realizing it. And I became a Jew as a grown-up by ceasing to be a Christian. In 1965 I was appointed a teacher of Jewish studies at Oxford. In 1969 the then-editor of the *Journal of Jewish Studies*, Joseph Weiss (another Hungarian), tragically died, leaving the journal without an editor. I offered my services and was appointed.

HS: *One of your specialties has been the historical Jesus and the background of early Christianity. Do you feel this peregrination of yours has given you a unique perspective?*

GV: I would like to think that as far as scholarly studies are concerned, this is irrelevant. But it is pretty obvious that what I've been through must have helped considerably, first and foremost to acquire the technical knowledge and to understand the viewpoint of an insider. As an insider, you know how the other fellow thinks. At the same time, you come to realize that there is an enormous amount of misunderstanding and blindness and confusion in both camps regarding one another that really prevents them from perceiving historic reality accurately. Perhaps I kid myself by thinking that I've performed something useful in producing a historically valid portrait of Jesus without preaching either to one or the other. I trust I am an objective and a detached historian. I don't want to convert Christians to Judaism. I simply want to learn and to provide knowledge to others who seek to understand things better.

I started off studying Bible. In 1950 I switched to do a doctoral thesis on the Dead Sea Scrolls. In studying the Dead Sea Scrolls, I realized that in order to work on the scrolls, one must become an expert in the study of the interpretation of the Bible in ancient Judaism, so I turned my interests to ancient Jewish Bible exegesis, which resulted in *Scripture and Tradition in Judaism*. So that was my second line of study. Then in 1965 I was invited to reedit and revise Emil Schurer's great three-volume classic, *The History of the Jewish People in the Age of Jesus Christ*. With two Oxford colleagues [Fergus Millar and Martin Goodman], I spent 20 years on this; we finally finished it in 1986.

I became more and more involved in the details of Jewish political, cultural, religious and literary history. As an offshoot, I wrote *Jesus the Jew* (Collins, 1973). When it came out, it sounded like a very provocative title. Today it is commonplace.

Everybody knows now that Jesus was a Jew. But in 1973, although people knew that Jesus had something to do with Judaism, they thought that he was really something totally different. In the past 20 years, interest in the historical Jesus has increased enormously.

Meanwhile I pressed on with the Jesus work. The second volume, *Jesus and the World of Judaism* (SCM Press), appeared in 1983; this incorporated a series of public lectures I gave called "The Gospel of Jesus the Jew." Just a few weeks ago, a third volume, *The Religion of Jesus the Jew* (SCM Press and Fortress Press, 1993), came out. It is entirely devoted to the religion Jesus preached and practiced.

HS: *Did Jesus intend to start a new religion?*

GV: Not as far as I can see.

HS: *What has been the reaction to your new book?*

GV: It is too soon to say. The reviews that have appeared so far are mostly positive, even from conservative Christian circles. The reactions have almost been overgenerous. The most detailed review appeared in the [London] *Times Literary Supplement* by the subdean of Westminster Abbey, Canon Anthony Harvey. He does not agree with me that Jesus did not want to found a church, but very largely agrees with most other things I say.

HS: *What does the canon agree with?*

GV: He simply says that my portrait of the religious Jesus is very "credible" and "even at times arresting." I think that he would concede that the religion Jesus preached was substantially different from what Christianity has become.

HS: *Can you characterize the two?*

GV: Jesus preached a totally God-centered religion, whereas

* Pertaining to the end of days or the end of time.

Christianity is Christocentric. Everything focuses on Jesus. But Jesus was not concerned with himself; he was concerned with how to bring himself and the people who listened to him into the kingdom of God, to be children of God. Everything in his teaching is entirely within Judaism. The religion he preached and practiced was an eschatological* Judaism. But this eschatological Judaism in the form he envisaged it obviously didn't happen; the kingdom of God did not come in his lifetime. His followers, still totally under his influence, expected this kingdom of God to come almost immediately in their lifetime, coinciding with the return of Christ, which was imminently awaited. Some Christians in Greece went so far as to give up their jobs; they stopped carrying on business because they believed the day of the Lord was at hand, even present. Some believed that Christ had already returned and that Paul had written a letter to this effect. Paul himself had to pour cold water on all the excitement (2 Thessalonians 2:1–12).

Quite clearly such eschatological enthusiasm can't last. When things don't happen as quickly as you had hoped, the excitement cools down and evaporates. The expectation of the return of Christ is still part of Christianity today. But it is expected to come toward the end of an enormously long future; so much so that in practical terms it has no impact on individuals in the main Christian churches. Jesus himself, however, envisaged this as happening very soon—in his time. So did his disciples and even their disciples. And then, very naturally, it abated—in the same way as happened with the Dead Sea Scroll community of Essenes. In the Habakkuk commentary from Cave 1, you find exactly the same thing. The "moment of God" was expected very soon. The classical Hebrew prophets had also believed that it would happen in the near future. When it didn't happen, members of the Dead Sea Scroll community were told to put up with this, to persevere and show that they believed in the words of the prophets and in the teaching of the Teacher of Righteousness.

HS: *It's a similar accommodation to the early Church's readjustment?*

GV: Yes, of course. If the Essenes had lasted as long as the Church has lasted, probably they would have developed in the same way—paying lip service to the idea, as is the case in mainstream Christianity today.

HS: *One of the problems for the layperson in getting an understanding of Jesus from modern historians using modern historiographical criteria is that we get so many different pictures. How does the layperson choose? Different scholars interpret Jesus as an ascetic, a preacher, a magician, a hasid [a teacher of outstanding devotion], a revolutionary, a Mediterranean peasant, on and on.*

GV: For me, he was an eschatological hasid.

HS: *Who expected the imminent kingdom of God?*

GV: Yes.

HS: *How can you reconcile all these different portraits of Jesus? The layperson who reads these different interpretations says to himself or herself, "How can I trust these scholars who disagree so much among themselves. I look to my own faith and my own faith tells me that Jesus was born of a virgin and arose from the dead after three days."*

GV: Partly the variety is due to the fact that our information is very sparse, incomplete and partly self-contradictory. Consequently, all these portraits are vague sketches and approximations. There is room for a fair amount of disagreement among scholars in the details. But they would nevertheless agree on certain main lines of the portrait. In addition, there are means to improve the portrait—by an ever greater familiarization with all things Jewish of the time. Most New Testament scholars claim they have made some study of the Jewish world of the period, but surely most of them must agree that the possibilities are still not altogether exhausted. By improving on that knowledge, I'm confident that the means to arrive at a more precise picture will be available.

HS: *In my contacts with New Testament scholars, I notice a great divide between those people who, on the one hand, are trained deeply in Greek and Hellenistic thought and, on the other hand, those who are trained in Hebrew and Aramaic and Semitic thought.*

GV: Yes. Absolutely, I am in agreement. And for a very good reason. This is the basic divide in the New Testament itself and in the earliest layers of Christianity. Everybody knows that Jesus was a Jew and that he preached to Jews; his first followers were Jews. If you want to reach Jesus, it is definitely through a better knowledge of first-century Judaism that you can achieve this. But of course Christianity, after the crucifixion, very soon moved out of this Jewish context into Syria, into Asia Minor, into Greece, into Egypt and into Italy—into a civilization the language of which was Greek and the culture and religion of which was Hellenistic. It was to people with such a background that early Christianity—from St. Paul onwards—was preached. The teaching of Jesus had to be remolded and translated so that people who had no knowledge of Judaism and to whom all the Jewish ideas were double Dutch could grasp it. At the first stage, the followers of Jesus thought that only people who first became Jewish could become Jewish Christians. But of course this didn't work, so the Jewish condition was discarded, and it was agreed that people could become Christians without passing through Judaism. All those men and women from Athens or Antioch or Ephesus or Rome or Alexandria had no idea what Paul and his companions were talking about when they used all those Jewish concepts. They didn't have the faintest notion what those concepts meant. All this had to be adapted for them so that they could reach Christianity by means of the Hellenistic links.

Most people, probably rightly, consider that in order to understand Christianity, you do it best through Paul. To understand Paul you have to do it through Greek ideas. So in one sense New

Testament scholars are divided between the Hellenists and the Judaists. They are divided because some are interested in Paul and some are interested in Jesus. To understand Jesus you have to go one way; to understand Paul—and the religion known as Christianity—you have to go the other. If you want to avoid the difficulty—and here I'm being provocative—that faces Christians, then you can take a shortcut and decide that it is Pauline Christianity that gives you an easy understanding of what Jesus was about. You can cut out the Jewish part. That is the traditional Christian path. But if you are more demanding and want to go back to the sources, you will realize that Jesus stood before Christianity. And if you want to discover Jesus, Paul is not really your best guide, as he was never associated with Jesus and probably never knew him.

HS: *If you ever make Bartlett's Quotations, it's likely to be for the statement you made about the Dead Sea Scrolls. I think it was in 1977 that you said, "The Dead Sea Scrolls are likely to become the academic scandal par excellence of the 20th century." What occasioned that remark?*

GV: It was occasioned by the realization that the editorial system then in practice was a total failure and that there was nobody who could ensure that there would be reasonable progress in publishing the large majority of the fragments. And that would be the scandal of the century. My concrete evidence for this was my certain knowledge that in the early 1970s genuine steps were made via the publishers of the scrolls, the Oxford University Press, at my instigation, to oblige the then-editors to commit themselves to a definite, reasonable, close date for the delivery of their finished manuscripts. That was in 1972. The then-director of Oxford University Press, Colin Roberts, the famous Greek papyrologist, got in touch with all the editors—who had also been instructed in that way by the editor in chief of the day, Pierre Benoit—and requested them to send to Oxford University

Press a very definite timetable. I know exactly what happened. Half of them didn't reply. The other half did reply and gave precise dates, which had all expired without any result by the time I made that statement.

Then I said to myself, "Unless something drastic is done, this scandal will happen." I still hoped at that time that somebody would shake things up. But there was a fatal flaw in the system inaugurated by [Roland] de Vaux [the first chief editor]: There was no ultimate supervising authority who could say, "You, Mr. X, you received so many texts on such and such a date; 20 years have elapsed, and you still haven't produced the goods; we're going to take this manuscript away from you and give it to somebody else." There was no such independent authority. In fact, the only authority was the editors themselves. Their vested interest was that nobody should interfere with their activity—or their inactivity. My oft-repeated saying came about through the concrete realization that the system had completely failed.

About ten years later, the new editor in chief-in-waiting—not yet confirmed—John Strugnell—and most of the other editors attended a symposium in London. At a public meeting in connection with the symposium, I urged Strugnell to do the easy thing for himself and for everyone else. The editorial work consisted of publishing the plates [the photographs] on the one hand, and the transcriptions, translations and notes on the other. I proposed that the two be divorced. Release the plates at once. This could be done in no time. To which the answer was a two-letter word—No. No explanation and no comment, except possibly, "Out of the question." It could have been done easily and then they could have taken their time thereafter and everybody would have been happier because people who were equipped to work on the texts would have been able to do so, as they can now.

HS: *You were really the first voice crying in the wilderness about the situation.*

GV: Yes, I suppose so.

HS: *Yet it wasn't taken up by other scholars, at least not very widely.*

GV: Not until a few years later. Then voices became louder, asking for access to the texts. And that was fair and totally justified. I still can't understand why what I now call the "secrecy rule" had to be imposed except that some people didn't want to be disturbed in their snail-paced nonactivity.

HS: *Are you satisfied with the situation today?*

GV: I personally am totally satisfied. I can't see what more could be done except publishing texts more quickly than is done now. But at this moment the benefit of the doubt should be granted. Instead of the original set of eight editors, there are about 60 now. There is hope that this time things will be done. And, in any case, anyone can have access to the original material, either through the various photograph collections or the fragments themselves. The world has completely changed during the last three years.

HS: *Yes, and so has the attitude of the new chief editor, Emanuel Tov.*

GV: Absolutely. This time freedom is there, and it will stay.

HS: *The Israel Antiquities Authority under Amir Drori has also now agreed with this change.*

GV: Absolutely.

HS: *Do you think that there are any big surprises left in the Qumran material?*

GV: This is the sort of question one should dodge because surprises are, by definition, surprising. They may come from a corner where you never expected them. But I have the gut feeling that if there will be surprises they will not be fundamental ones.

HS: *How about the possibility of more scrolls?*

GV: If you had asked me in 1946, "Will there be any more scrolls?" the answer would have been, "Of course not." For the last hundred years archaeologists have been searching from Dan to Beer-Sheva and from the Mediterranean to Transjordan, in every nook and cranny of the land, and they realized there was nothing there because such things couldn't survive. Then, suddenly, the scrolls were there. They can survive. So it would be foolish to say that it's impossible. It's perfectly possible. It is perfectly possible that there are still scrolls hidden. And possibly there are still some scrolls clandestinely owned. But beyond this it would be foolish to speculate.

HS: *Do you see a development in the biblical concept of the Son of God? Wasn't, for instance, the Israelite king referred to as the Son of God?*

GV: Yes, indeed. I listed at one time the various meanings that the words "Son of God" have in the Hebrew Bible, on the one hand, and in early post-biblical Judaism, on the other. And of course the one that does not exist is a Son of God who will be Son of God by nature.

HS: *You mean biologically?*

GV: Yes, biologically, as it were; that is to say, the idea that has become the teaching of Christianity at a certain stage in its development. But this doesn't appear in any Jewish text. In Jewish texts, from the Bible onwards, you have a very general concept of "Son of God." Every Israelite is a child of God. "Israel is my son, my firstborn" (Exodus 4:22). Every member of the Israelite nation is entitled to be considered as God's son or daughter. Later, the biblical concept is restricted only to good Jews; those who are not observant or faithful don't deserve to be called sons of God. Then you have specific sons of God, like the king, "You are my son, today I have begotten you" (Psalm 2:7). This is obviously a reference to the Israelite king. Through his elevation to kingly dignity, he becomes God's earthly representative, his son.

HS: *That certainly is an old concept, the idea that the king is divine.*

GV: Undoubtedly. That goes back to the dawn of the ages. It was in Mesopotamia, as well. Then you have the holy man referred to as Son of God.

HS: *Where is that?*

GV: There are many references in rabbinic literature declaring, "Rabbi so and so, my son, is right in teaching such and such," and so on. And you have the heavenly voice that is supposed to be the voice of God approving of somebody, and this somebody is elevated to the dignity of being called the Son of God. But obviously nobody imagined for one moment that they belonged to a very specific group of entities above the human frame and belonging to a divine category. This is symbolical, indicating somebody who is—let's put it in sort of a boring way—close to God. In the Synoptic Gospels, the phrase often appears in the sense attested in Judaism. In the story of the annunciation (Luke 1:26–38), Jesus is "called" the son of the Most High. Even Paul refers to Jesus, not as *being* Son of God, but as being *declared* Son of God (Romans 1:4). This is a far cry from the creed that says that Jesus is "consubstantial with the Father."

HS: *Some of the things you have said, especially about Jesus, are going to be shocking to some of our readers. Yet it will be standard, even consensus fare among scholars. How do you explain the relatively large chasm between the scholars' study and the layperson in the pew?*

GV: To begin with, it is certainly not my intention to upset anybody. For instance, in the preface of *The Religion of Jesus the Jew,* I *warn* readers that those who are untrained in the academic study of the origins of Christianity may find many pages of the book disturbing. So, if they do not want to be disturbed, they should not go on reading.

But to answer your question, I think the responsibility for the chasm between historians and the men and women in the pew lies mostly on the shoulders of the people in the pulpit who have failed to provide the persons in their charge with intellectual food suitable for educated grown-ups.

ILLUSTRATION CREDITS

Todd Bolen/www.BiblePlaces.com—98 (bottom)
Werner Braun—121
Lance Fairchild (top left)—89
Cyrus and Constance Gordon—161, 165
Jim Haberman—11-14
Marcus Halevi—41
Erich Lessing—74
Maryl Levine—101
National Portrait Gallery, London—163
Nordfoto/Jens Lymgby—89 (bottom left)
Patricia O'Connor-Seger—128
The Ophel Excavations (courtesy Dr. Eilat Mazar)—131
Zev Radovan—104, 107, 139
The Selz Foundation, Hazor Excavations (courtesy Israel Exploration Society)—99
Hershel Shanks—27
Pavel Shrago, Tel Aviv University—61
Rob Stockfield (top right)—89
Ilan Sztulman—119
Duby Tal/Albatross—63
University of Pennsylvania Museum/T4-1000—174
Yigael Yadin, *The Art of Warfare in Biblical Lands*—148

OTHER ENGAGING BOOKS FROM THE BIBLICAL ARCHAEOLOGY SOCIETY